Dickson County, Tennessee,

Will Book "A"

1804 – 1856

Transcribed by:

The Works Progress Administration
1936

With New Index by Samuel Sistler

Byron Sistler & Associates
1998

> ## *Notice*
>
> In many older books, foxing (or discoloration) occurs and, in some instances, print lightens with wear and age. Reprinted books, such as this, often duplicate these flaws, notwithstanding efforts to reduce or eliminate them. The transcript this book was printed from is a carbon copy typed on onion skin paper over 70 years ago. The print quality varied throughout the work---this would seem to be due to the wear on the carbon paper. The pages of this reprint have been digitally enhanced and, where possible, the flaws eliminated in order to provide clarity of content and a pleasant reading experience.

Originally transcribed by:

The Works Progress Administration (WPA)
1936

New material Copyright © 1998 by Samuel Sistler

With New Index by Samuel Sistler

Reprinted by:

Janaway Publishing, Inc.
732 Kelsey Ct.
Santa Maria, California 93454
(805) 925-1038
www.JanawayGenealogy.com

2006, 2012

ISBN: 978-1-59641-048-0

Made in the United States of America

DICKSON COUNTY, TN WILL BOOK A: 1804-1856

transcribed by Mrs. Alma Loggins and Mrs. Bessie Binkley for the Works Progress Administration, 1936

reprinted by Byron Sistler & Associates with new index by Samuel Sistler, 1998

Please note: This revised edition has three separate indexes. At the beginning of the book appears the original testator index prepared by the WPA in 1936. At the end of the text appear two separate indexes: first a list of every full name that appears throughout the text, and then a list of slaves, arranged alphabetically by their masters' surnames. Note that index page numbers refer to original page numbers (in parentheses along the left margin) and not those of the typed publication itself (in the upper right corner of each page).

The WPA transcript this book was printed from is a carbon copy typed on onion skin paper over 60 years ago. The print quality varied throughout the work—this would seem to be due to the wear on the carbon paper. We have made an effort to make all the print as legible as possible. This is a second generation copy of the original, and there will be a few places where the writing cannot be made out.

We would like to thank Jean Sugg and Chuck Sherrill of the TN State Library and Archives for their kind loan of the original book.

Byron Sistler & Associates

TENNESSEE

RECORDS OF DICKSON COUNTY

WILL BOOK A
1804-1856

HISTORICAL RECORD PROJECT
OFFICIAL PROJECT NO. 65-44-1445

COPIED UNDER WORK'S PROGRESS ADMINISTRATION

MRS. JOHN TROTWOOD MOORE
STATE LIBRARIAN & ARCHIVIST, SPONSOR

MRS. ELIZABETH D. COPPEDGE
DIRECTOR OF WOMEN'S & PROFESSIONAL PROJECTS

MRS. PENELOPE JOHNSON ALLEN
STATE SUPERVISOR

MISS MATILDA A. PORTER
SUPERVISOR FOURTH DISTRICT

MRS. ALMA LOGGINS
COPYIST

MRS. BESSIE BINKLEY
TYPIST

June 30, 1936

ORIGINAL WPA TESTATOR INDEX from 1936

A

Adams, Howell	16-17
Adams, Rives	28-29
Anglin, John	130-131
Adcock, Henderson	251 /154
Austin, A.J.	269 251
Armstrong H.W.	277-280-

B

Baker, John A.	37-38
Breedin, Epraim	60
Baker, John	71-72
Bledsoe, Barnibas	72-73
Brasher, William	120
Bugg, John	30-31
Baker, William	71-72
Bibb, Minorm	162-3-4-5
Brewer, John	162-6-7
Balthrop, Mary	158
Bell, Shadrick	169
Bell, Mary A.	178
Bill, R.F.	206
Bell, T. d.	208
Brown, J	212

C

Cathey, John R.	85-86
Cunningham, James	140-141
Choate, John	113-115
Carr, John B.	261-262
Caldwell, A.	281-282

D

Dickson, Joseph	1-2-3
Dickson, Lewis	17-18
David, L Claudius	27
Dunnegan, James	31-32
Davidson, Joseph	68-69
Drummond, Thomas	95-97
Davidson, George	101-102
Davidson, John	139-140
Duke, Robert	167-168
Dodson, J.M.	181

E

Easley, Moses	69-71
Ellis, Ransom	100-101
Evand, Jacob	155-56

F

Frances, Edward	8-10
Fussell, Moses	93-94
Freeman, Howell	126-127

G

Goodrich, James	45-49
Gilbert, William	75-78
Garrett, William Sr.	86-87
Goodwin, Peter	118-119
Goodrich, Sam	160-162
Gentry, Thos.	172
Gleaves, E	225
Groves, J	225
Garrett, Wm.	227

H

Hughes, David	5-6
Hudson, William	34-37
Hall, John	40-46
Humphreys, John	55-60
Hudson, Lucy	65-66
Hall, Joseph	87-88
Holland, James	112-113
Hughes, J. Ben	133
Hoging, Wm.	142-145
Hightower, Wm	153-154
Harris, B.	198
Hinton, R. B.	239
Hardin, J.	257-261

I

J

Jones, Reuben	19
Johnson, Samuel	19-20
Jorden, Seth B.	38-40
James, Joshua	44-45
James, Amos	74-75
James, Enoch	90
Jones, John	97-98
Johnson, John	116-118
James, Samuel	134-135
Joslin, James	159-160
Jackson, Epps	210

K

Kelly, Ebenezar	63-64

L

Loftiss, Milton	78-80
Leek, Henry	147-150
Lampley, Jacob	293

ORIGINAL WPA TESTATOR INDEX from 1936

M

Meek, Adam	7-8
Moulton, Sarah	10-11
McClelland, James	20-22
McAdoo, David	22-24
Marsh, Ann	74
Morrison, William	120-126
Matthews, Thomas	128-
Myatt, Burwell	132
Mitchell, George	254-5-6
Matlock, Wm.	275-276
Martin, John L.	286-7

N

Norris, William	11-16
Napier, Richard C	106-110
Nesbitt, John	145-146
Nesbitt, Robert	175
Napier, E. W.	183
Nesbitt, Jermiah	290-1

O

Overton, Gabriel	17-

P

Passmore, David	103-
Pinegar, Lenard	111-112
Pullin, A	199
Pritchard, R.	205
Porter, Wm.	237
Parker, Moses	243-244
Pendergrass,	246-47-48

Q

R

Richardson, Thomas	24-26
Rye, Solomn	32-34
Richardson, Jorden	49-55
Reynolds, John Sr.	80-83
Ross, George	88-90
Richardson, Elizabeth	98-100
Richardson, Lebius	104-106
Rape, Gurtavius	239-240
Richardson, Winnifred	283-4-5

S

Stone, William	3-4-5
Smith, Moses	6
Sugg, John	29-31
Sansom, Richard D.	83-85
Street, Moses	156-7-8
Slayden, Hartwell	177
Sanders, John	201
Strong, C	214
Sensing, M. G.	245-246
Speight, W.D.	252-253
Skelton, Archabald	262-264
Smith, Bartholmew	271-274
Shelton, Elaner	298

T

Turner, John	64-65
Thomas, Stephen	66-68
Tucker, John	119-120
Tubb, George	129-130
Thompson, Charles	131-132
Tidwell, James	135-136
Taylor, Daniel	146-147
Tidwell, Josiah Isiah	180
Tidwell, Benjamine	268

U

V

Vick, Elizabeth	267

W

Wilson, Adam	60-65
Walker, Elizabeth	91
Williams, John Daniel	94-95
Willey, John	115-116
Wiley, David	127-128
Whitwell, Ann	136-139
White, James	141-142
White, Joshua	150-151
Wiley, William	151-152
Wiley, Ann	171
Work, A.	204
West, Robt.	230
Willey, W.	241-243
White, Reubin	248-250
Wilkins, Alexander	265-66
Walker, Elizabeth	288-9
Woodward, Jesse	295-6-7
Wyatt, Burell	132

X

Y

Yarrell, Mary	133-134

Z

WILL BOOK A.
1804-1856

(JOSEPH DICKSON Last WILL and TESTAMENT- No. 1)

(1) In the name of God Amen, I, Joseph Dickson of the State of Tennessee and County of Dickson being sick of body but of perfect mind & memory thanks be to God for his mercies &c calling to mind the frailty of man and knowing that it is appointed for all human to die have thought proper to constitute, appoint, make and ordain this to be my last Will and Testament, Viz.

First- I deliver up my soul to Almighty God who gave it me and my Will and desire is that my body be intered in a gentel and decent manner who are hereafter to be named and as to my worldly goods after my funeral expenses and all my other lawful debts, are paid. I will and bequeath as follows, to wit,

First-To my beloved wife Jane Dickson I will and bequeath my young negro girl called Chloe to her sole use and disposal.

Second-To my beloved son Hugh Dickson, I will and bequeath my negro boy called Pharoah.

Third- To my beloved son David Dickson I will and bequeath my negro boy called Sam.

Fourth- To my beloved son Melton Dickson I will and bequeath my negro boy called Rowland.

Fifth- To my beloved son Joseph Dickson I will and bequeath my negro boy called Daniel.

Sixth- My Will and Desire is for my negroes Reddick, Almyra, Warwick, Dinah and Sylvia with their increase to be equally divided between my three youngest sons, Viz, Abner Robert and William Dickson

Seventh-My Will and desire is that my young negro fellow dalled Virgil be hired out to the best advantage for ten years successively and the money arising from said Hire, to be appropriated by my Executors to the best advantage in Cloathing and educating my said three youngest sons, Abner, Robert and William at the expiration of the said ten years the said negro fellow Virgil to be the property of my three sons Hugh, David and Melton Dickson.

(2) Eighth-My will and desire is that my old negro fellow called Harry be the property of my three sons Hugh, David and Melton Dickson and that he have choice which of them he will live with and the one he lives with to pay to the other two thirds of what he is supposed to be worth per annum.

Ninth-To my beloved Grand daughter Lucy, Jane, Pearale I will and bequeath the first child my young negro woman Clarry shall have

Tenth- My will and desire is that my young negro woman Clarry with her increase except the first child as aforesaid and the above named Negro woman Sylvia remain on the plantation with my wife until her death after which they are to be equally divided among my three youngest sons Abner Robert and William Dickson.

Eleventh- My will and desire is that my old negro woman Phillis remain on the plantation with my wife until her death after which she is to be supported by my sons Hugh, David and Malton Dickson.

Twelfth- To my beloved niece Elizabeth Dickson Daughter of James Dickson of No. Ca. I will and bequeath one good bed and furniture and should she remain with the family until she gets married she is to be furnished at the expence of my estate with a good genteen suit suitable to her station to be married in.

Thirteenth- To my beloved sons Hugh and David Dickson I will and bequeath each a good bed and furniture also to my sons Malton Joseph, Abner, Robert and William Dickson I will and bequeath to to each of them one feather bed and furniture as they respictively came to the age of twenty one years.

Fourteenth- My will and desire is that my negro man Cato be so disposed of my my executors as shall be most advantageous in provincing of land which Land is to be the property of my son Joseph Dickson reserving the one third of my said land for my beloved wife during her natural life to include the improvements if any on said Land.

Fifteenth- My will and desire is that the present stock of Horses with my waggon be so disposed of by my executors as shall be most advantageous in procuring subsistance for the family the present years and if any remains they are to remain with my wife for her use and the benefit of the younger children.

Sixteenth- To my beloved Daughter Ann Pearsall I will and bequeath a genteel mourning suit to be furnished at the expense of my estate.

Seventeenth- To my beloved son Michael Dickson I will and bequeath a genteel Mourning suit to be furnished at the expense of my Estate.

Eighteenth- I make, constitute appoint and ordain my three sons Michael, Hugh and David Dickson Executors to this my last will and Testament.

Signed, sealed, acknowledged published and declared to be his last will and testament before us 27th day of December A.D. 1803.
D. Stewart, John Stewart, James Stewart)   Joseph Dickson(Seal)

State of Tennesse, Dickson County, June Session 1804. Then was the within last Will and Testament of Joseph Dickson decd produced in open Court and proved to be such by the oath of Duncan Stewart a subscribing witness thereto and ordered to be recorded.
Test: David Dickson C.C.

(WILLIAM STONES Last Will & Testament No. 2)

In the name of God Amen. I William Stone Senr of the County of Dickson and State of Tennessee being very sick and weak though memory do make and establish this and no other to be my last will and and Testament revoking all others heretofore made.

Principally and first of all I recommend my soul to Almighty God who gave it and my body to the earth to be burried at the discretion of my Executors.

I will that my Executors hereafter named pay off my just debts.

I give and bequeath to my son Hardemon Stone all the money I paid for him to Nicholas Kernes, and others amounting one hundred and seventy five dollars, and no more.

Item- I give and bequeath to Bartholomew Smith the cow and calf that he had in possession in my Daughter Dorcus lifetime and no more.

Item- I give and bequeath to my Grand-son Mansford Smith son of Barthlomew and Dorcas one negro girl named Nicy, and no more.

Item- I will and bequeath to my son John H. Stone one negro boy named Adam and one horse he has already in possession and one steer of a dark colour, and no more.

Item- I give and bequeath to my Daughter Susanna one negro girl Printer, one cow and calf one feather and furniture, one saddle and bridle and no more.

Item- I give and bequeath to my daughter Dolly one negro girl named Pleasure one feather bed and furniture one cow and calf one saddle and bridle and no more.

Item- I give and bequeath to my son Marble Stone one horse of an Eagle Colour and fifteen dollars.

Item- I give and bequeath to my son Solomon Stone one horse worth Eighty dollars.

Item- I give and bequeath to my beloved wife Elizabeth Stone all the tract of land I now live on, with the Appurtenances thereunto belonging, two negro women each named Jenny, two negro boys Jess and Jerry and all the rest of my property during her life or widowhood and then to be divided equally between my sons William, Marble, and Solomon Stone.

(5) I do likewise appoint my beloved wife Elizabeth Stone, Executrix and Bartholomew Smith my trusty friend together with William Stone my beloved son Executor of this my last Will and Testament. In Witness whereof I have hereunto set my hand and affixed my seal this twenty sixth day of April in the year of our Lord One thousand eight hundred and five.

Signed, sealed and delivered in presence) William Stone (seal)
of James Foster, Thomas Hardemon, Jas. Martin.

State of Tennessee, Dickson County, June Term 1805, Then was the within last will and Testament of William Stone Sen'r produced in open Court and proved to be such by the oaths of James Foster a subscribing Witness thereto

Teste D. Dickson C.C.

(5) Recorded in Book A and page this 4th day of September in the year 1805.

D. Dickson C.D.C.

(DAVID D HUGHES No. 3)

Be it remembered this 24th day of September one thousand Eight hundred and four, that I DAVID HUGHS of Dickson County and State of Tennessee being weak of body but of sound mind and memory and calling to mind my Mortality do think fit to make and constitute this my last Will and Testament in manner and form following, hereby revoking and disannulling all other Wills by me made either in word or writing and to pronounce this to be my last Will, VIZ

First-I give my soul unto God who gave it and my Body unto the earth to be Burned in a decent manner as my Executor hereafter named, shall see write. And I Will that all my just debts and funeral expenses be fully paid.

Item-I give and bequeath to my beloved wife Mary Hughes all my estate during her life or widowhood, and at her decease, or marriage to be equally divided amongst my surviving children share and share alike I do likewise Will and constitute John Nesbitt & Robert Nesbitt Executors to this my last Will and Testament, In witness whereof I have hereunto set my hand and seal the day and year above written.

Signed, sealed and pronounced in) his
presence of Thomas Simpson, Isach Choate.) David D Hughes (seal)
mark

State of Tennessee, Dickson County, September Term 1805. Then was the within mentioned Will proven in Court by the oath of Isace Choate and ordered to be recorded.

Test D. Dickson C.C.

(6) (MOSES SMITH No. 4)

In the name of God Amen. I, MOSE SMITH of the State of Tennessee and County of Dickson being weak in body but sound of mind and memory do make and ordain this to be my last Will and Testament and do hereby revoke all other Will or Wills that may heretofore have been made.

In the first place I recommend my soul to God that gave it and my body to be decently burried at the discretion of my Executors.

Secondly-I desire all my just debts to be paid.

Thirdly-I lend to my beloved wife Susanna Smith all the remainder of my property of every kind or discription whatsoever to make use of in whatever manner she thinks proper during her natural life or widowhood.

Fourthly-After my beloved wife Susanna's death or intermarriage with the second husband it is my desire that my property be disposed of as the law directs.

Fifthly-I do hereby nominate and appoint my beloved wife Susannah Smith, Bartholemew Smith & William Stone Executors to this my last Will and Testament. In testimony whereof I have hereunto set my hand and seal this Eleventh day of July 1805.

Moses Smith (seal)

Test-John Daviss, James Robertson.

(7) (ADAM MEEKS WILL No. 5)

In the name of God Amen. I, Moses Meek considering all men are mortal and that its appointed for all men once to die I do make and ordain this my last Will and Testament.

First-I bequeath my Soul into the hands of the Supreme Power who gave it.

Second-That my just   should be paid at the discretion of my Executor, and

Thirdly-That land I bought from John Daviss I allow to be equally divided between my two sons Joshua and Moses Meek, And

Fourthly-I likewise do ordain that my son Moses shall pay unto his Sister Elizabeth One hundred dollars and likewise ordain my loving Wife Margaret to pay James Martin three hundred dollars for that piece of land I bought from him he making a deed of conveyance agreeably to contract and I likewise ordain that one of the negro boys should be sold which one my wife choses and the other one to be hers and at her disposal and likewise my waggon and Team with all the household furniture with that land I bought from James Martin to at her disposal only that she is to divide with my Daughter Agniss as she thinks proper only horse, saddle and bed and furniture at her marriage and the negro at her Mothers decease if she lives longest and likewise I do bequeath to my Daughter Jennet Genier, the sum of thirty dollars and all the remainder and seversions and portion thereof of the Estate either seal or pursuit that is not mentioned in this my last Will and Testament I do bequeath to my beloved wife, and lastly I do nominate and appoint my wife Margaret and my son-in- law James Martin Executors to this my last Will and testament.

Signed, sealed and delivered as my act and deed this 5th of November 1807.

(seal)

(8) State of Tennessee, Knox County, This day come before me Adam Meek and on his solemn oath saith that he said Meek wrote the annexed Will at the request of the said Moses Meek dec'd and that the said Moses divided and worded said Will as it is wrote and I read it to him three different times and he sd Moses was pleased with every part thereof and wanted to assign then but was requested to let that be until there would be more people who would be witnesses and it was afterwards neglected and the said Moses was in his proper sense and reason, as ever I saw him and further this deponent saith not.

Sworn to and subscribed this 11th November 1807.

Samuel Sample J.P.   Adam Meek

State of Tennessee, Knox County, I Charles W Cling, Clerk of the

Court of Pleas and Quarter Session of the County of Knox by John H Gamble my deputy do certify that Saml Sample before whom the within deposition was taken was at the time of the taking thereof and now is an Acting Justice of the Peace within the County aforesaid and that due faith and credit is and of right ought to be given his official acts as such. Given under my hand and seal of office in Knoxville this 15th day of November 1807.

                                          Charles W. Cherry by
                                          his deputy
                                          Jno. N. Gamble

(EDWARD FRANCES No. 6)

In the name of God Amen. I, EDWARD FRANCES of the State of Tennessee and Dickson County through the abundant mercy of Goodness and goodness of God tho weak in body yet of a sound and perfect understanding and memory do constitute this my last Will and Testament and desire it may be received as such by all.

I, Bequeath my Soul to God my Maker, besearching his most gracious acceptance of it through Jesus Christ our Lord. As to my worldly Estate.

(9) First-I bequeath to my dear and loving wife her bed and furniture one small pot and one oven and to dispose of them at her death as she sees cause. She is to have a part of the pewter during her life as will answer her necessities then after her death to be equally divided between my two sons, John & Gideon, she is to have the use of two iron pot racks during her life and after death they are to be one Johns the other one Gideons. It is my Will she should live in this house where I now live during her life. As to my land tenants I give and bequeath to my son John all that part of my lands that lies on the South side of the Creek where David Howell now lives, the other part on the North side of the Creek where I now live. I give and bequeath unto my son Gideon after my decease but he is not to be invested with power to sell or dispose of it in any wayform or manner whatever till he shall arrive to the age of twenty one years old. As to my household furniture there is two beds and furniture they are to be equally divided between my two sons John and Gideon, John to have one pot and Gideon to have one Kettle when he shall arrive to the age before mentioned. My farming tools are all to remain on the plantation for the use of the family till there is a call for a division then they are to be equally divided between my two sons John and Gideon. As to my stock of cattle and hogs I will that they remain on the plantation for the use and support of the family until there is a call for a division to be made then I will that they should be equally divided between my two sons John and Gideon except some few that I give to my wife. It is my will that she dispose of them as she may think fit.

(10) There is one sorrell mare it is my will and desire that she shall remain on the plantation for the use of the family as long as she lives. One Rifle Gun to remain on the place for the use of it. And I do here constitute my two neighbors Johathon Johnston and Henry Rape Executors of my last Will and Testament. In testemony whereof I have hereunto set my hand and seal the seventeenth of March in the year of our Lord one thousand eight hundred and twelve.

Witness present
Robert B. Stringfellow,
James D. Sharp

                                          her
                                      Edward X Frances
                                      mark

State of Tennessee, October Term, Dickson County 1813. Then was the within will proven in open Court by the oath of Robert Stringfellow and ordered to be recorded.

                                          Field Farrar Clark

State of Tennessee, Dickson County, November 8th-1813.-Then was the within Will recorded in Book A page 18-19.

            Field Farror, Clerk

(10)(11)(SARAH MOLTON No. 7)

  The last Will and Testament of SARAH MOLTON. In the name of God Amen. I, Sarah Molton being weak in body but sound in mind, and knowing that God Almighty hath appointed all to die I do make and ordain this my last Will and Testament as follows. First-I recommend my soul into the hands of him who gave it me and pray through the blessed Redeemer it may meet with a divine acceptance at the throne of Grace.

  2nd-I will that my body be decently intered and that the cost thereof be paid by my Executors hereafter mentioned out of such estate as I may leave.

  3rd-After my funeral expences and all my just debts are paid I give and bequeath unto my Grand-daughter Sarah Ann, Jane Molton, the daughter of my son Abraham my negro girl child named Anneritter now about four years old said negro child being the daughter of young Penny, to her and her heirs forever.

  4th-I give and bequeath unto my son Michael my negro woman young Penny with her increase except the one before given to Sarah Ann Jane Melton, to him and his heirs forever.

  5th-I give and bequeath unto my two daughters Jane Stewart and Patience Pearsell my negro woman Betty and her increase to them and their heirs forever.

  6th-I give and bequeath unto my daughter Elizabeth Simpson forty dollars to be paid her by my Executor hereafter mentioned within one year after my decease which sum in to be paid to herself and not subject to the claim or controul of her husband John Simpson and this Legacy to be paid by my two daughters, Jane and Patience to whom I willed Betty and increase if they refuse to pay the said Legacy or neglect to do it then I desire and direct my Executors to hire out said negro Betty until the said sum of forty dollars shall be raised.

  7th-I constitute and appoint my son-in-law Jermiah Pearsall and my son Michael Molton my Executors and to carry into effect this my last will and Testament.

  8th-I do by this Will revoke and disannul all other Wills by me heretofore made andwill that this only shall stand good in law.

  Given under my hand and seal this 14th of July 1812.

  Witness-Edward Pearsall, Danl H Williams)   his

                    SarahXMolton

                     mark

  State of Tennessee, Dickson County, July Term 1814-Then was the within last will and Testament of Sarah Molton dec'd produced in open Court and proved to be such by the oaths of Edward Pearsall and Danl H. Williams subscribing Witnesses thereto and ordered to be recorded.

  Test-Field Farror, Clerk.

(WILLIAM NORRIS No. 8)

  In the name of God Amen. I, WILLIAM NORRIS of the County of Dickson in the State of Tennessee being sick and weak in body but of sound sense, mind, and memory thanks be to the Almighty God do this third day of February in the year of our Lord one thousand and eight hundred and seven make and publish this my last Will and Testament, that is to say, I give my soul to Almighty God and by the merits of Jesus Christ I trust and believe to be saved and my body to be buried in such a decent and Christian like manner as my Executors herein after named think proper and as to my temporal estate and whatsoever else

God has been pleased to bestow on me I give and bequeath as follows-
My Will and desire is that my just debts be paid Imprinisio I give
and bequeath to my loving wife Jane Norris during her natural life or
(12) widowhood the land and plantation on which I now live together with
all the stock of Horses, Cattle, Sheep and Hogs and all the household
and Kitchen furniture and the plantation and utensels of every description, that is not here after given or bequeth or Legacyed away
by me likewise I lend my loving wife during her natural life or widowhood all my negroes, that is to say, Jude, Rose, Rachael, Jill and
Entnum with all their increase, but my will and desire is that my
loving wife raise and educate my children that is now under age and
under her tuition on the income and nett proceeds of the above discribed property, except the negroes.

Item-I give my beloved son Robert Norris my big old road wagon my
blacksmiths tools of every kind and new leathers for a bellows and
half the valuation of an eighty one gallon still to him and to his
heirs forever but be it remembered that he is to have no profits of
the above mentioned still nor remove her until the season of stilling
is over for the present year.

Item-I give my belove Son John Norris during his natural life all
the issues, rents and profits of one hundred acres of land on the East
side of Yellow creek known by the Puckett place for his maintainance
and support now the reason of this restriction is his being in a state
of insanity.

Item-I give and bequeath to the heirs of my deceased daughters Jane
Maxwell that is to say to her son Jess Maxwell when he shall arrive
of eighteen years of age Six silver dollars credit in the Store in
likewise her daughter Jane Maxwell Ten Silver dollars credit in a
story when she shall marry or arrive to fourteen years of age.

(13) Item-I give and bequeath to my beloved son Ezekiel Norris the one
half the value of ninety five acres of land on both sides of Yellow
creek which included the Mill and Mill seat together with the land
he is already in posession of on the East side of said creek including
the plantation known by the name of the Holland place but be it known
that he is to receive no profits of the increase of said Mill till
after the expiration of two years, when after that term of time he is
to receive half the profits of the Mill and land including the Mill
and land including the Mill. Likewise one Roan Horse called Julias
Calsar One feather bed and furniture, one cow and calf one Ewe and
lamb, a sow and pigs and half the valuation of an eighty one gallon
still but it is to be considered that he receives no profits on the
said still the present season, not remove her until the present season
expires all the said property to be to him and his heirs forever.

Item-I give my beloved daughter Nancy Dillihay together with what
I have already given her a Ewe and lamb and after my loving wifes dee
cease I give and bequeath her a negro girl named Rose to her ahd her
heirs forever.

Item-I give and bequeath to my beloved daughter Ellinor Norris, a
Sorrell Horse, Saddle and bridle, one feather bed and furniture two
Cows and Calves a Ewe and Lamb and Ten dollars worth of Iron castings
and Ten dollars worth of Pewter and delf stone or crockery ware. And
after my loving wifes decease I give and bequeath her a negro wench
named Jude but my desire is that if my wife please she may put her in
possession or give her up the said negro at her marriage or becoming
of full age to her and her heirs forever.

Item-I give and bequeath to my beloved son William Norris a horse
called Robuck, a Saddle and bridle one feather bed and furniture one
cow and calf one Ewe and Lamb, two sows and pigs and two stills, one
of forty three gallons and the other sixty six gallons and after my

loving wifes decease or widowhood I give and bequeath him the land a and plantation on which I now live. Also one negro gorl named Rachel also a set of new plough irons out of the iron now on hand to be made and paid for out of the next proceeds or profits of the estate with the necessary tacklines for ploughing and the one half of the edge tools on the plantation. Likewise my Will request and desire is that my son William Norris should take the care, management and the nursing of his brothers John Norris at which time when he takes the charge and care of his brother John, his brother John is to receive and have for his use as long as he lives one feather bed and furniture and a bedstead out of the Estate or its <u>Nett</u> proceeds as profits all the above given property to be to him and his heirs forever.

(14) Item-I give and bequeath my beloved Son Jesse Norris the one half the value of ñnety five acres of land on both sides of Yellow creek including the Mill and Mill seat but he is to receive no profits from the Mill until his Mothers decease. Also I give and bequeath him after his brother John Norris, decease, the land and plantation known by the name of Picketts place containing one hundred acres on the East side of Yellow Creek, but should his brother John die before he comes of age my Will and desire is that the rents and profits of the last mentioned lands be applied to the use of his mother and those of his sisters and brothers that remain single on this land Likewise a Horse Saddle, and bridle and after my loving wifes decease I give and bequeath him a negro boy named Entrum, to him and his heirs forever.

(15) Item-I give and bequeath to my beloved daughter Betsey Norris one Black mare colt called Providence one saddle and bridle one feather bed and furniture two cows and calves one Ewe and Lamb ten dollars worth of Iron Castings and Ten dollars worth of Pewter & delf stone or crockery ware and after my loving wifes decease I give and bequeath her a negro girl named Till to her and her heirs forever. Now my Will and desire is that all the money or cash on hand together with what may be collected by bonds and outstanding debts may be immediately put to interest by my Executors hereafter named and whenever the Orphan or Representative in law of <u>Col.</u> William Davis calls or demands the money given as an equivalent to him in the difference of the land by the Commissioners on the division that they may callect the money and pay him or his order, or his lawful applicant whatever may be due him or them after deducting the money advanced by me for his part of the charge in cleaning the land from installments, paying taxes as also including expences of every kind relative thereto. And the remaining money or cash in the hands of the Executors my Will and Desire is that it be equally divided between all my children.

Also my two Waggons not yet disposed of my will and desire is that they remain on the plantation I now live on for the use thereof with the gear thereto belonging. Likewise my will and desire is that Aster my loving wife's decease, all the kitchen, shelf and house cupboard ware of every kind be equally divided between my sons Ezekiel, William and Jesse Norris and all the remaining part of my estate not yet given or legacied away my will and desire is that it be equally divided after my wife's decease between all my children. Now my will and desire is that the income or profits of my stills be sold by my Executors on a reasonable credit for cash and the money arising put to interest and the <u>nett</u> amount of cash applied as the cash on hand or m money be collected on outstanding debts for the term of two years and after that term of time my will and desire is that my son William receive half the profits Lastly I constitute and appoint to this my last Will and Testament my beloved sons Robert Norris and Ezekial Norris my son-in-law Nathan Dillahay whole and sole Executors of this my last will and Testament Pronouncing, Publishing and declaring this to be my last Will and Testament revoking and making void all Wills or Wills by me family made. In witness hereof I have hereunto set my hand and seal in the presence of the subscribing witnesses the day and date above written.

Jno Humphreys)
Edward Swanson)
Isaiah Moore)

Wm Norris   (seal)

(16) State of Tennessee, Dickson County, February 10th 1820. Then was the within Will recorded in Book A page 21-22-23-24-25.

Field Farror, Clerk.

(HOWELL ADAMS No.9)

Wrote at the request of Howell Adams Esquire after being mortally wounded at the Battle of Muckfaw VIZ, My Will and desire is that all my just debts be paid, that all my children that is not married and left me when they marry shall have as much of my Estate as will be equal with these that have married and that they all, that is all my children, shall as they marry or come to age to act for them selves shall have three hundred dollars in good property or money to be raised out of my estate   that my wife Nancy Adams keep my estate together to raise my Children in her hands during her remaining my widow and if she should interminany that she have choice of the negro woman belonging to my estate should any of the negroes prove unruly it is my will that those that I have left to manage my Estate should sell them which I think he told me was his wife, his son William Adams, Hodge Adams and that the money that he the Testator had sued Benjamine Joslin for was not money belonging to his Estate it was his sons William Adams as it was his horse that was sold for the same, but the bond was taken in his name and further this Testator said not Sworn to before me this 10th day of Feb. 1814. Attest

Jesse G Christian

Cutbert Hudson

(17) (
(GABRIEL OVERTON No.10)

In the name of God Amen. I, GABRIEL OVERTON do constitute and ordain this my last will and Testament.

Item-I leave or lend to my beloved wife Elizabeth Overton all and singulor my estate personal and real during her remaining my widow at her death or intermarriage, that my Estate be equally divided between my three children Robert Overton, Elizabeth Overton & Moses Overton also the child that my wife is now pregnant with an equal proportion of my Estate. In Witness whereof I have hereunto set my hand and seal this 21 day of September 1814.

Test-
Cutbert Hudson)
James Hanna)

Gabriel Overton   (seal)

State of Tennessee, Dickson County, July Term 1815. Then was the last Will and Testament of Gabriel Overton was proven in open Court by the oaths of Cutbert Hudson and James Hannah and ordered to be recorded and certified.

Field Farrar   (Clerk)

State of Tennessee, Dickson County, March 9th 1820. Then was the within Will of Gabriel Overton deceased Recorded in page 28-

Field Farrar   (clerk)

LEVIN DICKSON or DIXON No.11)

Last Will and Testament of Levin Dickson.

In the name of Amen I, LEVIN DIXON of the county of Dickson and State of Tennessee being of sound mind and memory but weak in body remembering my mortality that man is born to die first resign my body to the dust and my soul to God from whence it came.

As to my worldly goods that God has been pleased to bless me with I wish to dispose of in the following manner, to wit, (Item 1) My Will is that my beloved Wife Abigail shall remain in posession of the plantation whereon I now live together with all my household and kitchen furniture and as much of my stock as herself and her Brother David Parker may think sufficient to raise my children on.

(Item 2) My will is that my negro boy Stephen remain in posession of my wife until my youngest son arrives at the age of eighteen years, then to be sold and the money equally divided between my surviving children.

(18) (Item 3) My will is that the balance of my property be sold at 18 months credit and the money together with all money now due me and all debts due me be put to interest.

(Item 4) My Will is that my Executor pay to my children severally as they arrive to full age or intermarry the sum of one hundred Dollars each.

(Item 5) My Will is that if my Mother dies before my wife that my wife take posession of my negro man Tom during her natural life at her death said negro Tom shall be amansipated and set free.

(Item 6) Lastly my Will is that my beloved wife Abigal and loving friend Daniel Parker, her brother be and are hereby appointed my true and lawful Executors and Executor.

In witness whereof I have hereunto set my hand affixed my seal this twelfth day of March in the year of our Lord Eighteen hundred and fifteen.

Daniel Hogan)
William Hodges)   July Term 1815   Lovin Dixon   (seal)

Then was the last will and Testament of Lovin Dickson power in open Court by the oaths of David Hogins and William Hodges and ordered accordingly.

Field Farrar, Clerk.

State of Tennessee, Dickson County March 10th 1820. Then was the last Will and Testament of Lovin Dickson Recorded.
Field Farror

(REUBEN JONES No. 12)

In the name of God Amen. I, REUBEN JONES being sick and weak of body, and calling to mind the mortality of this body and that it appointed for man to die and do constitute and ordain this my last Will and Testament.

Item-My Will and desire is that all my just debts should be paid,

Item-My Will and desire is that my wife Ester Jones keep all my
(19) estate personal and real to raise my children during her remaining my widow and at her death or intermarriage that it be divided among my five children, namely, John Jones, Thomas Jones, Elizabeth Jones, Nancy Jones, Seabum Jones, and also that the (child) that my wife is pregnant have an equal share with the rest and I appoint Joseph Manner and my wife Easter Jones my two Executors. In witness whereof I have set my hand and seal this 24th day of January 1815.

Test-
Cuthbert Hudson)   Reuben Jones   (seal)
Hugh Lewis   ) his death proven July Term 1815. Then was the last Will and Testament of Reuben Jones proven by Cuthbert Hudson and also the hand writing of Hugh Lewis deceased one of the subscribing witness

witness thereto.   Field Farrar, Clerk.

Recorded in Book A and page 30 this 11th day March in the year 1820.   Field Farrar, Clk.

(19) (SAMUEL JOHNSTON or JOHNSON No. 13)

Whereas Samuel Johnson of the State of Tennessee and County of Dickson is in a low state of health but having a sound mind and in the full exercise of his reason makes his last Will and Testament as follows. My negro Elick I leave to my dear Wife Polly while she lives and the beds and house furniture I give to my wife to dispose of as she pleaseth also one Cow and yearling heifer, and all my Hogs for her to support the family on. The said negro Elick after my Wifes death I leave to my three sons William Johnson, Dunkin Johnson, and James Johnson. Also I give my wife two mares a brown and a dunn. I also give fifty acres of land lying on the head of white oak Creek of Tennessee River, to my two sons Dunkin and James and after all my debts is paid out of the moneys due to me by notes obligations and amounts the balance of said moneys I want equally divided amongst all my children. Whereunto set my hand and seal this 25th of March 1816.

                                          Samuel Johnson (seal)

(20) Test-
William Givin) Executor, James King ows the fee William Johnson, January Term 1817. The last Will and Testament of Samuel
John Epperson) Johnson deceased was this day produced in open Court and proven by the oaths of William Givin and John Epperson and ordered to be received and recorded. Jany 7th 1817. Field Farrar, Clerk.

State of Tennessee, Dickson County, January 25th 1817, Then was the within Will recorded in Book A page 30-31.

                                          Field Farrar, Clerk.

(JAMES McCLELLAND No. 14)

In the name of God Amen. I JAMES McCLELLAND of the County of Dickson and State of Tennessee being in perfect health and body of perfect mind and memory thanks be given unto God calling into mind the mortality of my body and knowing that it is appointed for all men once to die do make and ordain this my last Will and Testament that is to say principally and first of all I give and recommend my soul into
(21) the hands of Almighty God that gave it and my body I recommend to the Earth to be buried in decent Christian burial at the discretion of my executors nothing doubting but at the general resurection I shall receive the same again by the mighty power of God and as touching such worldly estate wherewith it is pleased God to bless me in this life I give demise and dispose of the same in the following manner and farm.

First- I give and bequeath to Jane my dearly beloved wife all my movable property after my debts is paid whom I likewise constitute make and ordain the sale Execution of this my last will and Testament All and singular my lands so long as she lives a widow, likewise bequeath to my beloved son Frances one Dollar, likewise I bequeath to my dearly beloved Daughter Agness one hundred dollars which is paid to her, when my youngest son comes of age, that is Thomas, and to be paid by my four sons who I leave my lands to, that is my son William is to pay twenty five dollars and my son Nelson twenty five dollars and my son John twenty twenty five dollars and my son Thomas twenty five dollars, And I bequeath to my four sons, last mentioned above all my lands at my wife's death or at her marriage that the land is to be divided into four parts, my son William to have his part at the lower end where he now lives, my son Thomas next, my son John next my son Nelson next and last and I appoint Thomas Bullion Executor with my wife and I do hereby utterly disallow revoke and disannul all and every other former Testaments Wills legaces bequests and executors by me in any ways before named Willed and bequeathed, ratifying and confining this and no other to be my last Will and Testament. In witness whereof I have hereunto set my hand and seal this the twentieth day of August in the year of our Lord one thousand eighteen. James McClelland (seal)

Test- John West, Sally X West
             her
             mark

Court of Pleas and quarter Session April Term, 1819. Then was the last Will and Testament of James McClelland was proven in open Court by the oaths of John West and Sally West and ordered to be received and recorded.

Field Farrar, Clerk

State of Tennessee, Dickson County, January 18th 1821. Then was the within Will recorded in Book A page 31-32.

Field Farrar

(DAVID McADOO, No. 15)

In the name of God Amen. I David McAdoo Senr. of Dickson County and State of Tennessee, being at present in a low state of bodily he health but blessed be God perfectly sound in Judgement and memory and remembering that it is appointed for all men once to die and not knowing but the dissolution of my body may be nigh at hand. I do therefore make ordain and constitute this my last Will and Testament hereby disallowing, disannuling, and making void all former Wills and records of that kind heretofore made and acknowledged by me, acknowledging this and this only to be my last Will and Testament which is in form as follows:

First- I do with deep humility and resignation yield up my soul to God who gave it and who is the Father of all spirits and my body to the earth to be buried in a decent and Christianlike manner at the discretion of my Executors hereafter named, nothing doubting but the same soul and body will be united in the morning of the general resurection and as to such worldly substance wherewith the Lord has blessed me, I give, bequeath and dispose of in the following manner, VIZ:

In the first place I give and bequeath to my beloved wife Margaret McAdoo the dwelling house in which I now live together with all the privileges thereto belonging likewise the garden and all convenient buildings about the house to be for her only use and behoof during her natural life or widowhood and for the same term of time I allow her the privilege of using fruit at her own discretion of my orchards and likewise such Stock as she have occasion to keep and that at her own discretion during her natural life or widowhood as aforesaid I likewise I give and bequeath unto my said wife all my present Stock consisting in Horses, Cows, Hogs, Sheep, Geese &C likewise all my household furniture of every kind now in my posession or at least so much of the same as shall remain after my children who are now come of age shall have received their respective positions which I allow them to be for her use and the use of my children who are yet in a State of minority.

Item- I give and bequeath to my son John McAdoo one Dollar to be paid unto him within one year after my decease.

Item- I give and bequeath to my son Samuel McAdoo, one hundred and nineth Acres of land it being part of a tract originally granted to James Ives and Quiring lives with land which I gave to my son John on which he now lives and on his South side. I likewise give and bequeath to my son Samuel my sorrell Horse called Hector, a certain Cow and calf which I got of Zebider Hicks a saddle and bridle a bed and and furniture, a plough, ax matlock and weeding hoe likewise fifty dollars in cash, all to be delivered to him on demand.

Item- I give and bequeath to my Daughter Jane McClelland eighty acres of land it being part of said Ives tract and on the last end of said tract. I likewise give and bequeath unto my said Daughter Jane one dollar in cash, to be paid unto her within one year after my decease.

Item- I give and bequeath to my daughter Sarah Burkett fifty acres of land on the east end. I likewise give and bequeath to my said Daughter, Sarah one dollar in Cash to be paid unto her within one year after my decease.

Item- I give and bequeath unto my son David McAdoo the plantation w whereon I now live include the water Mill and all other improvements observing however, that his power is never extended so as to infringe on the rights and privileges already secured to his Mother from said plantation and he is only to be in full posession of the whole afore-premises at his Mothers decease or marriage.

Item- I give and bequeath to my said son David and to be delivered to him when he comes of age, one Horse Saddle and bridle, all the cultivating utensils and other tools together with Stock, and property to be given to him at his Mothers discretion.

(24) Item- I give and bequeath unto my daughter Mary McAdoo and to be delivered unto her when she comes of age, one bed and furniture at her Mothers discretion one Horse saddle and bridle in value equal to the one her sister, Sarah got, one cow and calf and one hundred dollars in other property.

Item- I constitute, ordain and appoint my dearly beloved Margaret and my son David McAdoo my whole and sole Executors of this my last Will and Testament, signed, sealed and acknowledged this twentieth & Sixth day of Febuary Annodomoni 1815, in the presence of Samuel McAdoo

   her
Thomas X Burkett   David McAdoo (seal)
   mark

Court of Pleas and Quarter Session April Term 1815. The last Will and Testament of David McAdoo deceased was produced in open court and proven by the oaths of Samuel McAdoo and Thomas Burkett and ordered to be received and recorded April 14th 1815.

                   Field Farrar, Clk.

State of Tennessee, Dickson County, March 15th 1817. Then was the last Will and Testament of David McAdoo Recorded in Book A page 33-34-35.

                   Field Farrar, Clk.

(THOMAS RICHARDSON No. 16)

Dickson County State of Tennessee. In the name of God Amen. I THOMAS RICHARDSON being weak in body but in sound mind and memory blessed be Almighty God for the same, do publish and make this my last Will and Testament in manner and form following, that is to say, First, to my beloved Wife Winnefred Richardson I give and bequeath all my singular stock of Cattle, Horses, Hogs, Sheep &C, and all my household furniture and all things pertaining to the premises whereon I now live for the purpose of raising and Schooling my children (25) and also for the said purpose she is to have the use of the plantation and premisis whereon I now live also the use of three negroes, that is March, John and Charlotte, during her natural life or widowhood and at her decease or marriage I give and devise to my son Thomas J

Richardson his heirs and assigns all that my Messuage or tenament whereon I now live with the Appurtenance lying and being in the County of Dickson and State of Tennessee containing by estimation one hundred and fifty acres and I also give and bequeath to my said son at my wife's death or marriage the above named fellow March. And to my Daughter Frances Richardson I give and bequeath at the death or marriage of my wife the above named negro fellow John, and to my Daughter Elizabeth Tatom I give and bequeath one negro man named Ben to be given up when his time for which he is now hired expired and negro girl Charlotte and her increase if any to be equally divided between my son Thomas J Richardson and my Daughter Frances Richardson and it is my will that she nor her increase if any should not be sold out of the family and to my Daughter Margaret Blount I having already provided for her by Deed of Gift I give and bequeath one Cow and Calf and I also give and bequeath to Elizabeth Tatom my Daughter and Sally Walker, each one Cow and Calf be it understood that Winnified Richardson my wife is to pay over the said Cows and Calves when she can conveniently spare them and I do hereby appoint my beloved Wife Winnified Richardson my sole Executors to this my last Will and Testament hereby revoking all former Wills by me made. In witness whereof I have hereunto set my seal this the first day of February in the year of our Lord one thousand eight hundred and fifteen.

(26) Signed, Sealed and delivered, to be the last Will and Testament in presence of us who have hereunto subscrubed our names as witness in presence of the Testator.

    Test-
    John Willey
    Abriam Caldwell   his
    JohJohn Mabin   Thomas X Richardson   (seal)
                                                  mark

I Thomas Richardson of the State of Tennessee and County of Dickson do this 20th May 1816 make and publish this Codicile to my last Will and Testament in manner following, that is say provided that if either of my children that is Thomas J Richardson should die before they come of age that whatsoever I have I have in Will to which this is Codicil left to either of them shall fall to the surviving one in as full a manner as if had willed such part solely to the one so surviving and lastly it is my desire that this my present Codicil be annexed to and make a part of my last Will and Testament to all interests and purposes. In witness whereof I have hereunto set my hand and seal this day and year above written.

                                          his
                                Thomas X Richardson   (seal)
                                      mark

Signed, sealed, published and declared by the above named Thomas Richardson as a Codicil to be annexed to his last Will and Testament in presence of Abiram Caldwell, John Willey, John Mabin.

Winnifrid Richardson comes into court and presents the last Will and Testament of Thomas Richardson and qualified as executrix thereto and gave bond with David Irvin Lebius Richardson in the sum of $ 3.000.

(CLAUDIAS DAVID L No. 17)
In the name of God Amen. I CLAUDIAN DAVID L. of the County of Dickson and State of Tennessee being low in health but of sound mind and memory blessed be God for the same do this eighteenth day of February in the year of our Lord one thousand eight hundred and sixteen

(27) make and ordain this my last will and Testament in manner following.

First-I give to Jacob Johnson, son of Isac Johnson the sum of four hundred dollars a part of which to be laid out in giving said Jacob Johnson his education the ballance he is to remain on his arrival to the age of twenty one years of age but should he not arrive to the age of twenty one years of age but should he not arrive to the age of twenty one years I give the balance of the four hundred dollars to my wife Elizabeth David L.

Secondly- I give and bequeath to my wife Elizabeth David L. the tract of land whereon I now live containing eight hundred and twenty four acres more or less. Also I give to my wife Elizabeth David L. the tract of land conveyed to me by William Segg containing two hundred and eighteen acres more or less known by the name of Cave Spring tract.

Thirdly- I give and bequeath to my wife Elizabeth David L. all my negroes together with all my other property real or personal after all my debts and legacies are paid off. In witness whereof I have set my hand and affixed my seal to this my last Will and Testament the day and date above mentioned.

Claudias David L. (seal)

Signed, sealed published and delivered by the said Claudias David L. the Testator as his last Will and Testament in presence of us who were present at the time of signing and sealing thereof-Thomas Hunter Jenet Copeland, D'ny S. Whitmill.

State of Tennessee, Dickson County, Court of Pleas and Quarter session April Term 1816. Then was produced in open Court the last Will and Testament of Claudias David L. and proven by the oaths of (28) Thomas Hunter and Jarret Copeland two of the subscribing witness thereto and ordered to be recorded.

Field Farrar, Clk.

(REVES ADAMS No. 18)

In the name of God Amen. I REAVES ADAMS of the County of Dickson in the State of Tennessee, being weak in body but of sound sense, mind and memory at the time yet knowing the uncertainty of the earthly life and that it is appointed for man to die and after death to judgement do make this my last Will and Testament in manner and form following:

First- I recommend my Soul to Almighty God that Gave it and by the merits of Jesus Christ I trust and believe to be saved, and my body to be burried in such decent and Christian like manner as my Executor hereafter named shall think proper and as for temporal estate, and whatsoever else God hath been pleased to bestow on me I give and bequeath as follows-My Will and desire is that all my just debts shall (29) be paid and my funeral expenses discharged Also my Will is that my loving Wife Sarah Adams as soon as she shall find it convenient sell the land on which we now live and make a deed to the same, and the money arising from the sole of the land with the addition of two hundred and fifty dollars to be collected and made out of my personal estate, that is not otherwise appointed and more if my wife deems it nesessary be applied to the payments of a tract of land which tract of land so purchased is to be and to remain to her during her natural life and at her decease the said tract of land to be sold and the money arising therefrom to be equally divided between all my children.

Item- I give and bequeath to my loving wife during her natural life a negro girl named Mary and at my Wife's decease if my son Howell Collen Adams is twenty years of age that then the said negro, Mary and all her increase be sold to the highest bidder on twelve months credit and all the moneys arising therefrom to be equally divided between all my children, to wit, Cinthy Adam, Lillah Adams, Sarah Adams, Benjamine Johnson Adams, William Adams, Thomas Adams, and Howell Calbier Adams, to be to them their heirs and assigns forever and the same measure to take place with the monies arising from the sale of the land and all the remaining part of my estate of every kind I give and bequeath my loving wife to raise and School my children and give to them as they marry or come of age as she can spare or thinks proper, and at her decease to be disposed of between my children share and share alike to be to them and their heirs and assigns for ever provided she remains a widow and should she marry I assign her the fourth part of the last mentioned property, and the remaining three fourths to be equally divided between my children.

    Lastly-I constitute and appoint my loving wife Sarah Adams whole and sole Executrix of this my last Will and Testament revoking and making void all will or wills by me family made, pronouncing and declaring this to be my last Will and Testament in the presence of the subscribing witnesses. In Testimony whereof I have hereunto set my hand seal the twenty-first day of August Annodomino 1870.

John Humphreys   Reaves Adams   (seal)
John Davidson
John Luke

    State of Tennessee, Dickson County, January Pleas & Quarter Session 1818. This day was proven in open court the last Will and Testament of Reves Adams deceased by the oaths of John Humphreys and John Davidson which was ordered to be recorded and certified accordingly.

                                               Field Farrar, Clk.

(JOHN BUGG No. 19)

    I, JOHN BUGG of the County of Dickson and State of Tennessee do hereby make my last will and Testament in manner and form following, that is to say-

    First-After the payments of all my just debts and funeral expenses.

    Secondly-I leave to my wife Elizabeth Bugg all my estate both real and personal during her natural life as understand and at her death as mamage to be equally divided between my son Willis Bugg and my daughter Chanie Bugg and my son Samuel Bugg, my daughter Elizabeth Bugg and my son Allen Bugg, to them and their heirs forever.

    Thirdly- to my daughter Mary Wall Seventy-five cents to her heirs forever. I give to my daughter Tennessee Loveacks twenty five cent to her heirs forever. I give to my daughter Winefred Hicks twenty five cents to her and her heirs forever. I give to my daughter Sally Richardson twenty five cents to her and her heirs forever, I give to my son Jermiah Bugg twenty-five cents to him and his heirs forever. I give to my daughter Dorcas Bugg twenty five cents to her and her heirs forever. I give to my son William Bugg twenty five cents to him and his heirs forever. i give to my son Henry Bugg twenty five cents to him and his heirs forever. I give unto my son Stiles Bugg twenty five cents to him and his heirs forever. And lastly I do appoint my friends Reuben Gunn and Charles Hedges my Executors of this my last Will and testament, revoking all other former wills or testaments by me heretofore made in witness whereof. I have hereunto set my hand and affixed my seal this 27th of June in the year of 1809.

Signed, Sealed, published and)
delivered as the last Will and)   his
testament of the above names,)   John X Bugg   (seal)
John Bugg in presence of us-   mark
William Gunn
Isaac Huges
Lewis Evans

    State of Tennessee, Dickson County, January Term 1818. Then was

(31) the last Will and testament of John Bugg proven in open court by the oaths of William Gunn and Lewis Evans and ordered to be certified accordingly.

              Field Farrar, Clk.

 State of Tennessee) March 2nd 1821
 Dickson County) Then was the last Will and testament of John Bugg recorded in book page 41-42.

              Field Farrar, Clk.

(JAMES DUNNEGAN No.20)

 In the name of God Amen. The last will and testament of James Dunnegan of the State of Tennessee and County of Dickson considering the uncertainty of this Mortal life and being of soung mind and memory do make and publish this my last will and testament in manner and form following, VIZ!

 First I give and bequeath unto my oldest son John Dunnegan one sorrell mare bridle and saddle which he now claims, one Cow and Calf I do also give and bequeath unto my Second Son William Dunnagan one sorrell mare and Colt saddle and bridle one Cow and Calf. I do give my sons John and William Dunnagan all my right and title of the Barbour tract of land to be equally divided between them. I do also give and bequeath unto my three younger Sons, Charles, James and Andrew Dunnagan the hundred acre tract of land whereon I now live together with the forty acres timbered land. Also the forty acre tract I bought of Wyatt Fussell to be equally divided amongst them when the youngest of them shall attain the age of twenty-one years. I also nominate and appoint my son Charles to have the care of said premises to manage with care and prudence for his own support, and also for support of his younger brothers and sister, VIZ, Elizabeth Dunnegan, Ailsey Dunnagan, Matilda Dunnagan, Susannah Dunnagan, during the term of their infancy or single life. I will each of them one Horse Bridle & Saddle one Bed and furniture. It is my desire that they should be put in posession of the above named property at the age of twenty one years or on the day of their marriage. It is furthermore my will and (32) desire that all the remainder of my personal property which is or may be hereafter accumulated from the profits of the said premises be equally divided between my three sons VIZ, Charles, James and Andrew, and my four daughters VIZ, Elizabeth, Ailsey, Matilda and Susannah. I do also nominate and appoint my son Charles Dunnagan of the State of Tennessee and County of Dickson, and William Edwards Senr. of the same State and County aforesaid sale Executors of this my last Will and Testament thereby revoking all former Wills by me made. In witness whereof I have hereunto set my hand and affixed my seal this 30th day of September 1818. Signed sealed published and declared by the above named James Dunnagan to be his last Will and Testament in the presence of us who have hereunto subscribed our names as witnessess in the presence of the Testator.

              James Dunnagan (seal)

Test-
Calvin W. Eason
Solomon Graham
Joseph J Eason

 State of Tennessee, Dickson County, October Term 1818. Then was the last Will and Testament of James Dunnagan deceased was proven in open Court by the oaths of Solomon Graham and Joseph J Eason and proven and ordered to be recorded.

              Field Farrar, Clerk.

State of Tennessee, Dickson County, March 2nd 1821. Then was the last Will and Testament of James Dunnagan recorded in page 42-43.
Field Farrar, Clerk

(SOLOMON RYE No. 21)

In the name of God Amen. I, SOLOMON RYE of the County of Dickson and State of Tennessee being in perfect mind and memory calling to mind the mortality of my body do make and ordain this my last will and Testament in the manner and form as hereafter followeth:

(33) First-I bequeath and give unto my beloved Solomon Rye the place and plantation whereon he now lives, beginning at a stake on William Hoopers north boundary line and runs northward to a large Chesnut tree, thence a northeast course to Edward Jones north west corner of his tract of land, thence along said Jones line South to the above said William Hoopers line to the above named Stake.

2nd- I bequeath and give unto my beloved son William Rye, a parcel of ground the place and plantation whereon he now lives, beginning at Stake on William Hoopers northward to a large Chestnut tree, thence north east to Edward Jones north west corner, thence West to a corner on Jesse Lumsdens line, thence South to the said Lumsdens South east corner of his tract of land, thence west with the said Lunsdens line to his South west corner, thence South up the creek to John Adames, South east corner thence East to the beginning on the fore mentioned Stake.

3rd-I bequeath and give to my beloved Daughter Sarah B Rye while living single the use of the houses and plantation with all privileges appertaining thereto with the upper field where I now live and have tilled and after her marriage or death they shall be as will has heretofore discribed and it is my will and desire that my son Solomon have use of the upper sugar orchard giving William Hoopers line. It is also my desire and will that both my sons Solomon and William have equal and free use of my apple and Peach Orchards.

4th-It is my will and desire that my household and kitchen furniture with tools, stock of every kind and every special of utensils both in and out be equally divided among my three surviving children that is to say Solomon, William and Sarah B.

5th-It is my Will and desire also that the heirs of my beloved Daughter Martha Weaver deceased shall have one dollar and the horse, Cattle and what property that was in their possession at the time of her decease &C.

6th-It is my will and desire that my Grand Daughter Dorcas Weaver Daughter of Martha Weaver deceased shall have twenty pounds of Feathers for a bed with case or ticking for the same which I expept prévious to the division of Solomon, William and Sarah B.

Lastly-It is my will & desire that my surviving children, VIZ, Solomon Rye, William Rye, and Sarah B. Rye be sole Executors and Executrix to manage all, and every part of my estate in the manner and form before directed by me and I do hereby decree, this my last Will and Testament revoking all others &C, given my hand this 15th day of August in the year of our Lord Eighteen hundred and eighteen.

Solomon Rye (seal)

(34) Test-
George Bowen
William Given
Sterling Dillihay

State of Tennessee, Dickson County, January Term 1819. Then was the within Will and Testament of Solomon Rye deceased produced in open court and proven by the oaths of George Brown and Sterling Dillihay and ordered to be recorded.

Field Farrar, Clerk.

Recorded in Book A and page 44-45-46 this 2nd day of March 1821.
Field Farrar, C.D.C.

(WILLIAM HUDSON No. 22)

In the name of God Amen. I WILLIAM HUDSON of Dickson County and State of Tennessee being of a low state of health but of a sound mind and disposing memory but calling to mind the mortality of the body and that it is appointed for man to die do make constitute and appoint this my last Will and Testament in manner and form following, to wit;

First-and principally, I give and bequeath my Soul into the hands of Almighty God who gave it and my body to the dust to burried in Christian burial at the direction of my Executors and as to what Worldly Estate it has been pleased God to bestow on me I give and bequeath in manner and form the following, to wit, I lend to my beloved wife Taffincous Hudson, all my estate except such as shall be hereafter named during her natural life.

Secondly-I give to my son Baker Hudson, one negro woman named Mary and her three Children Arizilla, Susan and Charles to him and his heirs forever.

Thirdly-It is my will and desire that my Daughter Elizabeth Marsh shall have the use of a negro boy named Jacob from and after the first day of February next during the life of my wife aforenamed and at her death the said boy to be returned to my estate for a division to take place of all my slaves, that is not otherwise disposed of.

Fourthly-I give to my son William Hudson, four negro slaves by name, Edith, Bronce, Thornhill and Carry to him and his heirs forever.

Fifthly-I give to my Daughter Polly F. Russell one negro girl named Filda to her and her heirs forever.

Sixth-I lend to my Daughter Taffenons Eason one negro girl named Viny, and her two children, Lucinda and Matilda to her and her heirs forever.

Seventhly-I give unto my son, Thomas C. Hudson one negro girl named Susan and also I give unto said Thomas fifty two acres of land in four small entries which hold bonds f or rights to him and his heirs forever.

Eightly-I lend to my daughter Carry M. Hudson one negro named Agnis and one Horse, bed and furniture of equal value of those given to my married Daughter, also one Cow and Calf to her and her heirs forever.

Ninthly-I lend unto my Daughter Nancy Hodgins one negro girl named Clory also one Horse, bed and furniture and one Cow and Calf of equal value of these already given to my other daughters to her and her heirs forever.

Tenthly-I I lend to my Daughter Judith J Hudson one negro girl named Eliza and one Horse and bed and furniture of equal value of those given to my other Daughters and one Cow and Calf.

Elaventhly-I lend to my Daughter Rebecca B Hudson one negro girl named Alsy also one Horse bed and furniture and one Cow and Calf of Equal ot those given to my married Daughters to her and her heirs forever.

Twelfthly-I lend to my Ten Children, namely Baker Hudson, Elizabeth Marsh, William Hudson, Polly F Russell, Taffanecous Eason, Thomas C Hudson, Carry M. Hudson, Nancy Hogins, Judith J Hudson and Rebecca B Hudson, all my negroes that have not been specially named in the Will the division of said property to take place at the death of their Mother also all the interest that I have in a suit against the heirs of William Baker decd. in the County of MecKlinburg and State of Virginia to be equally divided amongst the aforenamed Ten Children after Baker Hudson has paid one third part of the Expence of said suit.

Lastly-I give to my eight Children namely Elizabeth Marsh, Polly

(37) F. Russell; Taffenous Eason, Thos. C. Hudson, Cary M. Hudson, Nancy Hogins, Judith J Hudson, Rebecca B Hudson, all my household and Kitchen furniture together with the stock of all kind to be sold and equally divided at the death of their Mother, is my will and desire that all my debts be paid out of my present property. I do hereby appoint Taffenous Hudson my Executrix and William Hudson my Executrix and William Hudson and Thomas C. Hudson my Executors of this my last Will and Testament. In witness whereof I have set my hand and affixed my seal this twenty third day of January one thousand eight hundred and twenty one.

                  Wm. Hudson   (seal)

Signed, Sealed and delivered in presence of us.
Attest-
John Scott
Richardson Tatum
Solomon Graham

 State of Tennessee, Dickson County, April Term 1821. Then was the within Will and Testament of William Hudson deceased proved in open Court and was proved by the oaths of Richard Tatom and Solomon Graham, and ordered to be recorded.
                  Field Farrar, Clk.

 State of Tennessee, Dickson County, April 13th 1821. Then was the within will And Testament of William Hudson Recorded in Book A and pages 46-47-48-49.
                  Field Farrar, Clerk.

(38) (JOHN A. BAKER No. 23)
 In the name of God Amen. I, JOHN A. BAKER of the County of Dickson and State of Tennessee being very sick and   but in perfect mind and memory and calling to mind the mortality of man and knowing that it is appointed once for all men to die I do make and ordain this to be my last Will and Testament in manner and form following that is to say. I give and bequeath my soul to God who gave it and my body to be decently burried. And touching what worldly goods I possess as follows:

 First-I lend to my beloved wife Jane Baker all my estate both real and personal during her natural life or widowhood for the purpose of supporting herself and my youngest children. And at the death or marriage of my wife Jane it is my desire that whatever remains of my estate should be sold and divided amongst the six Children by name, Nelly Baker, Sally Baker, John Baker, Patsey Baker, Benjamine Baker and Nancy Baker to them and their heirs forever.

 2nd-My Daughter Margaret Evans five dollars to her and her forever
 3rd-I give to my Daughter, Polly Hedges, five dollars to her and heirs forever.
 4th-I give to my Daughter Betsy England five dollars to her and her heirs forever.
 5th-I give to my Daughter Jane Evans five Dollars to her and her heirs forever-
 6th-I give to my Daughter Ann Tatom five dollars to her and her heirs forever.
 7th-I give to my son Absolom Baker, five dollars to him and his heirs forever.

 Signed, sealed and published in presence of us 3rd. May 1820.
John Wright   John A Baker   (seal)
George Brozzell
James McKee

State of Tennessee, Dickson County, Court of Pleas and Quarter Sessions, October Term 1820. Then was the last Will and Testament of John A Baker produced in open Court and proved to be the same by the oaths of John Wright, George Brozzell and James McKee and ordered to be recorded.

              Field Farrar, Clerk.

State of Tennessee, Dickson County, April 17th 1821. Then was the last Will and Testament of John A Baker, Recorded in Book A page 49-50.
              Field Farrar, Clerk.

(SETH B. JORDEN No. 24)

In the name of God Amen. I, SETH B. JORDEN, being weak in body but of perfect sound mend and memory do constitute and appoint this to be my last Will and Testament truly revoking and disregarding all others by me made.

 Item 1- I will and devise all my just debts be first paid.

(39) Item 2- I lend my beloved wife Brittannia W. Jorden all the land in Harveys pruchase upon the North side of Leather wood Creek and East side of Yellow Creek during her natural life I do give her a Bed and furniture and my Burgamot Mare, I also give to her negroes Britt, Gin & Charity to her and her heirs forever.

 Item 3- I will & desire that all the lands I own on Yellow and Leatherwood Creek including what I lemt my wife be equally divided according to quality and quantity as near as can be between my three sons, John Augustus, George West & Robert West Jorden.

 I also give my Daughter Mary two thousand dollars to be paid out of the sales of my plantation in North Carolina to be laid out at the discretion of my Executors to buy land for her. I do give my four children before named all the remaining part of my negroes to be equally divided among them as they become of age and apply for their respective shares.

 Item 4th-My will and desire is that all my lands be sold and debts collected and all other property I have in Benfort and Hyde County North Carolina according to direction left with my brother George W. Jorden or for less if that cannot be obtained and the proceeds expended on educating my children if necessary if not to be put at interest for their good and as much used as in suitable. Item-I will and bequeath that all the rest of my property be sold at six months credit and that my wife receive an equal part with my children.

 Item- I hereby constitute and appoint my brother George W Jorden of Hyde County North Carolina my Executor in this my last Will to make sole and execute in every sense the property in North Carolina & I do furthermore constitute and appoint my good friend Robert West

(40) of Dickson County Tennessee to carry into effect the provisions before mentioned and as my sole Executor in Tennessee given under my hand and seal as the last Will and Testament at Mount Vernon on Yellow Creek, 14th April 1822.

              S.B. Jorden (SC)

Casidal To this my last will. I will and desire that my books be not sold but kept by my Executors and by him divided among my children according to his direction 14th April 1822.

              S.B. Jorden (S1)

State of Tennessee, Dickson County, Court of Pleas and quarter Session July Term (1st day of the month) 1822. This day appeared in open court Parry W. Humphreys, John H. Maralile and Bryan Latham who being duly sworn on the Holy Evangelist of Almighty God dispose and say not that they are well acquainted with the hand writing of Seth B Jorden the Testator of the within last Will and Testament having frequently seen him write his name in his lifetime and that they believe that the within said Will and Testament is in the own proper hand writing of the said Seth B Jorden and that the signature and seal thereunto is also in the own proper hand writing of the said Seth B Jorden. It is therefore ordered by the Court that the said last Will & Testament of the said Seth B Jorden proven as aforesaid be certified accordingly and admitted to record agreeable to act of assembly in such case made and provided. In testimony whereof I Field Farrar Clerk of said Court have hereunto set my hand at office, July 18th 1822.

Field Farrar, Clerk.

State of Tennessee, Dickson County, July 18th 1822. Then was the within last Will and Testament of Seth B. Jorden entered in the Book of Record for said County together with the certificate thereto annexed in Book A page 51-52.

Field Farrar, Clerk.

(40) (JOHN HALL No. 25)

In the name of God Amen. I, JOHN HALL of the County of Dickson and State of Tennessee being weak in body but of perfect mind and memory do this seventeenth of May Eighteen hundred & Twenty two make, ordain and publish this my last Will and Testament in manner and form following revoking all others by me made.

1st-It is my Will and desire that all my just debts be paid. It is my will that my son Joseph W. Hall have my negro man named Brick also four hundred and nineteen dollars which sum he has received of me for which he stands charged on my books said negro in left to him and his heirs forever.

He the said Joseph on the receipt of said negro shall pay to my Executors in cash. It is also my Will that my son Joseph Hall have my negro Woman named Penny and her child William said John paying one

(41) hundred dollars in cash on the receipt of said negroes to my Executors I also give to my son John Hall the sum of four hundred and fifteen dollars which sum he received of me and stands charged on my Books.

It is my will that my son Jesse Hall have my negro man named Joe also one hundred acres of land the place where he now lives on, also one hundred and ninety one dollars which sum he had received of me and s stand charged on my Books. It is also my Will that my Daughter Martha have the loan of my negro girl named Caty also one hundred acres of land which she now lives on, including the Duff tract and the residue to be made out of the tract formily belonging to Isaih Healy Beginning on a Gim stump Healeys old original corner running south so as to take two poles out side of Holloway Marrisets fence to a stake, thence west twenty poles to a stake thence South forty poles to a Stake, thence East twenty poles to Healeys old original line thence South with said line so as to include one hundred acres with the Duff tract.

It is my will that the said negro named Caty shall never be sold or traded but remain to Martha and her increase if any she has forever Also one hundred and forty seven dollars which she has received of me & stand charged for.

It is also my will that my Daughter Elizabeth M. Hall have the loan of my negro woman Jamima & her child Juliet also one hundred and fifty dolllars which amount stand charged against her on my books but on the receipt of said negroes she shall pay to my executors the sum of one hundred dollars in Cash said negroes to remain and never sold to her and her heirs forever. It is also my Will that my son David Hall have my negro boy named Edwarda also one hundred and eighty nine acres of

(42) land which family belonged to James Haley & also part to Isaiah Healey lying on both sides of Williamson & Yellow Creek also a horse which he claims&to have to have a twenty dollar saddle.

It is also my will that my son Joshua Hall have a negro girl named Amy also a tract of land known by the Mill Tract, containing one hundred and three acres, also a nineteen acre tract known by the name of the Mace Tract, also the Horse he claims and have a twenty dollar saddle. It is also my Will that my son Berrimon Hall have my negro girl Ester also one half of the tract of land I now live on holding in his share part of the cleared land but he have no share to the buildings or orchard during my wifes natural life or widowhood at my wifes death or intermarriage he will be allowed a full half share of said Tract of land in value. I also give him Colt he claims and to have a twenty dollar saddle. It is also my Will that my Daughter Susainna Hall have the loan of two negro Girls namely Hager and Lucinda also one Horse Briddle and saddle to be worth one hundred Dollars and also one bed and furniture & two Cows and Calves, the above said negroes never to be sold but to remain to her and her heirs forever.

It is also my will that my son Wesley Hall have my negro boy named Robert also the other half of my home tract of land on which I now live but not to have posession infull until the death of my wife or intermarriage the dwelling house, orchards and buildings to be kept for her support during life or widowhood-at her death or intermarriage the said tract as to value will be equally divided between my two last named sons. I also give Abraham a Horse saddle and bridle to be worth one hundred dollars.

2nd-It is my will that my beloved wife Susanna have during her life or widowhood every other species of my property not above named for the support and the five youngest children & for their education. At her death or intermarriage the whole of my property left in her hands to be equally divided between all my children. Should any of the little negroes die before my five children become of age it is my Will that the loss be made good out of my estate left in the hands of my wife. It is my will that my beloved wife be allowed two hundred dollars to be made out of the amount of sales of any of my property together with the three hundred dollars that will be due from my sons, Joseph & John & Daughter Elizabeth, in all five hundred dollars which sum to be appropriated to the purchase of a negro boy for the support of my wife & the raising my youngest children and at her death to be equally divided between all my children as my other property.

Lastly-And make and ordain my beloved wife Susanna and son Jesse Executors of this my last will and Testament. In witnes whereof I the said John Hall have to this my last Will and Testament set my hand and seal the day and year above written.

John Hall (seal)

Signed, sealed, published and declared by the said John Hall the Testator as his last will Testament in the presence of us who were present at the time of signing and sealing thereof.
Test-
William Morrison
Martha Douglass
Mark Reynolds

State of Tennessee, Dickson County, January Session 1823. Then was the within last will and Testament of John Hall deceased produced in open Court and proven to be such by the oaths of William Morrison and Martha Douglass subscribing witnesses thereto and ordered to be recorded.

Field Farrar, Clk.

Then was the last Will and)) State of Tennessee, Dickson County,
Testament of John Hall deceased) January 18th 1823.
recorded in Book A pages 54-55-
56-57.
Field Farrar, Clk.

(44) (JOSHUA JAMES No. 26)

In the name of God Amen. I, JOSHUA JAMES of Dickson County and State of Tennessee do make ordain and declare this instrument which is written for me to be my last Will and Testament revoking all others.

IMPRIMUS) All my debts of which of which there are but few and none of magnitude are to be punctually and speedy paid and the legatees hereafter bequeathed are to be discharged as soon as circumstances will permit and in the manner directed them.

(45) To my dearly beloved wife Aby James I give and bequeath the use profit and benefit of a certain negro girl named Fanny and a certain mare known by the name of Blaze one feather bed and furniture and bedstead the bed that we now lie on one small skillet and one Dutch oven namely our largest new oven for the term of her natural life or widowhood and at the expiration of her natural life or intermarriage the above mentioned negro girl with her increase if any and the bed and furniture and bedstead oven and skillet to be sold to the highest bidder and the money to be equally divided amongst my own children

The mare above mentioned to be at my wifes Will to do as she pleases with. To wit: William James, Thomas James, Amos James, Joshua James, Jamay James, Aby Tucker, Elijah James Jnr. heir of my son Elijah James Senr. Enoch James and Sally James.

Item-At my decease it is my will and desire that all the residue of my estate real and personal that is to say land negroes and property of every description to set up and sold to the highest bidder, and the money to be equally divided amongst above mentioned children.

In witness of all and each of the things herein contained I have set my hand and seal this 24th day of July 1820.
Archibald Pullen
John Stafford   (seal)
George X Powell
       his mark

N.B. It is my will and desire that my sons Amos James and Enoch James to be Executors to the within Will.
Test-
Archibald Pullen   Joshua James

State of Tennessee, Dickson County, July Session 1821. Then was the within last Will and Testament of Joshua James decd. produced in open court and proven to be such by the oaths of Archibald Pullen, John Stofford and Arch George Powell, subscribing witnesses thereto and ordered to be recorded.

Test, Field Farrar, Clerk.

State of Tennessee, Dickson County, March 25th 1823. Then was the last Will and Testament of Joshua James deceased, recorded in Book A Page 58-59.

Field Farrar, Clk.

(JAMES GOODRICH No. 27)

In the name of God Amen. I, JAMES GOODRICH of the State of Tennessee and County of Dickson being sound sense mind and memory thanks be to God do this 29th day of August in the year of our Lord one thousand eight hundred and eighteen make this to be my last Will and Testament, that is to say, I give my soul to Almighty God and by the merits of Jesus Christ I trust and believe to be saved and de- and my body to be buried in such decent manner and christian like as my Executors hereafter named may think proper, and as to my temporal estate and whatsoever else God has been pleased to bestow on me I give and bequeath as follows, VIZ:

My will and desire is that my funeral expences and my just debts be paid first.

(46) Item 1st- I give and bequeath unto my beoved wife Dorthy Goodrich my four negroes named Newborn, Anthony, Rose and Ridley, Also one good Horse saddle ~ bridle with her bed and furniture. I also lend unto my beloved wife during her natural life or widowhood and no longer all my lands on Yellow Creek also all my household and Kitchen furniture, plantation tools and stock of all kinds together with all my money notes and negroes which is not hereafter bequeathed.

Item 2nd- I give and bequeath unto my Daughter Mary Rushing my three negroes named Jane, Raccolina and Bob with all what I have already given her, also three hundred dollars to her and her heirs forever.

Item 3rd- I give and bequeath unto my Daughter Rebecca Hill my three negroes named Ester, Aggy and Jefferson with what I have already given her. Also three hundred dollars to her and her heirs forever.

(47) Item 4th- I give and bequeath unto my Daughter Sarah Bonds my negro girl named Filda with what I have already given her. Also three hundred dollars to her and her heirs forever.

Item 5th- I give and bequeath unto my Daughter Ellinor Hooper my negro girl Harriett with all what I have already given her. Also three hundred dollars to her and her heirs forever.

Item 6th- I give and bequeath unto my Daughter Elizabeth Stanfield my negro girl Sally with allwhat I have already given her. Also tr three hundred dollars to her and her heirs forever.

Item 7th- I give and bequeath unto my Daughter Nancy Sturdivant my negro girl named Lucy with what I have already given her. Also three hundred dollars to her and her heirs forever.

Item 8th- I give and bequeath unto my son George Jackson Goodrich my Wells, Creeklands and two negroes named Hezekiah and Mary. Also a good Horse, saddle and bridle and one bed and furniture and one Cow and Calf unto him and his heirs forever to have in possession when he arrives to the age of twenty-one.

Item 9th- I give and bequeath unto my son William H Goodrich my two hundred and ninety two acres of land that I bought of Alexander Dickson as agent for Alexander McGowen, and my two negroes named Edmond and Seloy. Also a horse, saddle and bridly and bed and furniture one Cow and Calf and unto him and his heirs forever for him to have in his possession when he arrives at the age of twenty one years.

Item 10th- I give and bequeath unto my Daughter Dorthy Goodrich my two negroes named Big Peter and Jenny and one Cow and Calf. Also three hundred dollars to her and her heirs forever for her to have in possession at the age of twenty-one or when married.

Item 11th- I give and bequeath unto my Daughter Patsey Goodrich my two negroes little Peter and Sealy and one Horse Saddle and bridle one bed and furniture and one Cow and Calf. Also three hundred dollars to her and her heirs forever, for her to have in possession at the age of twenty one or when married.

Item 12th- I give and bequeath unto my son James Goodrich my children tract of land and my two negroes named Billy and Cresey, one Horse, saddle and bridle, one bed and furniture and one Cow and Calf unto him and his heirs forever to have in possession when he arrives at the age of twenty one.

Item 13th- I give and bequeath unto my Daughter Charlotte Goodrich my two negroes named Young Dave and Linda, one Horse Bridle and saddle one bed and furniture and one Cow and Calf. Also three hundred dollars to her and her heirs forever to have in posession at the age of twenty one or when married.

(48) Item 14th- I give and bequeath unto my Daughter Alice Goodrich my two negroes named Mercda and Sarah and one Horse Saddle and Bridle one bed and furniture and one Cow and Calf. Also three hundred dollars

and her heirs forever, to have in posession at the age of twenty one or when married.

Item 15th- I give and bequeath unto my son John Goodrich my tract of land where I now live containing four hundred and forty acres. Also the lands I purchased of Ezekiel Norris and my two negroes named Tom, Clarrica, one Horse, saddle and bridle, one bed and furniture and one Cow and Calf to him and his heirs forever. To have in possesion at the age of twenty one.

Item 16th- My will and desire is that my Mother shall be maintained by my wife out of the loaned property as long as she sees proper to live with her.

Item 17th- My will and desire is that all the property that should be lost by death or otherwise that I have willed to my children, that is under age shall be made good out of the loaned property.

Item 18th- My will and desire is that when my youngest son arrives at the age of twenty-one there shall be an equal division of all the undivided property with my seven youngest children VIZ: Wm H Goodrich Dorthy Goodrich, Patsey Goodrich, James Goodrich, Charlotte Goodrich, Alice Goodrich and John Goodrich.

Lastly, Executors- I constitute and appoint to this my last will and Testament my beloved wife Dorathy Goodrich and my Truaty Friend Alexander Dickson whole and sole Executors of this my last will and Testament, declaring this and this to be my last will and Testament making void all other wills by me made. In witness whereof I have hereunto set my hand and seal in the presence of Darrel Y Harris and Robert P. Harris, James Goodrich.

James Goodrich (seal)

(49) State of Tennessee, Dickson County, Court of Pleas and Quarter session January Term 1824. Then was the annexed paper writing purporting to be the last will and Testament of James Goodrich decd. produced in open Court and Darrell Y. Harris and Robert P. Harris subscribing witnesses thereto haveing been duly sworn in open Court testified that the said James Goodrich then in perfect sane and disposing mind having heard the same read executed said paper writing as his last Will and Testament by signing his name thereto in their presence and that they the said Darrell Y. Harris and Robert P Harris at the request of the said James and in his presence subscribed the same as witnesses at the date of the said will whereupon it is ordered by the court that it be duly certified and recorded whereupon Dorthy Goodrich and Alexander Dickson having been duly qualified as Executors of said last will and Testament and having given bond and security satisfactory to the court it is ordered that letters testamentary issue &C.

Test-   Field Farrar, Clerk.

October 20th 1825. When recorded the above will in Book A Page 62-63.   Field Farrar, Clk.

(JORDEN RICHARDSON No. 28)

In the name of God Amen. I, JORDEN RICHARDSON of the County of Greenville Virginia do make and ordain this to be my last will and Testament as follows to wit:

Item-The slaves and other personal estate that I have heretofore loaned to my daughter Rebecca Mason, wife of William Mason, I now give the same to her and her heirs and assigns forever.

Item-The slaves and other personal estate that I have heretofore loaned to my daughter Frances Jackson wife of Coleman Jackson I now give the same with the increase of the said slaves to my said Daughter and to heirs and assigns forever.

Item- The slaves and other personal estate that I have heretofore loaned to my daughter Annie E. Marable, wife of Henry Marable wife of Henry Marable, I now give the same with the increase of the said Slaves to my said Daughter and to her heirs and assigns forever.

Item-I give and bequeath unto my son Stilh Richardson the following slaves, to wit, Edmond, Claburn, Dick, Fairry and her child Tempy, Amey and old Jude. Also all the stock and household furniture given him and household furniture given him and now in his possession to him and his heirs and assigns forever.

Item--I give to my Daughter Amey Richardson a negro girl by the name of Julia with her future increase and one bed and furniture c called hers to her and her heirs forever.

(50) Item-I desire my Executors hereafter named shall dispose of the two tracts of land I own and lying in Brunswick County, one tract containing four hundred and seventeen acres, the other two hundred and ninety acres at the price of not less than four dollars per acre, payable in three equal annul installments and when sold to execute a deed of bargain and sale to the purchases in fee simple in case my said Executors should not immediately dispose of the said land I desire the same shall be leased out until my Daughter Sally marries or arrives at the age of twenty one and then to dispose of the same in any way they may think most advantageous. The money arising from the sale of the aforesaid land and the lease thereof if leased at all I desire, may be equally divided between all my children namely, Rebecca, Frances, Amey, Nancy E. Sally and Stilh to them and their heirs forever.

Item- I give to my Daughter Polly one feather bed and furniture called hers to her and her heirs forever.

Item-I give to my Daughter Sally one negro girl named Phebe together with her future increase to her and her heirs forever.

Item- I desire my Executors hereafter named to dispose of such part of my personal Estate as they shall adjudge most advantageous for my estate and from the sales thereof pay all my just debts.

Item- It is my Will and desire that the residue of my estate be kept together for the support of my beloved wife and unmarried daughters and in case either of my said Daughters should marry I desire that she or they shall have allotted to her or them an equal portion of the slaves to be kept together after taking therefrom one third part to be assigned my said wife as dower in case all my said Daughters shall marry in this clause I wish it to be understood that the said
(51) estate is to be kept together as aforesaid during the natural life of my beloved wife and after her death two thirds of tthe said slaves and their future increase I desire may be divided amongst my said Daughters, Namely, Polly, Amey & Sally the portion of Polly to be taken possession of by my Executors who in this case are to be considered as trustees and out of the profits arising from the said slaves they are to furnish my said Daughter Polly with such necessaries as will support her comfortably, the other third part of the said Slaves to be considered as a part of the residue of my estate the share to be assigned my Daughter Amey and Sally, I give to them and their heirs forever.

Item-Where as I am entitled to an estate consisting of land and slaves at the death of Mary Richardson relect of my Father William Richardson deceased it is my will and desire that after the death of said Mary Richardson that the slaves that fall to me by her death be equal divided among my children namely, Rececca Frances, Nancy E. Stilh Amey And Sally and in case either of my asid children shall die before the happening of that event leaving a child or children it is my desire that they shall draw the same proportion to which their ancestors would entitled from this clause. The land to be sold by my

Executors on such terms as they shall adjudge most advantageous and the profits of the sale divided as the slaves all of which I give to them and their heirs forever.

Item-It is my will and desire that after the death of my wife the land whereon I now live shall be sold by Executors on one two and three years credit the proceeds of the sale of the said land together with all the rest and residue of my Estate not heretofore give away I desire may be divided relative to the Estate now in the possession of Mary Richardson and will be seen in the next preceeding clause (52) and furthermore it is my will and desire that after the death of my Daughter Polly that the slaves left in the hands of my Executors for her support and maintenance be divided in the same manners, to wit, among my children Rebecca, Frances, Nancy E. Stith Amey & Sally and the desendants of either of them as shall die before my wife. The desendant taking the part to which their ancestors would have been entitled to them and their heirs forever.

Lastly-I do hereby nominate constitute and appoint my beloved wife Eliza and my son Stith Richardson and my son-in-law William Mason, Executors of this my last Will and Testament. In testimony whereof I have hereunto set my hand and seal this seventh day of June 1800 and twenty. The interleneations and erosures in this Will made before assigned.

           Jorden Richardson (seal)

Signed, sealed, published and declared by the Testator as his last Will and Testament in presence of

        Edmunds Mason
          her
        Edison X Bailey
          mark

State of Tennessee, To Thomas Spencer and Benjamine Macklin Esquires know you that we trusting to your deligence and prudent circumspection require you at such certain times and places as you shall appoint to cause to come before you Edmund & Mason and Edwin Bailey Witnesses in behalf of Stith Richardson Executors of the last Will and Testament of Jorden Richardson, deceased in a certain controversey in our court of Pleas and Quarter Session for the County of Dickson depending between the said Stith Richardson Executors of the last Will and Testament of Jorden Richardson deceased and Henry (53) H Mariable and Ann E. Mariable his wife and them diligently examine toughing the same in solemn form on oath or affirmation and having received their examination as aforesaid you shall destinctly plainly and without delay send and certify the same enclosed together with this Writ to our Court of Pleas and Quarter Session to be held for the County of Dickson at the Court house in the town of Charlotte on the first Monday in October next, Witness, Field Farrar Clerk of said Court at office the first Monday in July in the year of our Lord 1824 and 49th year of the Independence of the United States.

           Test-Field Farror Clerk of
             said Court.

State of Virginia, Granville County, Sc. By virtue of the foregoing commission to us directed we Thomas Spencer and Benjamine Maclin Justices of the Peace for the County of Granville and State of Virginia have this day caused Edmund Mason and Edwin Bailey subscribint witnesses to the Will of Jorden Richardson deceased hereto annexed and in the said Commission mentioned to come before us at Sandy Grove in the County of Granville aforesaid on the first day of September 1824 and they having been first duly sworn on the holy evangelist of Almighty God attested the said Will in due form & reason that the said Jorden Richardson signed and published the writing aforesaid

(54) hereunto annexed as his last Will and Testament (but it appears to the deponent that the said Will has since the acknowledgement thereof changed or attend in this, to win in the devise to Amey Richardson a slave by the name of Julia has be substituted for the slave originally devised) that the said Jorden Richardson was in their opinion of sound mind and disposing memory and that the said Edmund Mason and Edwin Bailey subscribed their names thereto as witnesses in the presence and at the request of the said Testator given under our hands and seals this first day of September in the year Eighteen hundred and twenty four.

             Thomas Spencer J.P. (seal)
             Benjamine Madin J.P. (seal)

 State of Virginia, Granville County, To wit:
 I, Edmund Mason, Clerk of the County Court of Granville aforesaid do hereby certify that Thomas Spencer and Benjamine Madin whose signatures are annexed to the within certificate are acting Justices of the Peace in and for the County aforesaid duly commissioned and qualified as such and full faith and credit is due to their official acts. In testimony whereof I have hereunto set my hand and affixed the County seal this sixth day of September one thousand and eight hundred & Twenty four.
      (seal)   E. Mason, C.G.C.

 State of Virginia, Granville County, To Wit:
 I, Esaw Goodwyn presiding Justice of the Peace in and for the County of Granville aforesaid do hereby certify that Edmund Mason is Clerk of the said Court and that his Attestation as above in in due form. Witness my hand and seal this 6th day of September 1824.
          Esaw Goodwin P.J.P.

(JOHN HUMPHREYS No. 29)
(55) In the name of God Amen. I, JOHN HUMPHREYS OF the County of Dickson in the State of Tennessee being weak and feeble in body but of sound mind and sound in memory thanks be to divine providence do make this my last will and Testament revoking and making void all will or wills by me previously made. I recommend my soul to Almighty God and by the merits of Jesus Christ I trust to be saved for Christ is my hope and as for my temporal estate that the Lord has been pleased to bestow on me I give and bequeath as follows:

 My will is that all my just debts shall be paid and every necessary expence discharged in carring my will into complete effect.

 Impinnus, I give and bequeath to my son John Howard Humphreys a negro woman named Dorcus, a feather bed and furniture bedstead & cord. I have already let him have to him and his assigns.

 Item- I give and bequeath to Amos Reynolds in right of my Daughter Clarida whom he intermarried with one dollar and twenty five cents she dieing and left no issue. Likewise I give and bequeath to the said Amos Reynolds one dollar and twenty-five cents in right of his marriage with my Daughter Sophia whom he left in a state of pregnancy with her third child in and has remained from her ever since, therefore I consider him as not entitled to any more to him his heirs and Assigns.

 Item- I give and bequeath to my son Horatio Humphreys negro man named Waynick and a negro girl named Chonce, my surveyors, instruments and a feather bed and furniture with what I have already let him have to him and his assigns.

 Item-I give and bequeath to my son-in-law John T Patterson a negro man named Glaster toget her with what I have already let him have, to him, and his assigns and I give to his Daughter Polly White Patterson my grand Daughter my stane of red Cambrick Curtains and the Coverlet of the same in place of her dear deceased Mother my Daughter

Dilly.

(56) Item- I give and bequeath to my son-in-law Edward Holley my Whipsaw and to my Daughter Sophia the stand of curtains of mixed colors with the coverlet and as I do not think it safe to gift them with any special property as there are some obstacles, I give to all my daughter, Sophias male children that she now has or may have as well those she had by Amos Reynolds as those she had or may have since her marriage with Edward Holly the land and plantation whereon I now live or the products thereof, share and share alike with survivors.

Likewise, I give to all my daughters Sophia Hollys children male and female as above stated a negro fellow named Joe and a negro woman named Sara and her increase from the time I purchased her, but those lands and negroes are not to be put into the possession of any of the children until the death of their Mother, Sophia Holly and her husband Edward Holly and at their decease then the land to be divided as above and the negroes to be divided equally amongst all the children male and female or the products thereof share and share alike or the survivors of them. The above gifts to Edward Holly and my Daughter Sophia together with what they have received to them and their assigns.

Item-I give and bequeath to my Daughter Jenisha Brown one Dollar and twenty-five cents, Likewise I give and bequeath to my two grandsons John Humphreys Brown, and Asa Madison Brown, my Daughter Jenisa Brown, children a negro woman named Sabra and her increase from the 7th of January 1823 it being the time their Father Asa A Brown did Feloniously steal take and carry her away from me, to be equally divided between them but they are not to take possession of this negro woman or increase until the death of their Mother, and then they are (57) to take possession to be to them and their assigns.

Item- I give and bequeath to my son Stokely Humphreys my crosscut saw and grind stone with what he has already had in possession and as I do not think it safe to Gift him with any land and negro property as there are some disagreeable obstacles. I give to all his children that he now has or may have the land I purchased of Amos Lewis and what I may acquire joining it and two negroes, VIZ:

A negro man named Scippis and a negro woman named Annaky and her increase but these children are not to have possession of the land and negroes until the death of their Father and at his decease this property is to be equally divided between them all share and share alike or the survivors beginning with John Patterson Humphreys and ending with the last child my son Stokley may have to be to them and their assigns.

Item- I give and bequeath to my Grandson Clinton Reynolds a Horse saddle and Bridle, a feather bed, & furniture bedstead and card and a cow and calf out of the Cattle I last let my Daughter Sophia have to him and his assigns.

Item- I give and bequeath to my grandson John Severe Reynolds a Horse, saddle and bridly feather bed and furniture, Bedstead and card and a cow and calf out of the Cattle I last let my Daughter Sophia have to him and his assigns.

Item- I give and bequeath to my grand Daughter Carolina Reynolds a mare, Saddle and Bridle, a feather bed and furniture, bedsteas and card a Cow and Calf out of the Cattle I last let my Daughter Sophia have to be to her and her assigns. My will is that my negro woman Peggy be sold to the highest bidder for ready money and that the money arising therefrom be appointed to the payment of my just debts and (58) defraying and discharging all necessary expences in carring my Will into complete effect and as for my old negro woman Amy my will is t that she be permitted to live with which of my children she pleases but not as a slave and which ever she chooses to live with shall be bound to maintain her as long as she ~~live but she~~ lives but she shall be compelled to live with some of them. My farming utensils to remain on the farm for the use thereof and the remaining part of my estate of every discription that is not given or legacied away or ordered for sale my will is that it be equally divided between my children VIZ: John Howard Humphreys, Horatio Humphreys, and my son-in-law John Tapley Patterson, Edward Holly and Stokley Humphreys share and share alike as equal in value as possible by my Executors and their supervisors hereafter named to them and their assigns forever. Now the crop that I may die possessed of my will is that it be divided equally amongst the above named five devises to enable them to support the stock they may receive the first year. Now the property that is said each child has received is as follows.

(59) First-My son John Howard Humphreys has received a negro boy named Brisis a Horse, saddle, and bridle, and a hundred acres of land in North Carolina and my Son Horatio Humphreys a negro boy named Buckner a more saddle and bridle a Cow and Calf, three little Gilt sows and an occupant claim of an 100 acres. My son-in-law John T. Patterson a negro boy named Anthony a Horse saddle and Bridle a feather bed and furniture a Cow and Calf and a sow and eight pigs. My son-in-law Edward Holly, a feather Bed and furniture, a mare, saddle and Bridle and a Cow and Calf and an old mare in room of a sow and pigs. My Daughter Jenira received on her first marriage a feather bed and furniture, mare, bridle and saddle a cow and calf and a sow and pigs My son Stokley Humphreys a feather bed and furniture a mare saddle and bridle a cow and calf and three little Gelt sows. Now to the children that has not received a negro I have given them two each, in my will striving to make an equal dividion amongst them as possible. Now the reason of my gifting my son Horatio Humphreys with this negro girl Chana is on the account or incourequence of his son my little grand son Benjamine Humphreys who measurable has but the use of one of his Arms and in some measure his having so many children she has always been willed to him. Now my will is that when it shall please God to call me home that my children bury me on the North side of my dear wife's grave and have a small neat tomb erected over our graves out of rock and arched over and made white with good lime Morter and the expence defrayed or payed out of the monies arising from the sale of Peggy.

Lastly-I constitute and appoint my Trusty friend Howard W. Turner superviser and my son Horatis Humphreys and my son-in-law John T. Patterson and Edward Holly Executors to this my last Will and Testament revoking and making void all wills by family made, pronouncing and declaring this to be my last Will and Testament in the presence of the subscribing witnesses.

In testimony whereof I have hereunto set my hand and seal the sixteenth day of September Annodomino 1826.
Robert Whittledge
B.B. Carbon   John Humphreys   (seal)

State of Tennessee, Dickson County, Court of Please and Quarter Session January Term 1827. Then was the last within Will and Testament of John Humphreys decd. produced in open Court and proved by the oaths of Robert Whittedge and Daniel Billups subscribing witnesses thereto which was hhen ordered to be recorded. Then came John T Patterson, Horatio Humphreys, Edward Holly and Howard W. Turner, Executors named in said Will and qualified agreeable to law and gave bond and security in the sum of Ten Thousand Dollars.
                           Test-Field Farrar Clk. of
                           said Court

(60) State of Tennessee, January 2nd, 1827, Dickson County. Then was the last Will and Testament of John Humphreys decd. in Book A. page 69-70-71-72-73.

            Field Farrar, Clerk.

(EPHRIAM BREEDING No. 30)

 In the name of God Amen. Knowing that it is once appointed for all men to die. I am now sick in body but in perfect mind and senses, to wit: I make this my last will and Testament after all my debts are paid I give and bequeath to my wife Mary Breeding all my property to do as she sees proper, this 18th Feby. 1826.

Robert Duke
   her   Ephriam Breeding
Charlotte X Duke
   mark

 State of Tennessee, Dickson County, Court of Pleas and Quarter Session January Term 1827. Then was the last will and Testament of Ephriam Breeding decd produced in open Court and proved by the oaths of Robert Duke, and Charlotte Duke subscribing witnesses thereto and was ordered to be recorded.

           Test- Field Farrar Clerk.

 Then was the last Will and Testament of Ephriam Breeding decd. Recorded in Book A pages 73-74. Field Farrar Clk.

(ADAM WILSON No. 31)

 I, ADAM WILSON of the County of Dickson and State of Tennessee on the 9th day of August in the year of our Lord one Thousand eight hundred and twenty two being sick though of good sound mind and Judgment do make this to be my last Will and Testament in manner and form hereafter named.

 In the first place I give my soul to Almighty God in whom I hope to be saved.

 1st- After all my just debts are paid I give and bequeath my property as follows:

 1st- I give and bequeath to my belove wife Margaret Wilson two (61) hundred acres of land including the improved part & house during her natural life also all my property that I dont hereafter bequeath to my childred also I request of my Executors to purchase a negro girl for the use of my wife Margaret with the money Thomas Parkes is due me when collected.

 Item 2nd- I give and bequeath to my son Joseph Wilson sixty acres of land that I purchased of John Lewis.

 Item 3rd- I give and bequeath unto my son John Wilson sixty acres of land lying in the South east corner of my survey to begin at the beginning corner running west to Joseph Wilsons corner then No. So. as to include said sixty acres.

 Item 4th- I give and bequeath unto my son James Wilson my Stud Horse that he now claims and one-half of the land in value that I have given to my wife her lifetime.

 Item 5th-I give and bequeath to my son.

 Item 6th- I give and bequeath unto my Daughter Margaret Wilson one bed and furniture and all the bed clothing that she claims as hers and my roan mare & her two colts and one saddle.

 Item 7th-I give and bequeath unto my Daughter Nancy Wilson, one bed and furniture and all the bed clothing that she claims and my roan filly, saddly & Bridly and two Cows as the value of them-

 Item 8th- I give and bequeath unto my daughter Lucerria Wilson one bed and furniture and all the clothing that she claims and my sorrell mare colt and one saddle to be purchased for her and when my said

(62) Daughter Luwcena becomes of age and calls for her part of my estate it is my will and desire that my Executor or Executors shall sell as much of my Stock or any property that can be the best spand from the family so as to make my said Daughter Lucrenia part up equal in value with my other Daughters.

Item 9th- It is my will and desire that all my propert y, say, stock of every kind, farming utensils of every kind, household and kitbhen furniture my negro man Henry and a negro that I have requested to br purchased for the use of my wife her lifetime and every thing that is mine that I have not bequeathed shall continue in the family for the benefit of my wife Margaret Wilson and at her death all the said property that is not bequeathed shall be equally divided amongst all my daughters.

Lastly it is my will and desire that my two sons Joseph and John Wilson shall be my Executors to this my last will and testament. Signed and acknowledged to be the last will and testament in the presence of

Test-
Alexander Dickson
Chancey Depenport or Desinport

Adam Wilson

State of Tennessee, Dickson, last of Pleas and Quarter Sessions April Term 1824. Then was the within last will and Testament of Adam Wilson decd. produced in open court and proved by the oaths of Alexander Dickson and Chancey Depenport subscribing witness thereto and ordered to be accorded. Then came Joseph Wilson and John Wilson and qualified as executors of said Will.

Test, Field Farmar, Clk. of said court

State of Tennessee, Dickson County, April 26th 1827. Then was the last Will and Testament of Adam Wilson decd. recorded in Book A pages 74-75-76.

Field Farmar, Clerk

(63) EBENEYER KELLY No. 32)

In the name of God Amen I, EBENEYER KELLY of the County of Dickson in the State of Tennessee considering the uncertainty of this natural life and being of sound mind blessed by Almighty God for the samd do make and publish this my last Will and Testament in manner and form following, that is to say.

First-I give and bequeath to my beloved wife Rachall Kelly, during her natural live all and singular the profits and emotuments of the tract of land in the county of Dickson whereon I now live and after her decease I give and bequeath said land to my beloved nephew Nathan Foster of Kentucky his heirs and asigns forever.

Se condly-I give and bequeath to my said wife Rachall during her natural life all my stock farming tools that are or will be coming to me that thereby she may be enabled to pay all my just debts and to hav e something to support and cheus her in her old age and at her death I will that all that is left of the above named articles shall go to the proper use and behoof of the said Nathan Foster his heirs and assigns forever.

Thirdly- I will that my other tract of land of one hundred and thirty acres are in said County of Dickson should be kept in the hands of my Executors for the purpose of being sold for the support of my said wife Rachall provided that from age and that should be necessary and provided also that the other that the other bequeath that I have made her in this my last will and testament should prove insufficient for her support and after her death I will that all my estate both real and personal shall go to my said nephew

Nathan Foster whom with Abiram Caldwell I hereby revoking all former Wills by me made. In witness whereof I have hereunto set my hand and seal this 21st Feb. 1826.

                                               his
                                       Ebeneyer X Kelly
                                            mark

    Signed, sealed, published and declared by the above named Ebeneyer Kelly to be his last will and testament in presence of us who have hereunto subscribed our names as witness in the prisence of the Testators-
Thomas Richardson
(64) Joseph Willey
Polly Willey

    State of Tennessee, Dickson County, Court of Pleas and Quarter Session, July term 1827. Then was the within last will and testament of Ebenayer Kelly decd. produced in open Court and proven by the oaths of Thomas Richardson and Joseph Willey two of the subscribing witness thereto and was these orders to be recorded. Then came Nathan Foster one of the Executors named in said will and quallified according to law.

                                Test- Field Farmar, Clk. of
                                        said court
State of Tennessee, Dickson County, April 26th 1827. Then was the last Will and Testament of Ebeneyer Kelly deceased recorded in Book A page 76-77.

                                       Field Farmar, Clk.

(JOHN TURNER) No. 33
    In the name of God Amen. I, JOHN TURNER of Dickson County, State of Tennessee being in perfect mind and memory not knowing have how soon it please God to call me, I do make this my last Will and Testament.
    First- I do give and bequeath to my beloved wife Elizabeth Turner, the plantation whereon I now live together with all the personal property and thrrr negroes, VIZ, Peter, Loviea and mine during her natural life or widowhood but if she should marry or at her death for the above property to be equally divided between all my children. I also give and bequeath unto my Samuel Turner the land whereon he now lives. I give and bequeath to my William Turner, one horse out of the above property at the death of my wife I also give my wife fifteen dollars that my son Howard has on his hands. I futher appoint my son Samuel Turner and my wife Elizabeth my executors.
    Witness my hand seal this 28th June A.D. 1820.
Test-
Jessie May   his   John Turner   (seal)
Willis Norworthy, John X Dunning
                    mark

    State of Tennessee, Dickson County, Court of Pleas and Quarter Sessions Jan. Term 1824. Then was the within last Will and Testament
(65) of John Turner Senr. produced in open Court and proven by the oaths of John Dunning and Willis Norworthy subscribing witness thereto and ordered to be recorded. Then came Samuel Turner one of the executors in said will and qualified according to Law.
                                       Test- Field Farmer, Clerk
    State of Tennessee, Dickson County, April 26th 1827. Then was the last Will and Testament of John Turner Senr. recorded in Book A page 78-
                                       Field Farrar, Clerk.

(LUCY HUDSON No. 34)
    In the name of God Amen. I, LUCY HUDSON of the County of Dickson

(66) and State of Tenn. being low in health but of sound mind and memory knowing the certainty of death and the uncertainty of life do 1st desire to commit my body to the earth from whence it was taken to be burrried with decancy.

Secondly- I commit my soul to God who gave it, do this day make and constitute my last will and testament, to Wit, First: I desire that my lawful debts and contracts be paid out of my property is as following, VIZ, a negro woman named Nancy another negro named Mary 3, Madison 4, Emasuel 5th, George together with all my stock of every description with that of my household and kitchen furniture after my debts are paid. I wish for my Son Cluthlept Hudson and my daughter Susan Hudson and my son Christpher Hudson and my son Christpher Hudson equally to devide the residue between them without making of a sale. In testimony whereof I have hereto set my hand and seal this 15th day of March 1825.

Signed in presence of
David Gray
Merior Bibb
Edward Tidwell

          her
Lucy X Hudson   (seal)
        mark

State of Tennessee, Dickson County, Court of Pleas and Quarter Sessions, July term 1825. Then was the within last will and testament of Lucy Hudson decd. produced in open Court and proven by the oath of David Gray, Missor Bibb and Edward Tidwell and ordered to be recorded.

        Test- Field Farrar, Clerk of
        said Court

State of Tennessee, Dickson County, April 26th 1827. Then was the above last Will and Testament of Lucy Hudson decd. recorded in Book A Page 79.   Field Farrar, Clerk

(STEPHEN THOMAS No. 35)

In the name of God Amen. I, STEPHEN THOMAS of the County of Dickson and State of Tennessee considering the uncertainty of this Mortal life and being of sound and perfect mind and memory blessed be to God for the same do make and publish this my last will and Testament in manner and form following that is to say, First: I leave my Soul to God imploring his special blessings thereon for Christs sake.

Secondly-My Will and desire is that all my just debts be paid.

(67) Third- I will, leave and bequeath unto my two sons John C Thomas and William Thomas all my books, My watch and wearing apparel to be equally divided between them.

Fourth-I leave and bequeath unto my beloved Wife May Thomas all my land my negroes, horses, cattle, hogs with all my tools and plantation utensils and all my household and kitchen furniture with all other articles, debts dues or demands whatsoever not heretofore named or bequeathed during her natural life and at her death what may then be remaining of my said estate to be sold and equally divided between my three surviving sons, and Daughters and lastly I hereby nominate and appoint my beloved wife Mary Thomas my sole Executrix to this my last Will and Testament hereby revoking all former Wills by me made. But it is to be understood that my desire that my said Executrix be permitted to administer on this my last Will and Testament without giving any security for her performance.

In testimony whereof I the said Stephen Thomas have hereunto set my hand and seal this twentieth day of August one thousand and eight hundred and twenty four.

        S. Thomas   (seal)

Signed, sealed, published and declared by the named Stephen Thomas to be his last Will and Testament in the presence of us who have hereunto subscribed our names as witnesses in prisence of the Testator.

D. McAdoo
Robert Livingston

State of Tennessee, Dickson County, Coubt of Pleas and Quarter Session, July Term 1825. Then was the last Within last Will and Testament of Stephen Thomas decd. produced in open Court and proven by the oaths of David McAdoo and Robert Livingston subscribing witnesses thereto and ordered to be recorded.

Test-   Field Farrar, Clerk.

(68) State of Tennessee, Dickson County, April 26th 1827. Then was the last Will and Testament of Stephen Thomas decd. Recorded in Book A. pages 80-81.

Field Farrar, Clerk.

(JOSEPH DAVIDSON No. 36)

In the name of God Amen. I, JOSEPH DAVIDSON of Dickson County and State of Tennessee being of sound mind but of low state as to health do make and ordain this my last Will and Testament as follows, to w wit, I will and bequeath unto my beloved wife Elizabeth Davidson all debts dues and demands justly owing to my estate after the payment of my just debts, which I wish paid out of the first money collected from debtors. I also Will and bequeath unto my above named wife my house and Lands during her natural life or widowhood, together with all my household and kitchen furniture, plantation Utensils, Stock and Crop of every description for the support of herself and family. In case of my Wife Elizabeth marring again I wish an equal division of my property to take place and my beloved Wife to have an equal part agreeable to the number of my children to have a and to hold in fee simple and to bequeath or devise in any manner she may think proper, the property hereinafter named excepted I will and bequeath unto my son Aquilla when he shall arrive to the age of twenty one my negro boy Edd now about fourteen years of age, nevertheless I wish my wife to have the use of said Edd until my son should arrive at the age of twenty one for the support of herself and children and educating of them. I would be understood the boy Edd bequeaths to my son Aquilla is to be considered as so much of his part of my estate at the time of a final division as I wish an equal division of my property amongst my childrenngiving one no more than another, and I do hereby constitute and appoint my brother John Davidson and my brother-in-law Aquilla Tidwell my true and lawful Executors to execute this my last Will and Testament. In testimony whereof I have hereunto set my hand and affixed my seal this 6th day of November, in the year of our Lord 1824.

Joseph Davidson (seal)

Assigned sealed and delivered in presence of us,
Muckins Carr
Edward Tidwell
Sally Grigsby

State of Tennessee, Dickson County, Court of Pleas and Quarter Session, July Term 1825. Then was the within last Will and Testament of Joseph Davidson decd. produced in open Court and proved by the oaths of Muckins Carr and Edward Tidwell subscribing witnesses thereto and ordered to be recorded, then came John Davidson and Aquilla Tidwell Executors appointed in said Will and Qualified according to Law.

Test-Field Farrar, Clerk

State of Tennessee, Dickson County, April 26th 1827. Then was the last Will and Testament of Joseph Davidson dec'd. Recorded in Book A Pages 81-82.

Field Farrar, Clerk

(MOSES EASLEY No. 37)

(69) In the name of God Amen. I, MOSES EASLEY of the State of Tennessee and County of Dickson being very sick and weak in imperfect health of body but of and of perfect mind, and memory thanks be given unto God calling into mind the mortality of my body and knowing that it is appointed for all men once to die do make and ordain this my last Will and Testament that is to say, princepally and first of all I give and recommend my soul into the hands of Almighty God that gave it and my body recommended to the earth to be burried in a decent Christian burial at the discretion of my Executors nothing doubting but at the general resurrection I shall receive the same again by the mighty power of God and as touching such worldly estate wherewith it has pleased God to bless me in this life I give divise and dispose of the same in the following manner and form. First- I give and bequeath to Emialine my dear beloved wife this negro man named Elleck, also one roan mare, two Cows and Calves, six head of sheep fifteen head of

(70) hogs, one bed and furniture one chest, one loom, one wheel and cards two Pots, two ovens, two skillets, one pair of Dog irons one pot Rack one Plow and Gear, two hoes one axe, one Grubbing hoe, one Drawing knife, and Hand saw, also the land whereon said Easley has formerly lived to be the property of his wife until Eliza E. comes of age also his wife to give his three children good English Education this property to belong to his wife and the heirs of her body, also I give my well beloved Daughter Elizabeth Easley one tract of land containing Twenty acres where said Easley now lives, also nine acres then Twenty acres where said Easley now lives, also nine acres then Twenty acres on the North side of Big Harricane Creek also fifty acres to be saved on the West side of said Twenty acres money to be taken our of said estate to save the said fifty acres of land, one cupboard, one bed and furniture, one Flax wheel one check reel, one set of Cups & Saucers one set of Plates, one set of knives and forks. Also I give to my well beloved son James V. Easley one hundred acres of land lying on little Harricane Creek, likewise two hundred and fifty dollars, one Bed and furniture, all profits arising from said land, also I give my well beloved son John H. Easley one hundred acres of land lying in Ships bend on Duck river one bed and furniture and allprofits arising from said land, all property not named in the above Will to be sold next fall, the above named two hundred and fifty dollars to come out of the said property when sold and the balance to be divided equally with the three children. It is my wish for Reuben Comer to see to selling of the property, and dividing of the money as I have directed and I do hereby utterly disallow revoke and disannul all and every other former Testaments, Wills legacies bequests and Executors by me in any wise before named wille d and bequeathed. Ratifying and confirming this and no other to be my last Will and Testament. In witness whereof I have hereunto set my hand and seal this 27th of March in the year of our Lord one thousand eight hundred and twenty four.

Test-
Joel Massie
Michael Light
William H. Varnell

Moses Easley (seal)

State of Tennessee, Dickson County, Court of Pleas Quarter Session July Term 1824. Then was the within last Will and Testament of Moses

(71) Easley dec'd. produced in open Court and thereupon Michael Leight and Joel Massie subscribing witnesses thereto being duly sworn on the Holy Ebangelist made oaths that on the 27th of March 1824 the said Moses Easley, did in their presence sign with his own proper hand and publish the same as his last Will and Testament and that at the request of the said Testator they subscribed in his presence the said last Will and Testament of said Easley as Witnesses of the same and the same is ordered to be recorded.

Test-Field Farrar, Clerk of said Court.

State of Tennessee, Dickson County, April 27th 1827. Then was the last Will and Testament of Moses Easley dec'd. Recorded in Book A. pages 83-84-85.

Field Farrar Clk.

(JOHN BAKER NO. 38)

State of Tennessee, Dickson County, To all whom these may come, Greetings. Know Ye that this day came WILLIAM BAKER before me John Humphreys an acting Justice of the Peace for the County aforesaid, at the request of Rebecca Baker widow of Hohn Baker dec'd deposetha and sayeth that he was the dec'd person (VIZ) John Baker, a few days before he died and he called him the said William Baker and requested him to sit down by him and said I shall die I want to imform you how I wish my business to be done. I have sold my land to Doctor Frances V. Schmittou and the money when collected will be sufficient to pay all my debts and something over, and what is over I want my wife to know it and apply it to the benifit of herself and my children th in the best way she can and I have other debts due me and when she collects the money my desire is for my wife Beckah to apply it also to the benefit of herself and my children and as to my personal property as it is but little I do not wish her to be at any expence in administering on it but forher to keep it in her possession and make use of it for her maintanance and the raising of my children in the way she thinks most proper for I am satisfied that money due me will be more than sufficient to discharge all the debts I owe therefore I wish my wife to be at as little expence and trouble as possible for I have no doubt but my wife will do the best she can for self and children. Witness his hand and seal.

Subscribed and sworn to before me the 11th of April 1823.

(72) Jno. Humphreys J.P.

                        his
William X Baker
        mark

State of Tennessee, Dickson County, Court of Pleas and Quarter Session, July Term 1823. Then was the within verbal will of John W. Baker dec'd produced in open Court and proved as such by the oaths of William Baker and Frances V. Schmittou and ordered to be recorded.

Test-Field Farrar, Clerk of sd. Court.

State of Tennessee, Dickson County, April 27th 1827. Then was the verbal Will of John W. Baker deceased Recorded in Book A page 85-86.

Field Farrar, Clk.

(BARNIBAS BLEDSOE No. 39)

In the name of God Amen. I, BARNIBAS BLEDSOE of the County of Dickson and State of Tennessee being sick and weak in body but of sound sense and memory and knowing the uncertainty of this earthly life do make this my last Will and Testament in manner and form following revoking and making void all will or wills by me family made. First-I recommend my Soul to Almighty God who gave it in whom by the merits of Jesus Christ I trust and believe to be saved and my body to be buried in such decent and Christian like manner, as my Executor may think fit and as to my worldly goods and whatever else God hath

(73) been pleased to bestow on me I give and bequeathe in the following manner, VIZ, In the first place I lend to my beloved wife Rebecca all of my property such as house lands and negro woman named Dinah, House hold and furniture and stock of every kind during her natural life and after her death it is my Will and desire that the above mentioned property and all and every thing appurtaining thereto be named divided between my beloved children, VIZ, To my son Giles J. Bledsoe I give and bequeath fifty Dollars to make his portion equal to that already given to the rest of my sons. The reso of my property my will and desire is that it be equally divided between my beloved children VIZ, Ann Halley, Hamor Halley, Elizabeth Rue, Agnes Rue, Rebecca Wallace, Barney L. Bledsoe, Nancy Halliburton, Pinkney T. Bledsoe, Duncilla Whitehead, Giles J. Bledsoe, and Unity Jurnagin. The division to be made by my Executors hereafter mentioned.

Lastly I constitute my son Barny L. Bledsoe and Pickney T. Bledsoe whole and sole Executors to this my last Will and Testament. To this my last Will and Testament in the presence of the subscribing witnesses I have set my hand and affixed my seal satifying the same this --- day of December annodomino, one thousand eight hundred and twenty one.

William Reynolds
William Lewis

              his
              Barnibas X Bledsoe (seal)
                mark

State of Tennessee, Dickson County, Court of Pleas and Quarter Sessions, January Term, 1822. Then was the within last Will and Testament of Barnibas Bledsoe dec'd was produced in open Court and proven by the oaths of William Reynolds and William Lewis subscribing witness thereto and ordered to be recorded.

              Field Farrar, Clerk.

State of Tennessee, Dickson County, April 27th 1827. Then was the last Will and Testament of Barnibas Bledsoe recorded in Book A page 87-88.

              Field Farrar, Clerk.

(74) (ANN MARSH No. 40)

I, ANN MARSH of Dickson County and State of Tennessee considering the frailty of the body but of sound mind make my last Will and Testament in manner and form following, that is to say, 1st-To my son Gilbert Marsh, I give one negro man named Tony, a negro girl named Nancy and one feather bed to him and his heirs forever.

2nd-I give to my Grand son Mineyard Marsh one negro boy named Peter to him and his heirs forever.

3rd-I give to my Grand Daughter Fanny Shewmaker one negro girl named Ceely one feather bed to her and her heirs forever.

4th-Lastly I appoint my son Gilbert Marsh sole executor of this my last Will.

Signed, sealed and delivered in presence of us, January 10th 1822.

William Hudson
Richard Evans

              her
              Ann X Marsh
                mark

State of Tennessee, Dickson County, Court of Pleas and Quarter Session April Term 1825. Then was the last Will and Testament of Ann Marsh dec'd produced in open Court and proven by the oaths of William Hudson and Richard Evans subscribing witnesses thereto and ordered to be recorded.

              Test-Field Farrar, Clerk

State of Tennessee, Dickson County, April 27th 1827. Then was the last Will and Testament of Ann Marsh recorded in Book A page 88-89.

              Field Farrar, Clk.

(75) (AMOS JAMES-No. 41)

State of Tennessee, Dickson County, We the undersigned testify that the dec'd whilest on his death bed VIZ, He requested that Ten Acres of his land should be give to his son Joshua as his part of the estate and that this land lies in a survey to its self and that (James deceased) which property should be for the use of said given under our hands this 4th of July 1825.

         Test-Enoch James (seal)
         Abah his mark James (seal)

State of Tennessee, Dickson County, Court of Pleas & Quarter Session July Term 1825. Then was the within verbal will of Amos James dec'd produced in open Court and proven by the oaths of Enoch James and Abah James subscribing witnesses thereto and ordered to be recorded.

         Test- Field Farrar, Clerk

State of Tennessee, Dickson County Apl. 27, 1827. Then was the within verbal Will of Amos James Recorded County in Book A page 89-90
         Test-Field Farrar, Clerk.

WILLIAM GILBERT NO.42)

July the 18th 1827. In the name of God Amen. I, WILLIAM GILBERT of Dickson County and State of Tennessee being weak in body but of sound and perfect mind and memory blessed be the almighty God for the same, do make and publish this my last Will and Testament in manner and form following, that is to say, First of all I lend to my beloved (76) wife Nancy Gilbert the land and plantation whereon I now live until my son Henry Masison Gilbert comes to the age of twenty one years then one half to her during her natural life. Also I lend to my beloved wife one negro woman named Jude during her natural life and then I give the said negro Jude to my son Thomas Gilbert and his heirs forever. Also lend my wife one negro man named Jeffry until my son Nathan Gilbert come to the age of twenty five years and then I give the said negro Jeffry to my son Nathan and his heirs lawfully begottn of his -- then the said negro to return to my son Mabel Gilbert and his heirs forever.

I also lend to my Daughter Temperance Gilbert one negro girl named Mary during her natural life and then I give the said negro to her heirs lawfully begotten of her body for ever and if the said Temperance should die without a lawful heir then the said negro Mary I give to my son Nathan Gilbert and James Monroe Gilbert to be equally divided between them and their heirs also the increase of said negro. I also give all of my land on the West side of Jones Creek to my son Henry Madison Gilbert to his heirs, Executors, Administrators or assigns after the death of my wife. I also give my son Henry Madison one negro woman named Fanny and one negro boy named Smith to him and his heirs forever, but if he should die without an heir of heirs lawfully begotten of his body then the above named negroes is to return to William Gilbert, Nathan Gilbert, James Monroe Gilbert and be equally divided among them all. Also the increase of the said negro if any to be divided between William Gilbert, Nathan Gilbert, and James Monroe Gilbert and hi their heirs administrators and assigns forever (that is the first three) then if any increase after them the said Henry Madison Gilbert is to keep them to himself, his heirs, executors and administrators forever. I also give to my son Mabel Gilbert one negro girl named Monah to her heirs and assigns forever. I also give my son William Gilbert Ten Dollars. I give my son William Gilbert one hundred acres of my new Entry land on the west side of sawland also one cow. I also give my son Nathan Gilbert fifty acres of land entered under the law, also two hundred acres of my new Entry land, followed from Maufly and one feather bed and furniture. I give my son Henry Madison Gilbert one hundred acres of my new Entered land when my son Nathan pleases to let him have it also one feather bed and furniture. I also give my Daughter Temperance which she claims with propertfurniture. I also lend my wife all my household furniture, farming utensils and all of my stock after my debts are paid except what I haveeotherwise parted with. I give my son Henry Madison Gilbert, the horse which he now claims and one bridle and saddle. I also give my Daughter Temperance Gilbert one horse when my wife can best spare it. I inform my Executors to sell at private sale that which they think can best be spared to pay my debts. I also give my son William Gilbert six acres of land reserved for the Mill seat. I do utterly disallow revoke and disannul all and every other former Will or Wills made before this time named, ratifying and confirming this to be my last Will and Testament. In witness whereof I have set my hand and seal this day and dste above written.

(77) I do constitute and appoint my beloved wife Nicy Gilbert, Thomas G Gilbert and Mabel Gilbert my Executors.

Signed, sealed and declared in the presence of us,
William Armstrong
Henry R. Legget   William Gilbert   (seal)
Richard Cocke

State of Tennessee, Dickson County, Court of Pleas and Quarter session, January Term 1828. Then was the paper writing purporting to be the last Will and Testament of William Gilbert dec'd produced in open Court and proven by the oaths of Henry R. Legget and Richard Coke two of the subscribing witnesses thereto and the same was ordered by the Court to be recorded.

Test-Field Farrar, Clerk of said Court

State of Tennessee, Dickson County, July 15th 1828. Then was the last Will and Testament of William Gilbert Recorded in Book A page 90-91-92.

Field Farrar, Clerk.

(78) (MILTON LOFTIS No. 43)

January the 6th day 1825. In the name of God Amen. I, MARTIN LOFTIS of the County of Dickson and State of Tennessee considering the uncertainty of this mortal life and being of sound mind and memory blessed by the Almighty God for the same do make and publish this my last Will and Testament in manner and form following, that is to say First, my just debts is to bepaid, secondly, I bequeath to my loving wife Fereba Loftis all my estate both real and personal during her life or widowhood, then after her death I will to my son William Loftis, also that tract or parcel of land that he now lives on during his lifetime and after his death to be equally divided between his three children, to wit, William Samuel, M and Cintha Loftis, also to my son-in-law Andrew Beard I bequeath one dollar, also to my Daughter Phebe V. one horse. Also to my Daughter Rilla E. one horse. Also to my son Milton my three negro boys, namely, James Tony and Peter also the tract of land that I now live on containing one hundred and sixteen acres and half. Also the balance of the horses, cows, hogs and sheep. Also all my household and kitchen furniture and farming toold. Also all my household and kitchen furniture and farming tools. Also if I own my negro woman Milla at my death I will and bequeath her to my wife Fereba Loftis to dispose of as she pleases I

(79) also appoint Josiah Thornton my Executor and my loving wife Fereba Executrix of this my last Will and Testament hereby revoking all former wills by me made. In witness whereof I have hereunto set my

hand and seal the day and date above named. Signed, sealed published and declared by the above named Martin Loftis to be his last Will and Testament in the presence of us who hereunto subscribed our names as Witnesses in the presence of the Testator.

                                                  his
                                           Martin X Loftis   (seal)
                                              mark

Esther Thornton)
)
Reuben Thornton)

Josiah Thornton Adm'r.

Ferbe Loftis, Executrix)
) At the October Term of the County Court
    vs   ) of Dickson 1826, Josiah Thornton and Fer-
) ebe Loftis offered for Probate the annexed
E Smith & others   ) paper purporting to be the last Will and
) Testament of Martin Loftis deceased, where-
upon Elisha Smith and William Loftis opposed the probate of said paper offering that it was not the last Will and Testament of said Loftis and requested the Court that an issue of   be made which was according done which fact is to submitted to a Jury of the next Court whether it is the will of said Martin Loftis or not and the Executors say it is the last Will and Testament and of this the ---- put themselves on the County.

                                             J.P. Cheatham, atty for Smith
                                              & Co.
                                             Collier & Allen and the
plaintiff doeth the like.
                                             Cheatham for Ptff.

And at July Term 1827. The parties came as follows.
Josiah Thornton Executor &)
Pheribe Loftis Executrix for)   This day came the parties by
Martin Loftis, dec'd.   )   their attorneys and thereupon
)   come a Jury of good & lawful
    vs   )   men, to wit, Thomas C. Smith,
)   William Fentress, Ashburn Vanhook,
Elisha Smith and   )   William Adams, Mumford Smith,
William Loftis   )   Richard Murrell, James W. McCannon,
Absolum Baker, Nehemiah Scott, John Weakley, William Gunn, Jesse Alexander who being elected tried and sworn the truth to speak upon the issue joined upon their oaths do say this the last Will and Testament of Martin Loftis deceased. It is therefore ordered by the Court that said Will and Testament of Martin Loftis dec'd be admitted to record, as the law directs and that said Executor and Executrix be permitted to enter into bond and security and qualify according to law as Executors of the same. I, Field Farrar Clerk of Dickson County Court do hereby certify that the foregoing is a given true copy of the precedings had in said court on said Will. Given under my hand this 15th July 1828.

                                              Field Farrar, Clerk.

    State of Tennessee, Dickson County, July 15th 1828. Then was the last Will and Testament of Martin Loftis, dec'd. Recorded in Book A pages 93-94-95 T.

(810) (JOHN REYNOLDS SEN'R NO. 44)

In the name of God Amen. JOHN REYNOLDS SEN'R of the County of Dickson and State of Tennessee being old and weak in body but of sound mind and memory do this sixth day of July in the year of our Lord one thousand eight hundred and twenty five make and publish this my last Will and Testament revoking all other of my former Wills in manner and form as follows, First-It is my Will that all my just debts and funeral expence be paid out of my estate. Secondly-I wish my beloved wife Susannah Reynolds to have full and entire possession of the plantation I now live on including the small tract George Martin family lived during her natural life or widowhood. I also wihh she may be allowed an ample support for herself and my two children for the present year, out of what is already laid up, or may be made for that purpose, I also give Herever, her choice of any two of my work horses. I also loan her my negro man Gillis during her natural life or widowhood to further the support of herself andmy two children. I also loan her my negro man Isaac for the same purpose giving my Executors the right to retain them on the plantation or hire them out as they may desire most expedient for the interest of my children. I wish my Executors to retain in the family and in the posession of my wife during her widowhood every thing necessary to carry on the farm either in farming tools, stock of all kinds, household goods and kitchen furniture with my oxen and ox cart provided my just debts can be paid other wise. I also wish my Executor to dispose of all surplus property towards the payment of my just debts on the terms they may think most advnatagious for my heirs. It is my Will and desire my executors pay strict attnetion to the education of my children and that they remain under the direction of their Mother, during their minority or her widowhood. Should my wife marry again my Executor may continue my children with their Mother ob take them from her, using his discretion. It is my will that when my son Thomas Becomes he be allowed to have and forever to hold, as his own real right and property all the aforesaid tract of land as well as the Martin tract forever, but by no means shall be allowed to disinherit his Mother

(81) during life or widowhood. It is also my will that my Daughter Nancy have and forever hold as own property right a small tract of land of thirty five acres more or less known by the Pond tract provided said land be not otherwise disposed or before my death. It is my will and desire that should mywife marry again that an equal division of all my property be made, my land execepted, between my wife and my two children, my lands my wife willhave no share in, neither do I wish an accounts made of the Legacy bequeathed her forever, should any of the above named children, die before of age it is my will the surviving child have the dec'd childs share should Thomas and Nancy both die without an heir, or an heir begotten of their own body it is my will their whole both shares of my estate be equally divided between all my first wife s children, namely John and Mark Reynolds, Charlotte Livingston, Polly Wilson, Gilly Reynolds, Heaven Acary Dunnaway, Alley Smith, Eably McMurry and William Reynolds or their heirs this being the whold and every part and parcel that I allow any of my first wifes children and last named of my estate with what they have already received of me and no part of this provided Son Thomas, and Nancy or e either of them live to enjoy it themselfes on have surviving children

82 (to inherit their estate and as bef ore under no circumstance whatever shall my wife be disinherited from her peacable Inheritance and support on the land I now live on during her natural life or widowhood should my wife continue and die a widow it is my will and desire that the whold of my estate in her hand be given to Son Thomas and Nancy or their heirs forever if any surviving children they have if not to

be equally divided amongst my first wifes children as above named. Lastly I make and ordain my beloved wife Susannah Reynolds and my worthy friend Thomas Batson Esq'r of Montgomery County Executrix and Executor of this my last Will and Testament. In witness whereof I the said John Reynolds Sen'r have to this my last will and Testmanet set my hans and seal the day and year above written.

                                                John Reynolds (seal)

Signed, sealed published)
and declared by the said)
John Reynolds the Testator)
as his last will ant Test-)
ament in the presence of us who)
were present at the time of)
signing and sealing thereof.)

    State of Tennessee, Dickson County Court April Term 1828.
Susannah Reynolds Exer'x of
John Reynolds dec'd   ) Will conteste this day came the
) parties by their attorneys and
      vs   ) thereupon came a Jury of good and
) lawful men, to wit, James M. Ross,
France N. Schmittou   ) Moses T. White, Samuel Mitchel,
William T. Reynolds &   ) Matthew Crumpler, Raifred Crumpler
Mark Reynolds   ) John T. Williams, William Turner,
                                            Woodrow Daniel, William King, Benjamine
(83) Sanders, Thomas Brown, Daniel Moore, who being elected tried and sworn the truth to speak upon the issue uoined upon their oaths do say they find the Will in question to be the last Will and Testament of the said John Reynolds Sen'r. dec'd. whereupon it is considered by the Court that said Will be recorded.

                                             Test- Field Farrar Clerk.
    State of Tennessee, Dickson County, January 30th 1830. Then was the last Will and Testament of John Reynolds dec'd. in Book A. pages 95-96-97-98-99-100-101-102.

(RICHARD D. SANSOM No. 45)
    I, RICHARD SANSOM, being of sound sense and memory do make this my last Will and Testament hereby revoking all others, VIZ;
    First, Item 1-I offer up my soul to God who gave it and my body to be returned to its kindred earth.
    Item 2nd-It is my will and desire that all my just debts be paid.
    Item 3rd-It is my will and desire that my beloved wife Barbara have two of my negroes, Viz, Armsted and his wife Venis, my Gray horse and all my household and kitchen furniture.
    Item 4th-It is my will and desire that my Executors sell a small tract of land on Jones Creek adjoining a tract purbhased and now occupied by Thomas C. Smith towhich I have an equitabble right also my carriage and all my stock excepting the horse already disposed of at such time and places and on such terms of payment as their discretion may suggest and when the money is collected from said sales I vest my Executors with full power to appropriate the same to the purchase of other property or to loan it on interest for the benefit of my children.
    Item 6th-It is my will and desire that my Executors be vested with full power to sell any of the property left to my children which may in their opinion be unprofitable and invest the proceeds in other property for them or loan it on interest for their benefit.

Item 7th- Having, full confidence in the Justice and Justice and prudence of my Executors it is my will and desire that they have the entire management of the property of my children with power to move it from place to place until a division takes place according to them.

Item 8th- It is my will and desire that my two brothers David N. Samsom and William C. Sansom and my Uncle Henry A. C. Napier be my Executors.

Richard D. Sansom

(84) Witnesses:
Thomas K. Handy
B.C. Robertson

I, RICHARD D. SANSOM being of sound sense and memory do make this as a supplement to my last Will and Testament as follows Viz, It is my will and desire that my beloved wife Barbara be my Executrix in addition to my three Executors already appointed.

Richardson D. Sansom

(85) State of Tennessee, Dickson County, Court of Pleas and quarter Session July Term 1828, Tenth day of the month. Then was produced in open Court the within paper writing purporting to be the last Will and Testament of Richard D. Sansom dec'd which was proven by the oaths of Thomas K. Handy and Benjamine C. Robertson subscribing witnesses thereto and the same was ordered by the Court to be recorded. In testimony whereof I, Field Farrar, Clerk of said Court have hereunto set my hand at office this 10th day of July 1828.

Field Farrar, Clk.

State of Tennessee, Dickson County Court July Term 1828. Then was the last Will and Testament of Richardson D. Sansom Dec'd was recorded in Book A. pages 98-99.

Field Farrar, Clerk.

(85) (JOHN R. CATHEY No.46)
State of Tennessee, Dickson County, I, JOHN R. CATHEY calling to mind the imortality of all flesh and being feeble of body but sound in memory and understanding do ordain this my last Will and Testament hereby revoking all others.

1st- I give unto my beloved wife Peggy Cathey during her natural life or widowhood all my lands that I am now in possession of (except fifty acres lying above my son Archy Catheys which I give to my son Joshua Cathey) The balance at my wifes decease to be equally divided amongst my four younger sons, Viz, Daniel, Samuel Martin and John Cathey, also I give to my said wife all my personal property after all my legal debts are paid. Also I give unto my Daughters Jane and Dolly, one feather bed, one Cow and Calf to each when they come of age or marry.

2nd- I have give to my son George one filly to Archie one sorrell Horse, and to my Daughter May wife of William G. Austin a Cow and Calf and feather bed they are to have no more of the remaining property as I consider they have had their share and rather more when the rest are raised.

3rd- I do constitute and appoint Munsford Smith and Peggy my wife my sole Executors & ets to this my last Will and Testament. In witness hereof I sign and seal the same 10th day of July 1827.

Attest-John Forsythe

John R. his X mark Cathey (seal)

State of Tennessee, Dickson County Court July Term 1828. Then was the last within paper writing purporting to be the last Will and Testament of John R. Cathey dec'd produced in open Court and proved to be such by the oath of Jno. Forsythe a sub witness thereto and the same was ordered to be certified accordingly and recorded.

Test-Field Farrar, Clerk.

State of Tennessee, Dickson County, January 30th 1830. Then was t the last Will and Testament of John R. Cathey dec'd recorded in Book A. page 103.

6) (WILLIAM GARRETT Sen'r, No. 47)

Know all men by these presents that I, WILLIAM GARRETT Sen'r do make this my last Will and Testament, being low in body but possess a good reason being in my proper sense at this time I will my soul to God and my body to a decent burial. All of my property which I am in possession of I will and bequeath to my beloved wife Sary Garrett during her natural life or widowhood at the expiration of either, I will all the property which she is in possession of to be equally divided amongst my children so as to give my beloved son and Daughter, William and Sary Garrett my two minor children as much more that the rest as will make them equal with the rest of my Children who have accrued of my property prior to this time. Given under my hand this 3rd day of July 1828. I leave my beloved wife Sarah and my beloved son William Garrett Executors to this my last Will and Testament.

(87) Jacob Evans)   William Garrett, Sen'r.
W. Kiragan)
Henry B. Koen)

State of Tennessee, Dickson County Court, October Term 1828. Then was this paper writing purporting to be the last Will and Testament of William Garrett Sen'r. dec'd. produced in open Court and proved to be such by the oaths of William Kiragan and Henry B. Koen subscribing witnesses thereto and the same was ordered by the Court to be certified accordingly and recorded.

Test-Field Farrar, Clerk.

State of Tennessee, Dickson County, January 30th 1830. Then was the last Will and Testament of William Garrett Sen'r. dec'd. Recorded in Book A. page 104.

Field Farrar, Clerk.

(JOSEPH HALL No. 48)

State of Tennessee, Dickson County, In the name of God Amen. I, JOSEPH HALL being moderate health of body and sound in mind and memory and knowing that all men must once die do constitute and appoint this my last Will and Testament in manner and form following, to Wit;

In the first place I give my daughter Nancy one sheep of the she kind. I give to Henry Hall my grandson the tract or parcel of land lying East and North of what is called the hedge roe. In the next place I give my grandson Henry three girls Mary Susan & Sary the land lying South and West of said Hedge roe. Also I five one mare and filly. Also I give seven head of Cattle. Also I gove fifteen head of sheep. Also I give my stock of hogs to those said girls Mary, Susan & Sary. Also I further appoint my grand son Henry Hall Executor of this my last Will and Testament done this 22nd day of February 1828. Signed, sealed in presence of us

Attest-Robert Moore,)   his
    Robert Whitall)   Joseph X Hall   (seal)
                                                                          mark

Then was the within paper writing purporting to be the last Will and Testament of Joseph Hall dec'd produced in open Court and proved to be such by the oaths of Robert Moore and Robert Whitwell subscribing witnesses thereto and the same was ordered by the Court to be recorded.

Test-Field Farrar, Clerk.

(88) State of Tennessee, Dickson County, February 13th 1830. Then was the last Will & Testament of Joseph Hall dec'd., recorded in Book A. page 105.

Field Farrar, Clerk.

(GEORGE ROSS No. 49)

I, GEORGE ROSS of the County of Dickson & State of Tennessee, being of perfect mind and memory do make & ordain the following my last Will and Testament.

First-Igive & bequeath to my son James M. Ross all my landed Estate in the County of Dickson & State of Tennessee estimated at seven hundred and forty four acres more or less being the tract or tracts of land whereon I now reside and where James M. Ross resided now. And I further give to my son James M. Ross one negro man, Elijah, one negro woman Sarah, one negro boy little Elijah, one negro girl Charity one negro girl Martha, one negro woman Isbel, one negro man Gabe, one negro woman Phillis, one negro girl Caroline, one negro girl Milly, one negro girl Ealy.

Secondly-To my grandson, George R. Craft I give and bequeath one negro woman Ivvy, one negro girl Clarrisa, one negro girl Priscilla and one negro boy Sigh.

Thirdly-To my grand-daughter Sally West I give and bequeath one negro girl Lilo, one negro man Harry Walker, one negro woman Hanna and negro boy Dick.

Fourthly- I gige & bequeath to mygrand-daughter Harriet Outlaw one negro man little Harry, one negro girl Lucy.

Fifthly-I give and bequeath to my great grand-daughter Margaret Outlaw, one negro girl Cassandra.

Sixthly-Igive and bequeath to my grand-spn James Craft one negro woman Betty and her female child unnamed and one negro girl Harriet, one negro man Alston.

(89) Seventhly-To my Daughter Mary Drake I give and bequeath all the property she now has in her posession to which I have had a claim to dispose of as she may think fit. I further give her claim to dispose of as she may think fit. I further give her claim to one negro man Dave and one negro woman Milly-To my grand-daughter Sally Perry I give and bequeath one negro woman Nan. Toomy grand-daughter Lucy Eaton I give and bequeath one negro boy Major. To my grandson George George Drake I give and bequeath one negro boy Lewis to my granddaughter Pernella Williams, I give and bequeath one negro boy Jim. I further give my Daughter Mary Drake one negro man Haky. I further give my Daughter Mary Drake one negroman Haky.

Eightly-I give my grand-daughter Harriett Outlaw one negro man Peter.

Ninethly-I give and bequeath to my son James M. Ross two negro men Abraham & Mark.

Tenthly-To my grandson George R. Craft I give & bequeath to my one negro man Laurel.

Eleventh-I give & bequeath to mygrand daughter Sally Bacon, one negro girl Serena, To my son James M. Ross I give and bequeath one negro man Isaac. To my daughter Mary Drake I give & bequeath one negro man Yellow Harry. The right title claim and interest to the tractof land on which Jesse Craft now lives in Montgomery County Tennessee containing four hundred and twenty acres being in me & being my right I give jointly to my two grand sons George R. Craft & James Craft. To my sons in law Jesse Craft, Lewis Joslin and Benddict Bacon I give to each and severally the sum of fifty dollars to my son James M. Ross, Mary Drake, the children of my daughter Margaret Craft and the children of my daughter Jane Bacon I give an equal share in my undivided estate. Lastly, I appoint my son James M. Ross, George R. Craft and John H. Marable Executors to this my last Will & Testament. In witness whereof I have hereunto set my hand & seal the 18th October 1828.

                 George Ross (seal)

(90) Ack'd. in presence of us
George T. Cooksey, Robert Baxter, Daniel Moore.

 State of Tennessee, Dickson County Court, January Term 1830. Then was the annexed paper writing purporting to be the last Will and Testament of George Ross dec'd produced in open Court and proved by the oaths of George T. Cooksey, Robert Baxter & Daniel Moore subscribing witnesses thereto and ordered by the Court to be Recorded.

                 Test-Field Farrar, Clerk.

 State of Tennessee, Dickson County, February 20th 1830. Then was the last Will and Testament of George Ross dec'd recorded in Book A. pages 106-107-108.

(ENOCH JAMES No. 50)
 In the name of God Amen. I, ENOCH JAMES of the County of Dickson and State of Tennassee, do make ordain this my last Will & Testament revoking all other to which I being very weak in body but perfect in mind & memory. I ordain my well beloved wife one of my executors and Archibald Pullen my other Executor to manage all my business my desire is for my well beloved wife and my other executor to sell my land to pay all my debts for my executors to sell as much of the land to pay all my debts and if the land dont fetch enough to satisfy all my debts for my executors to sell as much of the other property such as they think best as will be sufficent to pay all my just debts then my pleasure is for my well beloved wife to have all the balance to do as he thinks best her lifetime or widowhood then my pleasure is if my well beloved wife should marry again then my pleasure is then for what property is left for it to be divided amongst my children and for my well beloved wife to have a childs part with the rest. In testimony whereof I set my hand and seal this 25th day of August in the year of our Lord 1830.

                 Enoch James (seal)

Test-James Carter (seal)
 John Stafford (seal)

 State of Tennessee, Dickson County, Court January Term 1831. Then was the within last Will and Testament of Enoch James dec'd produced in open Court and duly proven to be such by the oaths of James Carter and John Stafford subscribing witnesses thereto and ordered by the Court to be certified & recorded.

                 Test-Field Farrar, Clerk.

 State of Tennessee, Dickson County County, February 18th 1832. Then was the last Will and Testament of Enoch James dec'd recorded in book A pages 100-109

                 Field Farrar, Clk.

(91) (ELIZABETH WALKER No. 51)

In the name of God Amen. I, ELIZABETH WALKER of the State of Tennessee and County of Dickson considering the uncertainty of the mortal life and being in sound mind and publish this my last Will and Testament in manner and form following, Viz, that after my just debts being paid and funeral expences satisfied I will that my five living negroes, that is Deliah, Priscilla, Tennessee & Horton & their increase if any should be equally divided between my five living children that is John E. Walker, Sarah R. Walker, Margaret R. Williams, Mary S. Walker, Nancy V. Gilbert. But it is my Will if it be possible that the above named negroes and increase should remain in the family and not sold.

Secondly- I will that my tract of land of one hundred and 31/3 acres in the above named county of Dickson being the tract whereon I now reside, should be sold and also what stock of hogs cattle & etc. there may be sold and out of the money arising from said sale I give and bequeath to Vann S. Crews son of my deceased daughter Barbary H. Crews the sum of one hundred dollars to be held by my Executor hereafter named and to belet out on interest for the benefit of said Vann S. Crews the interest to be applied in his schooling or in any other way that shall appear most benificial for him by my executor until he arrives at the age of twenty one or until marryeth then to be paid over to him, both principal and interest or so much of the interest as shall remain. Also I give and bequeath to Elizabeth T. Crews and Sarah Ann B. Crews daughters of my deceased daughter Barbara H. Crews each the sum of fifty dollars to be paid by my executor to my daughter Sarah R. Walker, for the benefit of the above named Elizabeth T. Crews and Sarah Ann B. Crews as she may think best and if not expended on them before they arrive at the age of twenty one or marrieth then the whole or balance as may be to be paid over to them by Sarah R. Walker, or her legal representative. The reason that I have made this difference in the legacies of my grand daughters in schooling, clothing & etc. I also will that my daughter Sarah R. Walker and Mary S. Walker shall have over and above their part with my other living children all my household and kitchen furniture that I may be in possession of at the time of my decease. Now after the legacys to my three children above named is collected then (92) if there should be any moneys remaining of the sale of my land and stock as above such remainder to be equally divided amongst my five living children above named or their legal representatives. I do hereby constitute my son John B. Walker, sole executor to this my last Will and Testament revoking all former Wills by me made. Signed, sealed and delivered by the said Testator to be her last Will and Testament in our presents who at her request in her presents and in the presents of each other have subscribed our names as witnesses signed, sealed this 17th December 1825.

                Elizabeth Walker (seal)

Test-
A. Coldwell S.
Wm. Kiragan S.

State of Tennessee, Dickson County Court Jan'y Term 1830. Then was the last Will and Testament of Elizabeth Walker dec'd produced in open Court and proved to be such by the oaths of Abrham Coldwell and Wm. Kiragan subscribing witnesses thereto and the same was ordered by the Court to be certified and recorded.

                Test- Field Farrar, Clerk.

State of Tennessee, Dickson County Feb'y 18th 1832. Then was the last Will and Testament of Elizabeth Walker dec'd Recorded in Book A Pages 109-110-111.

                Field Farrar, Clerk.

(93)   (MOSES FUSSELL No. 52)

In the name of God Amen. I, MOSES FUSSELL of Dickson County and State of Tennessee being weak in body but of mind and memory considering the uncertainty of this mortal life do make and publish this my last Will and Testament in manner and form following that is to say after the payment of my just and lawful debts.

1st-I will and bequeath unto my beloved wife Lucy Fussell all of my estate both real and personal during her natural life.

2nd-I also will that after the decease of my wife Lucy Fussell that my slave man Ben, shall not be bound to serve any of my children but shall be at liberty to live with which of them he may think proper and that provision be made out of my estate for his support if necessary.

3rd-I give and bequeath to my Daughter Elizabeth Horner during her natural life the tract of land whereon she she now lives containing one hundred acres be the same more or less and after her decease to George Wyatt Horner and Picy Austin to be equally divided between them. I further give and bequeath to my Daughter the above named Elizabeth Horner, the sum of one dollar.

Fifthly-I give and bequeath to my son William Fussell the tract of land whereon I now live containing fifty one acres be the same more or less and all my working tools.

6th-The residue of my estate both real and personal which is not above mentioned, I will & bequeath to be equally divided between my daughters Sally Horner, Lucy Horner, Widow of James Horner dec'd and Patsey Dunnagan and I do hereby constitute and appoint my son Wm. Fussell and Mukins Carr Executors to this my last Will and Testament hereby revoking all former wills made by me. In testimony whereof I do hereto set my hand and seal this fifteenth day of October in the year of October in the year of our Lord 1830.

Signed, sealed and acknowledged in presence of
Eli Crow, John Dunnegan, Elizabeth Crow

                his
Moses X Fussell
                mark

State of Tennessee, Dickson County Court Ap'l Term 1831. Then was the within last Will and Testament of Moses Fussell deceased produced in open Court and duly proved to be such by the oaths of Eli Crow, John Dunnegan, subscribing witnesses thereto and ordered by the Court to be certified and Recorded.

Test-Field Farrar, Clerk

State of Tennessee, Dickson County Feb'y 18, 1832. Then was the within last Will and Testament of Moses Fussell dec'd Recorded in Book A. pages 111-112-113.

Field Farrar, Clerk.

(94)   (DANIEL WILLIAMS No. 53)

In the name of God Amen. I, DANIEL WILLIAMS of the County of Dickson and State of Tennessee being of perfect mind and memory calling to mind that man is once appointed to die and by these presents do make this my last Will and Testament in manner and form as follows, to wit:

1st-That all my just debts be paid which are but few.

2nd-Whereas my estate was by estimation worth nine thousand six hundred dollars, having twelve children which will make eight hundred dollars to each childs share. All of my married children after marriage to wit, Daniel H. Williams, Thos. Williams, Joseph Williams, Christian Scott, Mary Killabrew, Cassander Napier, Susannah Norworthy,

Jennetta Napier, Benjamine Williams, Henry B.H. Williams each of them have rec'd in good proerty eight hundred dollars as their share them and their heirs forever.

3rd-I give and bequeath to my son Richard Nixon Williams all of my land on the West side of Yellow Creek including of the Dod place.

4th-I give and bequeath unto my son Henry H.B. Williams all of my lands on the East side of Yellow creek not heretofore given to my son Rich'd N. Williams.

(95) 5th-I give and bequeath to my son James Williams a Land Warrant No. 1624 issued to me from the War Office the 7th day June 1830 for three hundred acres of land to him and his heirs forever. I also give a negro girl called Matilda all the residue of my property of every discription it is my will and desire should be equally divided amongst all of my children and for the executor of this my last Will and Testament revoking all former Wills. I do hereby nominate and appoint my beloved son Joseph Williams my Executor to Execute this my last Will. Witness my hand and seal this 5th day of October 1830.
In the presence of

Samuel X Brown (his mark W)   Daniel Williams   (seal)

John W Scott
William Scott

State of Tennessee, Dickson County Court October Term 1831. Then was the last within Will and Testament of Daniel Williams dec'd produced in open court and duly proven to be such by the oaths of Samuel Brown, John W Scott subscribing witnesses thereto and ordered by court to be certified and recorded.

Test-Field Farrar, Clerk

State of Tennessee, Dickson County Feb'y 18th 1832. Then was the last Will and Testament of Daniel Williams Recorded in Book A pages 113-114.

Field Farrar, Clerk.

(THOMAS DRUMMOND No. 54)

In the name of God Amen. I, THOMAS DRUMMOND of the County of Dickson and State of Tennessee being weak in body but of sound mind and memory and considering the uncertainty of this life and that it is
(96) appointed unto all men once to die and being desirous to make some disposition of the earthly treasure which it has pleased Almighty God to bless me do make and ordain this my last Will and Testament.

I give and commend my soul unto the Lord who gave it to me and I desire that my body shall be buried in a decent Christian like manner.

Item-It is my will that all my just debts be paid out of my property and that after my death my executor and executrix sell so much and such part thereof as may be necessary to pay the same.

Item-I declare it to be my will and desire that all my children have equal shares of my property including that which I have already given and in order that there may be no difficulty in ascertaining the share of each one I hereby declare that I have given to my son Zachius Drummons in money and property one hundred and ninety eight dollars and seventy cents. To my son Thomas one hundred and seventy dollars and twenty cents. To my daughter Elizabeth Shropshire one hundred and fifty nine dollars thirty seven and a half cents. To my daughter Patience Ragan one hundred and eleven dollars. To my daughter Peggy Rye thirty two dollars and to my son William eighty six dollars and fifty cents. To the balance of my children I have yet given noth-

given nothing.

Should it please God to permit me to live for any considerable length of time hereafter I intend to give to such of my children as have not had until all are equal such portions of my property as I can conveniently spare for which I will take of them receipts or make some account of it.

Item-At my death my will and desire is that my wife have all the property both real and personal to keep and hold during her life or widowhood and to sell or use so much thereof as may be necessary for the maintainance of herself and our children and leaving it to her direction to give to such of them as have had but little, so much and such portion of my property as will bring them equal with our son Zachius.

(97) Item-Upon the death of my wife my will is that all of my property real and personal besold and that the proceeds of said sale be so divided amongst my children as that each one have an equal share taking into view what they or any of them may have already had.

Item-In case my wife should think proper to marry after my death my will is that she have the use and benefit of the farm and place where we now live in conjunction with my youngest son James M during her life.

Item-I do hereby appoint my beloved wife Peggy my Executrix and to my son Zachius and my friend Alexander Wilkins Executors of this my last Will and Testamet. In testimony of all which I hereunto set my hand and affix my seal the 30th day of March 1831.

```
                                              his
In the presence of                 Thomas  X  Drummond    (seal
John Montgomerty S.                       mark
Richard Waugh S.
```

State of tennessee, Dickson County Court, October Term 1832. Then was this the last Will and Testament of Thomas Drummond dec'd produced in open court and proven to be such by the oaths of John Montgomery and Richardson Waugh subscribing witnesses thereto and ordered by the by the Court to be certified and recorded.

Test-Field Farrar, Clerk

State of Tennessee Dickson County Clerks Office Nov. 1st 1832. Then was the last Will and Testament of Thomas Drummond dec'd Recorded in Book A. page 115-116.

Test-Field Farrar, Clerk of Dickson County Court.

(JOHN JONES No. 55)

In the name of God Amen, or be it remembered that I John Jones of the State of Tennessee and Dickson being weak in body and perfect mind and memory or you may say thus considering the uncertainty of this mortal life and being of sound & etc blessed be Almighty God for the same do make and publish this my last Will and Testament in manner and form following:

(98) That is to say first I want as much of my perishable property sold as will pay all my just debts. I give to Thomas Jefferson Jones one young sorrell horse price of thirty dollars and my next son Josiah Jones, Joshua Jones, John Jones Jr. William Jones, James Madison Jones I want that these my sons to have a horse at the year of nineteen equal in value to thirty dollars. I give and bequeath to my beloved wife Jane Jones all my land and perishable property during her life time or widowhood and then to be equally divided among all my Ars. I hereby appoint Jane Jones sole Executrix of this my last Will and Testament hereby revoking all former Wills by me made. In witness whereof

I have hereunto set my hand and seal this the twenty third day of April in the year of our Lord one thousand eight hundred and thirty two. Signed, sealed, published and declared by the above named John Jones, to be his last Will and Testament in the presence of us who at his request and at his presence have hereunto subscribed our names as witnesses to the same.

Simon Myers   John Jones (seal)
William Morris

State of Tennessee, Dickson County Court, January Term 1833. Then was the within paper writing purporting to be the last Will and Test- of John Jones dec'd produced in open Court and proven to be such by the oaths of Joshua White Simon Myers and William Morras subscribing witnesses thereto and ordered by the Court to be certified and recorded.

                                Test-Field Farrar, Clerk of said Court.

State of Tennessee Dickson County Clerks Office Feb'y 12th 1833. Then was the foregoing last Will and testament of John Jones dec'd Recorded in Book A. pages 116-117.

                                Test-Field Farrar, Clerk.

(99)(ELIZABETH RICHARDSON No. 56)

In the name of God Amen. I, ELIZABETH RICHARDSON of the County of Dickson and State of Tennessee foreseeing the certainty of death and being of sound and disposing mind and memory do publish make and ordain the following as my last Will and Testament that is to say.

Item-It is my Will and desire that after my funeral expenses are paid that my Executor herein after named should pay all my just debts.

Item-It is my will and desire that my daughter Polly Richardson shall have my Bureau and Trunk and Bedstead and Bed, Two pair of sheets, one pair of Blankets and half dozen silver tea spoons and all my wearing apparal.

Item-I hereby give to my Grandson Jorden W.A. Richardson of my son Stith Richardson one Silver Tea Pot, one large Silver Ladle, and half dozen silver table spoons, one Silver Ladle, and half dozen silver table spoons one Rim and Castor one large Glass Bowl, one silver Watch and Claybank coloured horse and one sorrell colt.

Ttem-I hereby give to my grand daughter Elizabeth Jackson daughter of Doctor Coleman Jackson, one bed, two pair of sheets, one pair of blankets and one ounterpin.

Item- The residue of my Estate whether the same consists of property or debts due me at the time of my death due by bond or otherwise I give and bequeath to my grand children Jorden W.A. Richardson, Hartwell Henry Richardson, Rebecca Ann Richardson, Mary A. Richardson, Edward Richardson, Thomas E. Richardson and   Richardson, sons and daughters of my son Stith Richardson to be among them equally divided or expended in their maintainance and education as my Ex. to may deem best my said Executor being hereby diredted to apply the same to said purpose and no other.

Item-I hereby appoint my said son Stith Richardson my sole Executor and hereby direct that he shall not be required to give any security for the administration of my estate.

In witness whereof I hereby make, publish and declare this to be my last Will and Testament hereby revoking all former Wills by me made, this 11th day of October 1832. Witness my hand and seal signed sealed, published and declared in presence of us,

John H Marable S)
Joseph Kimble S.)   Elizabeth Richardson (seal)

(100) State of Tennessee, Dickson County January Term 1833. Then was the paper writing purporting to be the last Will and Testament of Mrs. Elizabeth Richardson dec'd produced in open Court and proven to be such to be such by the oaths of John H. Marable and Joseph Kimble subscribing witnesses thereto and ordered by the Court to be certified and recorded.

                                       Test-Field Farrar, Clerk of said Court.

State of Tennessee, Dickson County Clerks Office Feb'y 12th 1833. Then was the last Will and Testament of Elizabeth Richardson dec'D Recorded In Book A pages 117-118.

                                       Test-Field Farrar, Clerk.

(RANSOM ELLIS No. 57)

In the name of God Amen. I, RANSOM ELLIS of the County of Dickson and State of Tennessee being weak in body but of sound mind and memory do make and ordain this my last Will and Testament in form following, to wit:

First-It is my Will and desire that my Executor hereafter mentioned shall pay all my just debts and funeral expenses out of my estate.

Secondly-I give and bequeath unto my beloved wife Nancy W. Ellis one negro woman named Milly with her future increase dispose of in such manner as she may think proper to her and her heirs forever.

Thirdly-I lend to my wife the tract or parcel of land which I have lately purchased in the County of Dickson during her natural life or widowhood or until my youngest child shall arrive at the age of twenty one years. In the event of the death or intermarriage of my wife or my youngest child ariving at the age of twenty one years my will and desire is that my Executors sell the land on such terms as they shall think best and the money arrising from such sale to be divided between my wife and children all of which I give to them and their heirs forever.

Fourthly- I lend to my wife Nancy W. Ellis all the residue of my Estate of every discription during her life or widowhood or until my youngest child shall arrive at the age of twenty one. It is my will and desire that the portion of the Estate loaned my wife shall be equally divided between my wife and my children all of which I give to them and their heirs forever.

Lastly- I hereby constitute and appoint my brother Thomas Ellis and my worthy friend Willie Balthrop Executors of this my last Will and Testament with power to execute the same. In testimony whereof I have hereunto (revoking all former wills by me made) set my hand and seal this second day of July in the year of our Lord Eighteen hundred and thirty two.

                                       Ransom Ellis (seal)

Signed, sealed and published
as his last Will and Testament
in the presence of Stith Richardson,
John Drye.

(101) State of Tennessee, Dickson County Court April Term, 1833. Then was this paper writing purporting to be the last Will and Testament of Ransom Ellis dec'd which was proven to be such at the last October Term of this Court by the oaths of Stith Richardson one of the subscribing witnesses thereto and at this Term by the production in open Court of the deposition of John Drye the other subscribing witness to said Will which was then ordered by the Court to be so certified and recorded. Then came Willie Balthrop one of the Executors named in said Will and entered into bond and security satisfactory to the Court and qualified according.

                                       Test-Field Farrar, Clerk

Recorded in Book A. page 119 this 17th April 1833.
F. Farrar, Clk.

(102) (GEORGE DAVIDSON No. 58)

Be it known that I, GEORGE DAVIDSON of the County of Dickson and State of Tennessee being in a low state of health but of sound memory and in my propertsenses make this my last Will and Testament, as follows, to wit. After my death my body to be buried in a decent manner and my Estate to be divided in the following manner (that is to say) All the land granted to me by the State of Tennessee I leave to my son George Davidson and all my farming tools I also leave to him the said George Davidson. And to my wife Elizabeth Davidson I leave a certain sorrell mare and one feather bed, bedstead and furniture and also all my household and kitchen furniture. I leave my wife Elizabeth during her natural life andlikewise she the said Elizabeth is to have her maintainance on theland during her natural life or widowhood and to my daughter Jane Clark I leave one sorrell horse colt and three head of cattle now in the possession of her husband Richardson L. Clark and alsotwo sons and the balance of my stock of hogs and mare colt. I leave to my son George Davidson and all my flock of Sheep to be equally divided between my wife Elizabeth my Daughter Jane Clark and my son George Davidson and the balance of my stock of Cattle I leave to be divided between my wife Elizabeth and Davidson Executrix and my son George Davidson Executor. In testimony whereof I have hereunto set my hand and seal this 10th day of July in the year of our Lord 1823.

George Davidson (seal)

Witness: James Teas
Matthey Gilmore S.
James Gilmore S.

State of Tennessee Dickson County Court Term 1823. I, Field Farrar, Clerk of said Court do hereby certify that at said Term of said Court the within last Will and Testament of George Davidson dec'd was produced in open Court and proven to be such by the oaths of James Gilmore and Matthew Gilmore subscribing witnesses thereto and ordered by the court to be so certified and recorded. Given under my hand at Office this 12th day of November 1833.

Field Farrar, Clerk of said Court.

(103) (DAVID PASSMORE No. 59)

In the name of God Amen. I, DAVID PASSMORE of the County of Dickson and State of Tennessee being in my proper senses calling to mind that we are all born to die thanks be to God for it I give up my soul in the care of God and my body to moulder in the Clay. I do make and ordain this my last Will and Testament (that is to say) Principal and first of all I give to my beloved Daughter Mary Reader, a certain tract of land containing one hundred and fifty acres lying on the waters of Four mile in said County whereon I now live. I also give to my beloved daughter Elizabeth Black a certain tract or tracts of land lying on the head of Four Mile containing thirty acres also one tract lying on Beaverdam Creek containing fifnetpen and 3/4 acres in the said County I also give unto my Grandson William Black son of Elizabeth Black fifty acres of land in Hickman County lying on Blue Creek the waters of Duck River. I also want my negro woman Jane, and all my personal property, Household and Kitchen furniture sold and after my just debts are paid and then divided it equally between my two daughters that is to say Mary Reader and

Elizabeth Black except one bed and furniture I leave to Nancy Blacks oldest Daughter of Mary Malvina last of all whom I leave appoint William Gentry and James Hicks my Executors of this my last will and Testament hereby revoking all former will by me made. In witness whereof I have hereunto set my hand and seal the day and date afore written in the year of our Lord one thousand eight hundred and thirty four.

Feb'y 20th 1834. Signed)
sealed and delivered in)   David Passmore   (seal)
the presence of us)
Test- Davidson Crink
        his
John L X Hicks
     mark

State of Tennessee, Dickson County Court April Term 1834. I, Field Farrar Clerk of said Court do hereby certify that at said Term of said Court (& seventh day of said month) the within paper writing (104) purporting to be the last Will and Testament of David Passmore dec'd was produced in open Court and proven to be such by the oaths of Davidson Crink and John L. Hicks subscribing witnesses thereto and ordered by the Court to be so certified and recorded. Given under my hand at office this 7th day of April 1834.

                                Field Farrar, Clerk.

(LEBIUS RICHARDSON No. 60)

In the name of God Amen. I, LEBIUS RICHARDSON of the County of Dickson and State of Tennessee being old and frail but of sound mind and memory have a desire to settle my estate to settle my estate as I wish it to be disposed of after my death do this 20th February one thousand eight hundred and twenty nine do make publish and confirm this my last Will and Testament ruleing all other former Wills and is in manner and form as follows.

1st-It is my will and desire that just debts and funeral expences be paid out of my estate.

2nd-I lend to my beloved wife Frankey during her life or widowhood the land and plantation whereon I now live together with my negro man Caster, and my negro woman Chancy and and one horse saddle and b riddle, one bed and furniture three cows and calves, six head of sheep and twelve head of hogs and as much of my household and kitchen furniture as she may think necessary for her use, and two ploughs and gear two axes and two weeding hoes for the purpose of raising and schooling my two youngest children. It is also my will that she have one years provision laid out for her out of the stock on hand and at her death or intermarriage it is my will that the land I lend her, and the stock and plantation utensils be equally divided between my two youngest sons, namely John and Stephen Daily. I also will that at her death or intermarriage my son John have my negro man Caster and my son Stephen Dailey have my negro woman Chancy and the household furniture to be equally divided between John and Stephen Daily. I leave to my son Thomas all thaat I have heretofore put in his posession, namely the land on which he lives which I have deede d to him, one horse, briddly and saddle, one bed and furniture one Cow and Calf, two head of sheep, two sows and pigs all of which he has already received. I give to my son Lebbius Wilkins one hundred and thirty acres of land adjoining that I deeded to my son Thomas, one Horse, one Cow and Calf, one bed and Furniture, two sows and pigs, four head of sheep. I give to my daughter Eliza Tatom one hundred acres of land lying on the head of Rocky Creek laid off on the South side of the tract of four hundred acres also all that I have heretofore put in her possession.

(105) I give to my son James Joy one hundred and fifty acres of land adjoining that I gave my daughter Eliza also one Horse, one cow and calf one bed and furniture six head of sheep, six head of hogs also all that I have heretofore put in possession. I give to my daughter Polly Knon one hundred and fifty acres of land more or less adjoining that I gave my son James, also one Horse, a one Cow and Calf, one bed and furniture one chest six head of sheep one spinning wheel and one pair of cords.

I give to my son John, one Horse, one Cow and Bed and Furniture together with property before named at his Mothers death or intermarriage and if he dies withour a lawful heir all his property shall return to Stephen Dailey.

I give to my son Stephen Dailey one Horse, one Cow, one Bed & furniture together with the property before named at his Mothers death or intermarriage and if he dies wihhout a lawful heir all his property shall return to John. The residue of my Estate I wish to be sold and the money equally divided among all my children.

Lastly, I make and ordain my sons Thomas Richardson, Lebius W.
(106) Richardson and John Richardson, Executors to this my last Will and Testament. In witness whereof I have hereunto set my hand and seal. Signed, sealed and delivered in the presence of us this 20th day of March 1829.

                                                       his
                                     Lebius X Richardson (seal)
                                          mark

A. Coldwell S.)
John B. Walker, S.)
Allen Nesbitt, S)

State of Tennessee, Dickson County Court October Term 1833. I, Field Farrar, Clerk of said Court do hereby certify that at said Term of court the within paper writing purporting to be the last Will and Testament of Lebius Richardson dec'd was produced in open Court and proven to be such by the oaths of A. Caldwell, John B. Walker, and Allen Nesbitt subscribing witnesses thereto and the same was ordered. Given under my hand at Office this 7th day of October 1833.

                                     Field Farrar, Clk.

(RICHARD CLAIBORNE NAPIER No. 61)

I, RICHARD CLAIBORNE NAPIER of Dickson County and State of Tennessee being of sound mind and perfect memory make and publish this my last Will and Testament in manner and form following:

First,- It is my request that all my just debts be paid as early as possible in order to which I desire that my Executors hereinafter named shall proceed to sell either at public or private sale on such credits as to them shall seem most to the interest of my estate all or any such portion of my real estate as they may deem best, except my store Houses and Lots on Union and College streets Nashville, and the tracts of Land on Harpeth river where my family have lately resided and the tracts of land in Robertson Bend of Cumberland River in Davidson County whereon Hannah Napier now lives.

Secondly- I desire that my Executors shall in like manner sell the following slaves, to wit, Negro woman Mary also Negro men, Charles, Speedley, Ivin Tasberry, Stephen Shelby Daniel Morehead and indeed any other of my slaves, that my Executors shall think it for the interest of my family and estate to sell whether for the payment of my debts or otherwise, and sell whether for the payment of my
(107) debts or otherwise, and whereas it is my desire to do equal and im impartial justice to my wife and each of my children as nearly as may be a small exeception in favour of my beloved wife.

Thirdly- I desire that my two youngest children, to wit, Leroy W. Napier and Charlotte Mary Napier, may have such a support in money or property act off to each of them for their education and support until they come of age or marry out of general Estate exclusive of what I shall hereafter devise to them as my Executors may deem just and right in order to place them on an equality with any two oldest children.

Fourthly- I give to my beloved Wife Charlotte Napier all my household and kitchen furniture, my Good Watch (which at her death I wish given to one of my children) My shot gun now in possession of Thomas Overton, My Rifle Gun which James R. Napier used for a number of years, my paisent riding Horse, saddle and Bridle and also such Books as she may have bought for her own use exclusive of her legace herein after mentiones.

It is my will and desire and I hereby direct my Executors after the payment of all my just debts to give to my beloved wife Charlotte Mary Napier, each the sum of nine thousand dollars in money or property as may be bought by my Executors to be most adwantageios to the interest of all my family and that the Robertson Bend tract of land and a part of my stock of every discriptipn and farming utensils to carry on said farm also negro woman Cloe and girl Hannah about four years old and boy Henry about six years old be given to to my two children Leroy W. Napier and Charlotte Mary Napier in part payment of the said sums of nine thousand dollars equally between my said two children according to quality, quantity and value. I also give to my son Leroy W. Napier my chain and compass extra not to be valued to him in the division of my estate.

(108 I give to my son James R. Napiers children the sum of nine thousand dollars which I advanced to their late Father during his lifetime which devise is exclusive altogether of a tract of land which I bought of their late Father lying on Nails Creek of the waters of Turnbull Creek which their said Father conveyed to me in his lifetime and which I now own.

I give to my son Madison C. Napier the sum of nine thousand dollars which I have advanced to him inclusive of all accounts that he has heretofore or may now have against me for whatever purpose or claim which nine thousand dollars I have advanced to him in part in a house and Lot near the Town of Nashville heretofore conveyed by me to him at the price of Five thousand Dollars & the balance I have paid him in money and such other things as he desires to the amount of the balance of Nine thousand Dollars.

I also direct my executors to pay to Hannah Napier the sum of seventy five Dollars per annum during the time she remains the widow of my son James R. Napier.

It is my will and desire that after the paymen of the said sums of Nine thousand dollars each to my said wife, my son Leroy W. Napier and my Daughter Charlotte Mary Napier, as herein befor directed that all the rest and residue of my estate both real and personal be equally divided into five shares share and share a like between my wife one fifth, the five children of my son James R. Napier one fifth to be divided among them in equal shares and to the survivor or survivors of them should any of them die before they arrive at the age of twenty one years. To my son Madison C. Napier one fifth. To my son Leroy W. Napier one fifth and to my Daughter Charlotte Mary Napier one fifhh to them and their heirs forever.

(109) And whereas I have confidence in the integrity of Peyton Robertson and Benjamin Sharp Jun'r. I hereby appoint them Executors to this my last Will and Testament and request that the Court will not require of them any security whatever for their faithful performance.

Hereby revoking all former Wills by me made.
In Testimony whereof I have hereunto set my hand and affixed my seal this sixth day of March in the year of our Lord one Thousand Eight hundred and Thirty four.

R.C. Napier   (seal)

Signed, sealed, published and declared by the within named Richard Claiborne Napier to be his last Will and Testament in the presence of us who have hereunto subscribed our names as witnesses in the presence of the Testator and at his request.

T.H. Claiborne
Titus Hale
Thomas Overton

I do immediately after signing the body of the foregoing as my Will and Testament hereby add the following as a codicil thereto to wit;

It is my will and desire and I do hereby give my Executor Benj'm Sharp Jun'r heretofore named as compensation for his trouble in executing my will the sum of Twelve Hundred Dollars per year, together with all such necessary expences in hiring a clerk or clerks together with other reasonable expences as may be found necessary in attending to the same. Witness my hand and seal the day and date above written.

R.C. Napier   (seal)

Acknowledged in like manner before us,
T.H. Claiborne
Titus Hale
Thomas Overton

(110) I, Richard C. Napier of Dickson County and State of Tennessee do this fourteenth day of March one thousand eight hundred and thirty four make and publish this Codicil to my last Will and Testament as follows, to wit:

Whereas I have sundry debts due me from persons in insolvent circumstances and it cannot reasonably be expected that the full amount of said debts or claims will be collected. I therefore authorize and empower my said Executors to compound and compromise with debtors and receive such a part of such debts or claims as they shall think to the interest of my estate andto give full and complete receipts and acquittance to such debtors as aforesaid at their discretion. It is my desire that this my present Codicil be annexed to and made a part of my last Will and Testament to all intents and purposes.

In witness whereof I have hereunto set my hand and affixed my seal this day and date above written.

R.C. Napier   (seal)

Signed, Sealed, published and declared by the above named Richard C. Napier to be his Codicil to his last Will and Testament in the presence of the Testator and at his request.

Titus Hale
Thomas Overton

State of Tennessee, Dickson County April Term 1834. Then was the last Will and Testament of Richard C. Napier Dec'd produced in open Court and duly provento be such by the oaths of Titus Hale and Thomas Overton suvscribing witnesses thereto and the same was ordered by the Court to be so certified and recorded. Then came Peyton Robertson and Benjamine Sharp Jun'r. the Executors named in said Will and qualified accordingly and that they have Letters Testamentary. In testimony whereof I, Field Farrar, Clerk of said Court have hereunto set my hand and affixed the seal of said Court done at office in Charlotte this 9th day of April A.D. 1834.

Field Farrar.

State of Tennessee, Dickson County, July 21st 1834. Then was the foregoing last Will and Testament of Richard C. Napier Dec'd Recorded in Book A. pages 124, 125, 126, 127.

Test- Field Farrar.

(111) LEONARD PINEGAR No. 62)

In the name of God Amen. I, LEONARD PINEGAR of the State of Tennessee and Dickson County being convinced of the certainty of death and being in perfect mind and memory do make this my last Will and Testament (to Wit)

1st- I give and bequeath unto my beloved wife Susannah Pinegar all my real and personal property, that is my land and negro girl Mary, together with all my stock of every kind my household and kitchen furniture of every what ever except one filly called Tibb which I give to my son Joseph Pinegar for his present use and benefit. In connection with every species of property as above named I give her (Susannah) all my money in hand together with all that is dur me by note or otherwise out of which I wish all my just debts paid-All with the exception as above to be by Susannah used as her legal right and interest during her widowhood, only should, or as my children marries I wish her to give to them as she my wife deems expedient. Should my wife intermarry I wish her then to take her part agreeable to Law and the balance equally divided between my children. In testimony whereof I have hereunto set my hand and seal this 12th day of February 1835.

Leonard Pinegar (seal)

Signed, Sealed & etc)
in presence of)
William Pinegar)
David Gray)

As a part of the aforementioned Will and Testament I wish I wish to make an alteration relative to my land and in connexion with the young mare give my son Joseph Pinegar a part of my Land (To wit) 223 acres lying down the creek known by the name of the Ross place all the divided as before mentioned. In testimony whereof I have set my hand and seal this 12th day of Feb'y 1835

Leonard Pinegar (seal)

Signed, sealed & etc)
in presence of)
William Pinegar)
David Pinegar)

(112) State of Tennessee, Dickson County, September 16th 1835. Then was the above last Will and Testament of Leonard Pinegar Dec'd Recorded in Book A. pages 128 and 129.

Test-Field Farrar.

(JAMES HOLLAND No. 63)

The last Will and Testament of JAMES HOLLAND OF The State of Tennessee and Dickson County I, the James Holland considering the uncertainty of this mortal life and being of sound mind and memory blessed be Almighty God, for the same do make and publish this my last Will and Testament in manner and form following, that is to say,

First, I give and bequeath unto my beloved son Hardy Holland the Twenty acre tract of land where he now live also I give and bequeath to my second son Mark thirty acres of land where I now live. I give and bequeath to my second daughter Sally one hundred acre tract of land being part of the survey taken up by my son Mark reserving of about four acres where I have improved. Also I give and bequeath to my son Mark one Rifle Gun. I give and bequeath to my son Mark one Rifle Gun. I give and bequeath to my second daughter Sally single woman above named two cows and their heifers. Also all the household furniture and all the money I have is to be hers above named at my death. Also she is to have her choice of one horse beast out of six head. I give and bequeath to Patsey Bruer my grand daughter and John and John my grown son all my corn and Bacon that I have if they stay and remain with Sally my Daughter as she   to deal out to them as necessary and share equally of the same w h them. Now all the re- mainder of my property that is to say Hor   s, Cattle, Sheep, Hogs and of Stock whatever, these my two sons Hard   and Mark to divide or cause to be divided between themselves as   hey think best. Now of all I possess or hold I do give and beque   h to my Daughter Delia and Mary my first and third daughters fiv   dollars a piece. Now this my last Will and Testament hereby revokin   all former Wills by me made. In Witness whereof I have hereunto   t my hand and seal this 12th day of February 1835.

Signed, Sealed, published and declared   y the above named James Holland to be his last Will and Testament   n the presence of us who have hereunto subscribed our names as wit   sses.

Test-Charles W. Brown S.   J   es X Holland   (seal)
     Isaac Glannery S.

(113)   Now in the presence of the above witne   es I, James Holland do appoint my oldest son Hardy to be Executo   of my above last Will and Testament.

    State of Tennessee, Dickson County, Co   t of Pleas and Quarter Sessions, April Term 1835. Then was the w   hin last Will and Test- ament of James Holland dec'd produced in   n Court and duly proven to be such by the oaths of Charles W. Br   , Isaac Glannery subscrib- ing Witnesses thereto and ordered by the   ourt to be so certified and recorded. Given under my hand at Office this 6th day of April 1835.
                                         Field Farrar, Clerk.
    State of Tennessee, Dickson County, September 16th 1835. Then was the foregoing last Will and Testament of James Holland dec'd., re- corded in Book A. Page 130,131.
                        Test-Field Farrar

(JOHN CHOATE No. 65)
    State of Tennessee, Dickson County, In the name of God Amen. I, JOHN CHOATE being weak in body but in sound mind and memory blessed be Almighty God for the same do publish and make this my last Will and Testament in manner and form following, that is to say first to
(114) my beloved Eleanor Choate I give and bequeath all of my household and kitchen furniture except such as I have disposed of and also four negroes, that is Mary, Verge, Nancy and Alsia and also my stock of horses, cattle, sheep and hogs except such of each as I may dis- pose of and also it is my desire that my son John H. Choate never disposses my beloved wife of the premises that I now live on which

I have given to him by deed of gift and it is my will that she have the use and benefit of the above mentioned negro and their increase be equally divided between all of my children and I also give and bequeath that my Peter Choate and Squire J. Choate, two tracts of containing one hundred acres each, which includes my old plantation where I have formerly lived which land I want equally divided between my two sons that is Peter Choate and Squire J. Choate, the division line to run from my north boundary line of the two tracts and run south with a hollow which divides the cleared land on my old tract so as to give the east division a cave spring is on that tract of land, the east division of said two hundred acres I give and bequeath to my son Peter Choate and the west division of said tract I give and bequeath to my son Squire J. Choate. And I do hereby appoint my beloved Eleanor Choate my sole Executor to this my last Will and Testament, hereby revoking all former wills by me made. In witness whereof I have hereunto set my hand and seal this nineteenth day of August in the year of our Lord Eighteen hundred and thirty four.

             his
           John X Choate (seal)
             mark

(115) Signed, sealed, published and declared to be his last Will and Testament in presence of us who have hereunto subscribed our names as witnesses in the presence of the Testator.

           Test-William S. Coleman S.
             Luke Matlock S.
             John H. Choate S.

 State of Tennessee, Dickson County, Court of Pleas and Quarter Sessions January Term 1835. Then was the within last Will and Testament of Choate deceased produced in open Court and duly proven to be such by the oaths of William S. Coleman, Luke Matlock and John H. Choate subscribing witnesses thereto and ordered by the Court to be so certified and recorded.

           Test-Field Farrar, Clk.

 State of Tennessee, Dickson County, September 18th 1835. Then was the foregoing last Will and Testament of John Choate dec'd Recorded in Book A. Pages 133,134.

           Test-Field Farrar, Clk.

(JOHN WILLEY No. 66)
 In the name of God Amen. I, JOHN WILLEY of the County of Dickson and State of Tennessee being weak in body but of sound mind and perfect memory-Blessed be Almighty God for the same do make and publish this my last Will and Testament in manner and form as followeth, that is to say. First, I give and bequeath to my beloved wife Polly during her natural life all the personal property I am now in possession of except such as I shall hereafter give and specify in this Will. To my Daughter Polly I give a horse called Jolly and one good feather bed and one Cow and Calf. And to my daughter Elizabeth I give one horse called Shap one good feather bed and one Cow and Calf. And to my son Washington I give one mare and Colt called Fanny until the colt become three years old then the mare to be returned to my wife provided the colt should live so long if not he is to keep the mare also one feather bed and Cow and Calf. and to my Daughter Frances Heaven I give one Cow & Calf. And to my son John I give one Cow and Calf. These several devices I will that my

(116) I give one Cow and Calf. These several devices I will that my wife do comply with, be giving each of my children the property herein given to them when they shall require it of her. I also will that my beloved wife have the use and benefit of the plantation whereon I now live and at her decease I will that the plantation and all the personal property that she shall leave be sold and the money arrising from said sale to be equally divided amongst all my children. I do hereby appoint my wife Polly and my brother William Willey Executrix and executor of this my last Will and Testament hereby revoking all former wills by me made. In witness whereof I have hereunto set my hand and seal this 18th of August 1823.

John Willey (seal)

Signed, sealed, published and declared by the above named John Willey to be his last Will and Testament in the presence of us who have hereunto subscribed our names as witnesses in the presence of the Testator.

Lebius W. Richardson
Allen Nesbitt
A. Coldwell

State of Tennessee, Dickson County, Court of Pleas and Quarter Sessions, October Term 1835. Then was the within or annexed last Will and Testament of John Willey deceased produced in open Court and p proven to be such by the oaths of Allen Nesbitt and A. Coldwell subscribing witnesses thereto which was ordered to be recorded.

Test-Field Farrar, Clk.
By his Deputy Tho. J. Kelly

State of Tennessee, Dickson County. hen was the foregoing or annexed last Will and Testament of John Willey deceased recorded in Book A. Pages 134,135.

(JOHN JOHNSON No. 67)

The last Will and Testament of JOHN HOHNSON of the State of Tennessee and Dickson County. I, John Hohnson considering the uncertainty of the mortal life and being of sound mind and memory blessed be Almighty God for the same do make and publish this my last Will and Testament in manner and form following, that is to say, First, I give and bequeath unto my beloved wife during her life or first widowhood the house and houses where I now live and also the farm and Mill for the same. She is to take the charge and care of my three youngest sons, that is to say, Thomas M. Johnson and Stephen B Johnson. I do give and bequeath to my beloved wife Anny one negro man by the name (117) of William Bedford also one negro boy by the name of Joe and one negro girl by the name or Jenny. Also I give to my wife one Mare named Kit and one horse by the name of Jack and one yoke of Steers and two Cows and Calves, two beds and also as much household furniture as will be necessary for her comfort in life, also all the crop that is now on the farm, and the gang of hogs thats at the Mill. All to be hers for her and three above named sons for their support. All and I wish my son Thomas H. Johnson to have a certain bay mare by the name of Fly and also one Cow and Calf and bed and furniture and one saddle. And I also give to my son Joel S. Johnson one filly and my saddle and also my saddle and also one Cow and Calf also bed and furniture. And also give to my son Stephen B Johnson one filly and saddle to be worth fifteen dollars and also one bed and furniture. I, John Johnson do give and bequeath to my daughter Patsey, single woman one mare called Diamond, one Cow and Calf, two bed and furniture.

(118) I, John Johnson do give and bequeath to my daughter Cholaty one Judgement of sixty seven dollars and seventy five cents on Richard Batson, and now as to all the rest of my negroes are to be valued and equally divided to all my children, that is to say, Polly Hudson, Patsey, John, William, Charloty, Thomas, Joel, Stephen, also all the land or lands belonging to me are to be sold and divided equally as they think best that is to say all other land besides what I left my dear wife Anny. And lastly as to all the rest, residue and remainder of my personal estate goods and chattels of what kind so ever, to be sold and equally divided to each and every one of my children. And hereby I do appoint my beloved Wife Anny Johnson, sole executrix of this my last Will and Testament hereby revoking all former Wills by me made. In witness whereof I have hereunto set my hand and seal this August 17th 1835.

John Johnson Sen'r (seal)

Test-
Charles W. Brown S.
Benjamine Holland S.

State of Tennessee, Dickson County, Court of Pleas and Quarter October Term 1835. Then was the foregoing last Will and Testament of John Johnson dec'd produced in open court and proven to be such by the oaths of Charles W. Brown and Benjamin Holland which was ordered to be recorded.

Test-Field Farrar, Clk.
By his Deputy Tho. Kelley.

State of Tennessee, Dickson County, Then was the foregoing last Will and Testament of John Johnson dec'd recorded in Book A. pages 136, 137.

Test-Field Farrar, Clk.

(PETER GOODWIN No. 68)

In the name of God Amen. I, PETER GOODWIN of the County of Dickson and State of Tennessee being in a low state of health but of perfect mind and memory do this day make my last Will and Testament, to Wit:

1st-I give to my beloved wife Sally Goodwin all my estate both real and personal during her natural life or widowhood and after her death to be divided as follows.

(119) I give to my five youngest children, Lucy Goodwin, Sal Goodwin, William Goodwin, Peter Goodwin, John Goodwin after the death of my wife all of my real and perishable property consisting of land, Horses, Cattle, Hogs, Household and kitchen furniture together with my farming tools of every kind to be sold and equally divided amongst the five youngest above named children and lastly I appoint Thomas Merrell and George W. Tatom sole Executors of this my last Will and Testament.

his
Peter X Goodwin (seal)
mark

Signed, sealed and delivered in the presence of us this 29th day of November in the year of our Lord one thousand eight hundred and thirty four.

Test-James Thedford
George W. Tatom

State of Tennessee, Dickson County, Court of Pleas & Quarter Sessions January Term 1835. Then was the foregoing last Will and Testament of Peter Goodwin dec'd produced in open Court and proven to be and proven to be such by the oaths of James Thedfore and George W. Tatom subscribing witnesses thereto and which was ordered to be recorded.

Test-Field Farrar, clk.
By his Deputy Tho. Kelly.

State of Tennessee, Dickson County. Then was the foregoing last Will & Testament of Peter Goodwin deceased recorded in Book A. page 139.

Test-Field Farrar, Clerk.

(JOHN TUCKER No. 69)

In the name of God Amen. Be it remembered that I, JOHN TUCKER of the County of Dickson and State of Tennessee, being weak of body but of sound mind and memory, you may say this, considering the uncertainty of mortal life and being of sound mind Blessed be to God for the same do make and publish this my last Will and Testament in manner and form following, that is to say, I give and bequeath unto my children, that is to say James M. Tucker, Jane, Lewis, Louisa, C. Tucker, William C. Tucker, Mary Anne. I wish my property sold and equally divided between them all after making the youngest equal with James and Jane which said James has had $113.75 and Jane has had $47.50 and an equal division after my just debts are paid. I appoint James M. Tucker and John Hicks as Executors to my Will. Given under my hand and seal this day signed in the presence of us August 15th 1835.

John Tucker (seal)

Test-Wm. Gentry S.
James Hicks S.

(120) State of Tennessee, Dickson County, Court of Pleas & Quarter Sessions October Term 1835. Then was the foregoing or annexed Will and Testament of Joh Tucker dec'd produced in open Court and proven to be such by the oaths of William Gentry and James Hicks subscribing witnesses thereto and which was ordered to be recorded.

Test-Field Farrar, Clk.
By his Deputy Tho. J. Kelly

State of Tennessee, Dickson County. then was the foregoing or annexed last Will and Testament of John Tucker dec'd recorded in Book A. Pages 137,138.

Test-Field Farrar, Clk.

(WILLIAM BRASHER NO. 70)

Being in my right mind and proper senses, on this the twelfth day of October in the year of Our Lord One thousand eight hundred and thirty two I make my last Will and Testament. I, first will and bequeath my soul to God and my body to the earth in a decent manner.

2nd-I will all my just debts to be paid.

3rd-I will and bequeath to my beloved Nephew William B. Simmons one horse, bridle and saddle, and one bed and furniture.

5th-I will & bequeath to my beloved Nephew William B. Simmons one horse, bridle and saddle, and one bed and furniture.

4th-I will & bequeath to Lovy Council one bed and furniture.

5th-I will and bequeath to Minerva Malugen one bed and furniture.

Lastly-I will and bequeath to my brother in Law Jacob Evans all the remainder of my Estate Real and Personal, and Jacob Evans, I leave Executor of this my Will. No security of him required.

William Brasher

Test-William Shelton S.
William E. Slayden

(WILLIAM BRASHER No. 70)

State of Tennessee, Dickson County, Court of Pleas & Quarter Sessions January Term 1836. then was the foregoing last Will and and Testament of William Brasher brought into open Court and proven to be such by the oaths of William Shelton & William E. Slayden subscribing witnesses thereto which was ordered to be recorded.
Test-   Field Farrar, Clerk.

State of Tennessee, Dickson County. Then was the foregoing last Will and Testament of William Brasher, recorded in Book A. page 138.
                    Test-Field Farrar, Clk.

(WILLIAM MORRISON No. 71)

In the name of God Amen. I, WILLIAM MORRISON of the County of Dickson being now grown old and knowing that is the lot of all men to die and being weak of body but of sound and disposing mind do make and publish this my last Will and Testament making such disposition of the effects which it has pleased God to bestow on me in such as is most just and pleasing to me revoking all other Wills ever by me made, and is in manner and form following:

(121) Item 1st-My Will and desire is that my body be buried in a decent and christian like manner on the farm where I now live and by the side of my daughter Charity Nolen and to be done at the expence of my estate.

Item 2nd-After the payment of all my just debts which are but few my will and desire is that my beloved wife Rachel Morrison have the sole use and benefit of my house and farm whereon I now live if she thinks it most desireable to continue there for and during her natural life also all necessary household and kitchen furniture and farming utensils & etc. which I particularly wish my Executors hereinafter named to see to that she has and enjoys, also the following stock, one bay mare called Loosy and my sorrell horse or other of her choice should one or either or both of those horses die before sale on my property and such of my other stock of cattle say cows, hogs and sheep as be may be necessary for her comfort and support together with my Daughter Betsey and my grand Daughter Betsey Melinda Nolen who I wxpect to reside with my wife during her life. I do wish my wife to retain either my ox cart or old waggon, and for her support through life and better comfort and she choosing to do so I wish my wife to have and take her choice of any two negroes I now own but should they prove to be refractory or disobedient my Executors are requested to sell such negro and my wife to be supported on such sale and otherwise I wish my executors to use his own discretion and make such disposition of a refractory or disobedient servant as he may think best for the benefit of my heirs- wife during her life having due regard to the interest of my heirs to whom it is to go after her death. Now that there be no misunderstanding of this division my whole object is under all and my circumstances for my Executors to see that my beloved Wife shall have a home and
(122) all the necessary comforts of life so long as she lives. Also all the necessary repairs on my house to be done and paid for out of my estate.

Item 3rd-My beloved Daughter Elizabeth lives with me and who has been a dutiful child to me my will and desire is that she remain on the plantation with her Mother during the life of wife. After the death of my wife I give to her one tract of land of one hundred acres on the east and and north east of the tract I live on for which I hold a Grant. Also my Daugnter Elizabeth has some property about the house such as bed, wheels & cards with every article of clothing, chest & etc. I allow her to keep. Also after the death of my wife it is my desire that my Daughter Elizabeth Morrison and my grand Daughter Betsy Malinda Nolen, share and share equal in all the household good, kitchen furniture, Horses, cattle, hogs, sheep & etc. with one plow hoes, and an axe which was left for the support of my wife to their own use and each of their uses forever, desiring Daughter Elizabeth to take charge of Grand Daughter Betsey M. Nolen and make a generous divide such Horses, cattle & etc. household goods and kitchen furniture they being all I allow my Daughter and Grand Daughter until we come to a general division among the whole of my children.

Item 4th-It is my will and desire that my son William Morrison for himself and heirs, continue to have and to hold and forever enjoy the tract of land he now lives on containing two hundred and three acres also a late entry of one hundred acres adjoining the other on the east and northwest every other species of property he may have received of me being all and the full amount of all I allow William on single division.

(123) Item 5th-It is my will and desire that my Daughter Rachel Patterson I loan to her during her life one negro girl named Ann, which she now has in possession and after her death I wish the negro Ann with her increase to go to my grand children, William and Polly Patterson to them and their heirs forever. I also have given to Polly Patterson a young sorrell mare to her and her heirs forever,,but do not allow to Robert and Rachael Patterson on a single division one cents more nor on a general division without charging Robert and Rachael Patterson with $300. which my estate will be credited with in their share on a general division,

Item 6th-It is my will that my daughter May Weakley be allowed no other part or share on single division than she has already received of me before my death, her balance of share shall be in general division of my estate amongst the whole of my children that she will be entitled to receive with the other heirs.

Item 7th-It is not my will that three children of Robert and Peggy Dickson deceased be entitled to receive on single division as legal heirs or be allowed more than they have received of me in their parents lifetime of my estate unless I think proper, and right to do so in my lifetime and before my death but will be allowed a full share in the general division, no charge to be brought forward against them for the negro girl I gave to my Daughter Peggy Dickson as she died the negro girl died at the loss of my estate and not that of Robert Dickson deceased nor the expence of his heirs.

Item 8th-To my Daughter Jane Reynolds I give and bequeath all the property she took home with her when she left home and for the for-- sook my house for the sake of Solomon Reynolds, Bed clothing, chest Wheel cards, two cows and calves and one steer. I have also loaned Solomon Reynolds and Jane his wife a large fine mare called Flash also a young horse, only on good behavior which is the whole and
(124) every cent worth I allow them of my estate forever, unless daughter Jane should have surviving children if so the loaned mare and young horse I give unto the children being all I allow them of my estate forever, unless also Solomon Reynolds should die and leave his wife Jane a widow in that case it is my will and desire that my Executors allow her in the general division to draw an equal share with my other children and no otherwise & should Daughter Jane die before her husband having no children living the loaned property must return to be divided with the rest of my estate among my other children.

Item 9th-Now all and every species of my property not disposed of of by my will otherwise it is my desire that it be so disposed of under the direction of my executors as they may think most advantageous for my heirs, selling all my negroes with the exception, should my wife seleet one or two as she may desire to be retained by her during her life time and after her death such negro or negroes as she may choose to retain will be sold also as likewise the tract of land on which I now livw and to be retained by her during her natural life shall at her death be sold and the proceed of such sale of negroes & lands to be secured by note with good security payable in specie and every species of my property not specially devised in this will to be sold and the money arrising from the sole or otherwise to be equally divided between my children as follows, to wit, Mary Weakley, Betsey Malinda Nolen in place of her Mother Charity Nolen dec'd to the heirs of Robert and Peggy Dickson dec' to wit, Joseph Morrison Dickson, Robert Patton Dickson, and Rachael Ann Elizabeth Dickson, those three children will be entitled to their Mothers full share, Elizabeth Morrison, William Morrison Jun'r. Rachael Patterson, taking from her equal share with the others the amount of three hundred dollars the price of the negro girl Ann as my other children have received no negro of me if any balance Rachael will be entitled to receive it. My Daughter Jane Reynolds being left out. But it is my desire that should my daughter Jane Reynolds outlive her present husband Solomon Reynolds it is then my sincere wish and desire that she be allowed as full share as one of my heirs and share equally with my other children as above named all of which I sincerely desire my Executors to see carried into full effect.

(125)

Item10-Upon further reflection & beliving that the 7th Item of this will does not exactly do justice to Robert 7 Peggy Dickson children I therefore rescind that clause and direct that my Executors pay over to their Guardians the sum of eight hundred dollars gross which is to be their full share of all dividends arising to them out of my estate.

Item 11- It is my Will and desire that all notes, bonds & deeds due to the Estate at my decease be by my Executors immediately collected the money arising therefrom and the money which I may have in possession at my death be immediately distributed to my children equally, the Executors taking from each a proper receipt from the amounts severally paid and when it is coming to a minor or minors or as is in the case of Robert & Peggy Dicksons children that it be paid over to the Guardians of such minor or minors.

Item 12-I do hereby appoint my worthy friends Robert West and George W. Jorden to be the Executors of this my last Will and Testament. Given under my hand and seal this 25th day of July in the year of our Lord one thousand Eight hundred and thirty five (the word "two" in Item 2nd. interlined before signed) Signed and sealed in presence of Thomas McMurry S.

H.W. Turner S.   William Morrison   (seal)

(126)

Then was the foregoing last Will and Testament of William Morrison dec'd produced in open Court and proven to be such by the oaths of Thomas McMurry and H.W. Turner, subscribing witnesses thereto which was ordered by the Court to be recorded.

Test-Field Farrar, Clk.
By his Deputy Tho. Kelly

(HOWELL FREEMAN No. 72)
In the name of God Amen. I, HOWELL FREEMAN of the County of Dickson and State of Tennessee, forseeing the uncertainty of death and being

of sound mind and disposing mind and memory do publish make and ordain the following as my last Will and Testament, that is to say:

First Item-It is my will and desire that after my funeral expences are paid that my Executor hereinafter named shall pay all my just debts.

Item-One Bedstead, Bed and furniture one Cow and calf, one dinner pot, one oven, and lid and one skillet all of which I give to her and her heirs forever.

Item-It is my will and desire that my Executors hereinafter named shall sell my estate real and personal at public sale, and the proceeds arising from said sale together with all moneys I may have, either in cash ordue me by bond otherwise shall be equally divided amongst my said wife Hannah and my six children, Viz, Bureall, William, Jeramiah, Freeman, Polly Burton wife of Ambrose Burton, Martha Self, wife of Abraham Self, and Elizabeth Massie wife of John Massie all of which I give to them and their heirs forever.

Item-I hereby appoint my son-in-law Abraham Self sole Executor of this my last Will.

In witness whereof I hereby make, publish and declare this to be my last Will and Testament hereby revoking all former Wills by me made, this 15th day of October 1835. Witness my hand and seal.
Signed, sealed and declared and
published in presence of us   Howell Free man   (seal)
Stith Richardson
John Hinson
Jermiah Underwood

(127)   Dickson County, June Term 1836. Then was the foregoing last Will and Testament of Howell Freeman dec'd produced in open Court and proven to be such by Oaths of Stith Richardson, John Hinson and Jeramiah Underwood, subscribing witnesses thereto which was ordered by the Court to be recorded.
                                Test-Wm. Hightower, Clk.

(DAVID WILEY NOQ 73)
State of Tennessee, Dickson County Dec'r. the 29th 1836.
In the name of God Amen. I, DAVID WILEY of the State and County aforesaid being weak in body but of sound mind and ordain this my last Will and Testament in manner and form as follows, to wit:

In the first place I bequeath my soul to God who gave it and my body decently buried. First, my just debts must be paid and my body decently buried. First my just debts must be paid and then I give a the land and houses where I live and the benefits arising from it to belong to my Father Wm. Wiley and my Mother, Ann during their natural lifetime and then my property of all kind during their lifetime then I would wish my land sold and all kind during their lifetime then I would wish my land sold and sold and all my property on twelve months credit then I bequeath sold Fifty Dollars to my brother Jonathan Wileys son Garton Wiley, then I give Fifty Dollars to my brothers Ebnenezer son Lowson Wiley, then I give Fifty Dollars to my brothers Ebenezars youngest son Adderson, Jasper Wiley then give all the balance of my property and the interest I have of my Fathers estate to my brother Ebenezers son Jesse Wiley that is if he stays with my Father and Mother and does for them during their life, if not, I would wish my Father to dispose of that part as he thinks proper and I would wish my Father to dispose of that part as he thinks proper and I hereby appoint David Frasher, my Executor to carry this my last Will into effect and declare this my last Will and Testament the year and date above written. Signed and sealed in the presence of us.

                                                                        David Wiley (seal)

Josiah Thornton

Elizabeth X Myatt (her mark)

(128) I certify that the foregoing is a true copy of the last Will and Testament of David Wiley.

                                                                   Wm. Hightower, Clk.

(THOMAS MATTHEWS No. 74)

    I, THOMAS MATTHEWS being of sound and perfect mind and memory do make and publish this my last Will and Testament in manner and form following.

    1st- I will that all my just debts be paid.

    2nd- I also will and bequeath that my loving wife Emilla Matthews have all of my estate to support her and my children during her life or widowhood, if she marries the property to be sold and the money equally divided between her and the children, to wit, My Daughter Lellia Matthews and my son Andrew Jackson Matthews and George R. Matthews.

    3rd- I appoint my loving wife Emillia Matthews, and my friend George T. Cooksey my Executors to this my last Will revoking all other Wills by me made. In testimony whereof I set my hand and seal this 28th day of April 1834.

                                                             Thomas X Matthews (seal) (his mark)

Attest- Selman Edwards S.)
        William Shelton S.)
Creel Shelton.)

    State of Tennessee, Dickson County, Court of Pleas & Quarter Sessions, April Term 1835. Then was the within last Will and Testament of Thomas Mattews dec'd produced in open court and duly proven to be such by the oaths of Selman Edwards, Wm. Shelton, & Creel Shelton subscribing witnesses thereto and ordered by the Court to be so certified and recorded. Given under my hand at Office this 6th day of April 1835.

                                                 Field Farrar, Clk. of said Court

    State of Tennessee, Dickson County, Sept'r 16th 1835. Then was the foregoing last Will and Testament of Thomas Matthews dec'd. recorded in Book A. page 132.

                                                 Test- Field Farrar.

(129) (GEORGE TUBB No. 75)

    In the name of God Amen. I, GEORGE TUBB of the County of Dickson and State of Tennessee being in perfect mind and memory though weak in body do make this my last Will and Testament in manner and form as follows, to wit:

    I will and bequeath to my beloved son Richard Tubb, two negroes a negro man called young Tom, and a negro woman named Nicy, and to my beloved son Nathan Tubb I will and bequeath two negroes a negro man named old Tom and a negro woman Milly and to my beloved son James Tubb I will and bequeath three negroes a negro woman Hager and boy named Solomon & a negro girl named Hager, and to my beloved Daughter Elizabeth Coleman I will and bequeath two negroes, a negro named Prince and a negro woman named Tener, and to my beloved daugter Martha Middleton I will and bequeath two negroes, a negro woman named Mary and a negro boy named Carroll and it is my will and de-

desire that if Martha Middleton's situation is such that she cannot keep her negroes that the negro woman Mary shall not be sold out of the family. I will and bequeath to my beloved Grandson Daniel Tubb, a note of hand that I hold on William Gilbert and my beloved Grandson, George Tubb. I will and bequeath a note of hand, that I hold on John Coldwell and it is my will and desire that the tract of land that I now live on and crop and all of my perishable property consisting of Horses, Hogs, Cattle and Sheep and my household and my household and kitchen furniture to be sold on a twelve months credit and the money to be equally divided between my Grand Children that is, to Pheba Cooksey's children, Isaac Tubbs children and Mary Davidsons children have one hundred dollars to be divided among them more than the other Grand children, and what money I now have after my debts are paid to begin to the above named grandchildren I wish to have it understood that what I have willed to the above named children. That is Phoeba Cookdeys children one fourth of the amount of my sale and what money I have and also I appoint my son Nathan Tubb & W. S. Coleman, my executors of this my last Will and Testament. In witness whereof I have hereunto affixed my hand and seal this the 17th day of October 1836.

Signed, sealed and published in presence of
Test-Daniel Leech
  James Loggins

(130)

              his
            George X Tubb (seal)
              mark

 I, William Hightower Clerk of the County Court do hereby certify that the foregoing is a true copy of the last Will and Testament of Geo. Tubb, as presented by his Executors Nathan Tubb and W.S. Coleman.

            Wm. Hightower, Clerk.

(JOHN ANGLIN No. 76)

 In the name of God Amen. I, JOHN ANGLIN of the State of Tennessee and County of Dickson being weak in body but of sound and perfect mind and memory, blesseed be Almighty God for the same do make and publish this my last Will and Testament in manner and form following, that is to say, First I give and bequeath unto my beloved wife, Elizabeth Anglin, the land and possessions where I now live, also my negro woman Phebe and negro boy William Henry, also all my horses and cattle and all my other stock, household and kitchen furniture and farming tools, my just debts first to be paid, to hold during her life or widowhood then to be divided as follows. I do give and bequeath to my four sons, Cornelius, William, Aaron and George Anglin the sum of one dollar each. also give and bequeath to my two daughters, Nancy & Margaret a new saddle each. I also give and bequeath to my daughter Sally C. Anglin my negro woman Phebe. I also give and bequeath to my son John Anglin my negro boy William Henry, and if said Phebe should have any mory children to be equally divided between my two youngest children, Sally C. Anglin and John C. Anglin, and lastly to all the rest residue and remainder of my personal estate goods and chattels of what kind and nature whatsoever I give and bequeath the same of my said youngest children Sally C. Anglin and John C. Anglin. I hereby appoint Jacob Rucker and Elizabeth Anglin my wife my sole Executors to this my last will and Testament, hereby revoking all former wills by me made. In witness whereof I have hereunto set my hand and seal the 11th of March in the year of our Lord 1828.

             his
           John X Anglin (seal)
             mark

(131) Signed, sealed, delivered and published by the above named John Anglin to be his last Will and Testament in the presence of us who have hereunto subscribed our names as witnesses in the presence of the Testator.

Archibald Ponder
Nicholas Dudley
Willis Dudley

I do certify that the above is a true copy of the original Will as presented by the above executrix.

Wm. Hightower, Clerk.

(CHARLES THOMPSON No. 77)

In the name of God Amen. I, CHARLES THOMPSON, being of sound mind and perfect memory do make and publish this my last Will and Testament in manner and form following.

Item 1st-It is my will and desire that all of my property of every description remain in the hands of my bloved wife Mary, to be applied in manner and form as I shall hereafter state.

Item 2nd-For the love and affection that I have to my beloved helpless children namely, Nancy, Sally and John and Charles I give all my property of every description including all of my land to them during their natural lives and be it further understood that as they die the property is to desend to the balance of the above named children during their natural lives and it is my will and desire that the said property should be kept alone for the use of said property should be kept along for the use of said children by my wife and my son James Thompson to support them in their helpless situation and at the final decease of all of the above named children then it is my express will and desire that should there be any thing remaining of the said property that my beloved son James Thompson should have it for his troble and attention to his above named sisters and brother.

I do by these presents nominate and appoint my wife Executrix and my son James Thompson Executor to this my last Will and Testament. In testimony whereof I hereunto set my hand and seal this 29th day of January 1834.

(132) Witness-   Charles Thompson (seal)
Ester E. Williams
Daniel H. Williams

I certify that the above is a true copy of the original Will.

Wm. Hightower, Clerk.

(BURWELL MYATT No. 78)

In the name of God Amen. I, BURELL MYATT of the County of Dickson and State of Tennessee being weak in body but of sound mind and memory and considering the uncertainty of this mortal life and being sound judgment blessed be almighty God for the same do make and publish this my last Will and Testament in manner and form following, viz, First I give and bequeath unto my beloved wife, Polly Myatt, all my estate of land and negroes and stock of all sorts my household furniture farming utensils of all sorts to have and to hold during her life or widowhood and after that I want the property of all sorts sold and divided equally except the land I give and bequeath unto my son Eldridge Myatt all the land lying in the West side of my spring branch where I now live and the balance of my land I want divided equally with beloved wife and daughters, I also here-

hereby appoint my beloved wife Polly Myatt, my sole Executrix of this my last Will and Testament hereby revoking all former Wills by me made. In witness whereof I have hereunto set my hand and seal the 2nd of August 1828.

           Burell Myatt

Signed, sealed, published and declared by the above named Burell Myatt to be his last Will and Testament in the presence of us who have hereunto subscribed our names as witnesses in the presence of the testator.

           Kindrick Myatt
             his
         Daniel D. George
            mark

I do hereby certify that the foregoing is a true copy of the original will as appears of record in my Office.

           Wm. Hightower, Clerk.

(133) J. BEV. HUGHES No. 79)

Being infirm of body but entirely sound of mind and knowing that it is appointed that all men shall die, I make this my last Will and Testament.

1st- I wish my affectionate Mother to have five hundred Dollars should there not be that sum, now in hand the first collected to go to her, till full amount received.

2nd- The balance due me after paying my just debts to be paid over to my Father and he equally divide it among my brother & sisters, My Bro's & Sist's Martha B. Ragland, William Granville Hughes, Edwin Madison Hughes, Nancy Newton Hughes, Lemuel Horace Hughes, I wish my Father to have my mare, saddle & Bridle, my sister Nancy to have my Gold Watch. Any and all other property found on hand to be equally divided among my brothers and sisters.

Signed, sealed in the presence of) J. Bev. Hughes
J.R. Hudson
Wm. Carter

I, Wm. Hightower, Clerk of the County Court do hereby certify that the foregoing is a true copy of the original Will of J. B. Hughes as appears of Record in my Office.

           Wm. Hightower, Clerk.

(MARY YARRELL No. 80)

In the name of God Amen. I, MARY YARRELL, widow, being weak in body but of sound and perfect mind and memory do make and publish this my last Will and Testament in manner and form following, viz, that is to say:

First- I give and bequeath to my beloved Nephew, Nathan Gilbert my negro man named Martin his heirs and assigns to have and to hold him his own forever, he the said Nathan Gilbert paying for each and every year, seventy dollars during the term or three years to my nephew William Gilbert.

Item 2nd- I give and bequeath my negro woman named Matilda her freedom at my death when the said Matilda pays over to my Executors the sum of one Hundred Dollars for the expences of my adopted niece Rosanna Gilbert and my niece Tempy Edwards which will be fifty dollars each when the hundred dollars is divided equally between them Then the said negro woman to be free the residue of her days.

Item 3rd- I give and bequeath to my adopted niece Rosanna Gilbert fifty dollars which sum my Executors will pay her from the hire of of Matilda also one of my best feather beds and bedding for the same, one cow and calf, and my side saddle.

Item 4th- I give and bequeath to my niece Tempy Edwards fifty dollars arising from the hire of Matilda.

Item 5th- My wish and request is that all of my personal and movable property shall be sold at public sale after my death except the property reserved as before memtioned and the money arrising from the sale of the same to be equally divided in three equal parts then equally divided among my nephews and nieces theye children of brother William Gilbert, Nicholas Gilbert and (134) James Gilbert and also a note on mybrother William Gilbert dec'd to be divided among my Nephews and Nieces the children of Wm. Gilbert, Nicholas Gilbert and James Gilbert-when collected in the manner as the money arising from the sale of my property. I do nominate and appoint my Nephew Nathan Gilbert and Mabel Gilbert my Executors. As witness whereof I have hereunto set my hand and seal this 6th day of March in the year of our Lord 1831.

            her
           Mary X Yarrell (seal)
            mark

Signed, sealed and delivered
in presence of witnesses
Caleb Evans
  her
Mary X Suither
   mark

Tennessee, Jones Creek-Dickson County, March 6th 1831. I, William Hightower, Clerk of the County Court do hereby certify that the foregoing is a true copy of the Will of Mary Yarrell as proven in open Court in my County.

           Wm. Hightower, Clerk.

(SAMUEL JAMES, No.87)

In the name of God Amen. I, SAMUEL JAMES do make and publish this my last Will and Testament hereby revoking and making void all other Wills by me at any time made. First I direct that my funeral expences and all my debts be paid as soon after my death as possible out of any money that I may die possessed of or may first come into the hands of my Executor. Secondly, I give and bequeath to my son James and Daughter Polly, sixty acres of land whereon I now live both to be equal in the land also to be equal in all the rest of my property exeept one bed that I give unto my daughter Pharnata for her kind attention to me. Lastly, I do hereby nominate and appoint John Cunningham my Executor. In witness whereof I do to this my Will set my hand and seal this 25th day of May 1838.

           Samuel James (seal)

Signed, sealed and published in
our presence and we have subscribed
our names hereto in the presence of the
testator this 25th day of May 1838.
W. Hand
  her
Aby X Williams
   mark

I, William Hightower Clerk of the County Court of Dickson

(135) County, certify that the foregoing is a true copy of the Will of Samuel James proven in open Court and recorded in my office Feb'y 8th 1839.

William Hightower, Clk.

(JAMES TIDWELL, No. 82)

In the name of God Amen. I, JAMES TIDWELL, of the County of Dickson and State of Tennessee, being in a perfect and sound mind but in an inferior state of health do make and ordain this to be my last Will and Testament as follows, Viz.

1st- My will is that my wife Mary Tidwell, shall have five negroes during her natural life or widowhood namely, Taner, Easter, Sam, Calvin, Anna. I wish her to have the house and land I now live on likewise all my stock of every description I wish at the death of my wife Mary Tidwell that all the property then remaining to be sold and the money to be equally divided or the property to be divided equally. Rebecca Lampley to have the one fourth part. Frances Tidwells heirs one fourth to
(136) be kept in the hands of my Executors and to be paid out to them as they come of age. I wish the Court to have no jurisdiction over their parts of my Estate. John Tidwell to have one fourth part. Mary Spencers three children James, Daniel and William to have one fourth to be managed by my Executors as in above directed.

Lastly- I do hereby nominate constitute and appoint my son John K. Tidwell and Joseph Lampley my true and lawful Executors to this my last Will and Testament to carry the same into execution hereby annulling and revoking all other Wills by me heretofore made. In testimony whereof I have set my hand and affixed my seal this twenty second day August one thousand eight hundred and thirty nine.

Signed, sealed and delivered in presence of us,
John B. Carr
Ruffin Perry
James Tidwell

I, William Hightower, Clerk of the County Court of Dickson do hereby certify that the foregoing is a true copy of the Will and Testament of James Tidwell and proven in open Court and recorded in my office on the 29th day of October 1839.

Wm. Hightower, Clerk.

I, Wm. Hightower, Clerk of the County Court of Dickson do hereby certify that the foregoing is a true copy of the Will and Testament of James Tidwell and proven in open court and recorded in my Office on the 29th day of October 1839.

                               Wm. Hightower, Clerk.

(136) (ANN WHITWELL No. 83)

In the name of God Amen. I, ANN WHITWELL of Dickson County and State of Tennessee being of sound mind and memory solemnly make and declare this my last Will and Testament.

To it: I will and bequeath to Blount W. Bell and James Finley both of County and State aforesaid all those negroes slaves for life which were conveyed by John I. Bell to Ann Whitwell by bill of sale bearing date fourth day of May eighteen hundred and thirty seven, and regularly registered among the records of Davidson County on the ninth day of May in the year 1837 in Book Z, pages 200,201 as by reference to said records will more fully appear viz, Hannah aged forty six years, Sam aged twenty seven years, Caroline aged twenty three years. Pope aged eighteen years, Drue aged fifteen years, Drue aged fifteen years, William aged twelve years, Jude the daughter of Hannah aged four years, Susan nine months, Sarah aged twenty seven years, Jude the daughter of Sarah, three years, Reuben aged forty one years, Penny aged forty four years, Lucy aged sixty one years, Patsey aged twenty five years, Phillis aged twenty one years, Cambridge aged thirty seven years, Tom aged seven years, together with the following negroes also slaves for live not included in said bill of sale, to wit, Virgil aged eleven months, Tempy aged eight months and Lucy aged seven months. In trust however for the following purposes which i strictly enjoin the said Trustees to carry into effect according to my last wishes, to wit, I will and bequeath to the said Trustees one negro boy named Drue now aged sixteen years, and one negro boy named Virgil aged eleven months. In trust for my grandson John P. Bell the son of John I. Bell and of my daughter Nancy S. Bell. Also one negro boy named William now aged thirteen years and one negro girl named Tempy aged eight months, In trust for my grandson Thomas Drue Bell the son of John I. & Nancy S. Bell as aforesaid. Also one negro boy named Tom now aged eight years and one negro girl named Lucy aged seven months. In trust for my Grandson Montgomery Bell, the son of John I. and Nancy S. Bell as aforesaid. Also two negro girls, to wit, one named Jude now aged four years, the daughter of Hannah and one also named Jude aged four years the daughter of Sarah, In trust for my Grand daughter Marceanna Bell the daughter of John I. Bell and Nancy S. Bell as aforesaid. And I further will and desire that the said Trustees shall deliver up to such of the above mentioned Legatees shall deliver up to such of the above mentioned Legatees the negroes severally bequeathed to them upon their arrival at the full age of eighteen years and sooner if in the sound discretion of the said Trustee it may be proper, and expedient to do so. And I fully bequeath the said negroes to the

(138) said Trustee In trust for the full use and benefit of the said Legatees and their heirs executors and benefit of the said Legatees and their heirs executors and assigns forever. And I further will and bequeath all my negroes not heretofore disposed of by this instrument to the said Trustees. In trust, that is to say the hire, services and money resulting and flowing from the use of said negroes to be appropriated and expended, to and for the sole support and maintainance of my daughter Nancy S. Bell, (not with standing her coverture) during her life and without being in any wise subject and liable to the debts management power or control of her husband John I. Bell

75

or any after taken husband and her receipt alone from time to time to be a sufficient discharge for the same. And if from the management of said negroes by the said Trustees their profit, hire, and services should realize a sum more than sufficient for the support of the said Nancy S. Bell, then the further profits and balance of the avails accruing from the use of said negroes, are to be devoted and appropriated to the support, Eduaation and maintainance of the minor children of the said John I. Bell and the said Nancy S. Bell and for the support of such of the negroes who are too young to work or who may be too old to work and it is my further will and desire that the said Trustees after the death of the said Nancy S. Bell will divide theaforesaid negroes bequeathed to them as before mentioned in the following manner, Penny, old Bucky, Patsey, Phillis a and Cambridge among my eight grand children sons and daughters of the said John I. Bell and Nancy S. Bell together with the increase of said negroes equally, to wit, Blount W. Bell, Elizabeth West Finley, Mary Ann Bell, Jane P. Bell, John P. Bell, Thomas Drue Bell, Marceanna Bell and Montgomery Bell, and it is my particular desire that these negroes with their Increase shall be equally divided according to value among my eight grand children as aforesaid after the death of the said Nancy S. Bell, and for this purpose I bequeath to the said Trustees the above mentioned negroes In trust to be divided with their increase equally among my eight grand children as aforesaid after the death of my daughter Nancy S. Bell.

(139)

In testimony whereof I have hereunto set my hand and seal, this the 27th day of August in the year one thousand eight hundred and thirty-nine.

Ann Whitwell   (seal)

Test-
J.R. Huson
Elizabeth J. Richardson.

I, Wm. Hightower clerk of the County of Dickson do hereby certify that the foregoing is a true copy of the last Will and Testament of Ann Whitwell proven in open Court by the oaths of J.R. Hudson on the 4th of Nov'r. 1839 and ordered by said Court to be recorded.

Wm. Hightower, Clerk.

(JOHN DAVIDSON No. 84)

In the name of God Amen. I, JOHN DAVIDSON sen'r being of sound mind but in a low state as to health do make and publish this as my last Will and Testament. First, I desire that all my debts be paid as soon as possible out of the first money that comes into the hands of my beloved wife or my Executor. Second, as to what property we have we in the bond of affection have labouped for it lovingly we have enjoyed it and now with a glad heart do I will and bequeath all that I may die possessed of whehher it be lands, cpop of any kind household and kitchen furniture or fowls of all kinds and all my stock of all kinds to my beloved wife during her natural life or widowhood for the support of herself and family. Third, having given my son Henyy one Cow and Calf, one horse, one bed " furniture I now will and bequeath unto him one dollar. Fourth, having given my son Joseph two horses I now will and bequeath unto him one dollar. Fifth, having given my daughter Sarah, one cow and calf, one bed and furniture one saddle. I now will and bequeath unto her one dollar. Sixth, having given my son David one horse, one yoke of oxen, and one hundred and forty dollars I now will and bequeath unto him one dol-

(140)

dollar. 7th, having given my son John one horse one Cow and Calf one bed furniture I now will and bequeath unto him one dollar. Eight, having given mydaughter Mary one Cow & Calf one bed & furniture I now will and bequeath unto her one dollar. Ninth, I will and bequeath unto my son Elijah one horse, Tenth, I will and bequeath unto my son James one sorrell mare. Eleventh, I will and bequeath unto my son William one Colt. Twelfth, I will and bequeath unto my daughter Matilda one Cow & Calf, one bed & furniture. Thirteenth, I will and bequeath unto my daughter Peggy, one Cow & Calf one bed & furniture. Again I will and bequeath unto my two sons, James & William the tract of land on which I now live containing one hundred and forty two acres and my part of the two hundred acres of school land by Grant No. 6630, and date the eleventh day of January 1826 and all that I hold of the forty acre tract that brother Abraham Davidson deeded tome and dated Oct. the 16th 1828 and all the above mentioned land I wish to be equally divided between my two above mentioned sons. Nevertheless I wish my beloved wife Violet Davidson to have the use of said land during her natural life or widowhood and all the other bequests made to her at her decease to be divided with those that may have the care or charge of her. Lastly, I do hereby nominate and appoint my son Elijah Davidson my Executor. In witness whereof I do to this my will set my hand and seal this the 3rd day of September 1839.

John Davidson (seal)

Attest- B. Tidwell
John Porter

I, William Hightower, Clerk of the County Court of Dickson County do hereby certify that the foregoing is a true copy of the original will of John Davidson Sen'r. copied and filed in my Office this day. Given under my hand this 10th day of December 1839.

Wm. Hightower, Clerk.

(JAMES CUNNINGHAM No. 85)
In the name of God Amen. I, JAMES CUNNINGHAM, do make and publish this as my last Will and Testament hereby revoking and making and making void all other Wills by me at any time made.

First-I direct that my funeral expences and all my just debts be paid so soon after my death as possible out of any money that I may die possessed of or may first come into the hands of my executors.

Secondly-I give and bequeath unto my beloved wife my sorrell horse and her saddle and briddle, also one bed and furniture and my pup.

Thirdly-I then wish my Executors to sell all the balance of my estate both real and personal.

Fourthly-I give and bequeath to my beloved brother Thomas Cunningham three hundred dollars in money. I give and bequeath to all the rest of my brothers and sisters, to wit, John Cunningham, Willis Cunningham, Nathaniel Cunningham, Anna atterson, Elizabeth Carroll, Mary Wilson, Amy Hagwood, Nancy Hamilton five dollars each.

Fifthly- I then wish my wife Sarah Cunningham to have all the balance of my estate except what will pay the expences of my executor.

Sixthly and lastly-I hereby nominate and appoint John Cunningham my Executor. In witness whereof I do to this my last will set my hand and seal this 5th day of December 1839.

Signed, sealedand published in our presence, and we have subscribed our names hereto in the presence of the Testator this the 5th day

5th day of December 1839.
Thomas Poyner
Jas. Daniel
Elizah W. Cunningham

James Cunningham (seal)

I, William Hightower, Clerk of the County Court do hereby certify that the foregoing is a true copy of the original will of James Cunningham on file in my office given under my hand this 11th day of January 1840.

Wm. Hightower, Clerk.

(JAMES WHITE No.142)

(142) In the name of God Amen. I, JAMES WHITE of Dickson County and State of Tennessee being of sound mind and memory do make and ordain this my last Will and Testament in manner and form following.

First-I recommend my soul to God who gave it in hope of a joyfull resurection of the same, and my body to be decently buried and as what worldly goods it has please God to bestow on my I dispose of as follows, to wit, I give and bequeath to my two sons John and James T. White, my land with all its appurtenances provided they decently support my wife Polly white off of the same to them their heirs and assigns forever. I also leave to my son Crage White fifteen dollars to Charles White thirty five dollars, Chapman White five dollars, Nancy McLaughlin five dollars Polly Ann Hail five dollars, Sally Harris five dollars, Marhta White a Cow and Calf, bed and five dollars. The residue after paying all my just debts I leave to my above mentioned son James T. White after settling the estate agreeable to the above mentioned will.

Item-I do constitute and appoint my son James T. White my whole and sole Executor of this my last Will and Testament reserving all Wills heretofore by me made. In witness whereof I have hereunto set my hand and seal this 22nd of September 1838.

James White (seal)

Signed, sealed and delivered in presence of
E. Harris
William Harris Jr.

(142)

(WILLIAM HOGINS No. 87)

(143) In the name of God Amen. I, WILLIAM HOGINS of the County of Dickson and State of Tennessee, being weak in body but sound in mind and taking into consideration the certainty of death and the shortness of time do make and constitute this my last Will and Testament.

First-I resign my breath into the hand of God who gave it and then give up my body to be buried decently in the earth from whence it was taken at the discretion of children, relatives and friends.

Secondly-I give and bequeath unto Morgan H. Hogins the tract of land known by the Eason tract beginning at the creek at William Walker Hogins deceased and running westward through the plantation with the cross fence, to where it strikes the hollow, then with said Hollow to the back line. Also an equal part of 150 acres tract and a ten acre tract. Also Jim a good feather bed and furniture & bedstead one cow and calf and as much cupboard ware and kitchen furniture as I give to Eleanor his sister, a Bureau worth $25..00 a set of chairs.

3rd-I give to the minor child of Wm. W. Hogins dec'd the balance of the tract of land lying (eas on tract) above the cross fence North and the balance of the 150 acres tract and ten acre tract and 128 acres of land in the name of Morgan Hood and the Mother of said child is to have the use of said land above given to said child with the exception that said child is to be supported from said land until the said Child becomes 21 years of age or during her widowhood. Sam I give to Wm. W. Hogins before said Hogins died together with his proportionate part of Horses, Cattle and household and kitchen furn- 4th I give unto Abram C. Hogins all my land lying in the fork of the creek that I own and Jack a negro boy, and the mare that he now claims, and a chance to raise a colt if he sees fit from off of the proceeds of the farm and a cow and calf and as much household and kitchen furniture as I have given to Morgan H. Hogins. 5th, I give unto Eleaner Phillips my Daughter Lucy a black woman and her two children a mare and colt, cow and calf, and her household and kitchen furniture she has already received. 6th, I give unto my daughter Sally, Clary and her two children and as good horse as the rest has had with a bridly and saddle, a cow and calf, bed and furniture and bedstead also the bed that her grand-mother gave her and household and kitchen furniture as is given to the rest. 7th, I give unto my daughter Polly Matilda and her child and Prince and as good a as the rest with a bridly and saddle, a cow and calf, bed and furniture and bedstead, also the bed that her grand Mother gave her and such household and kitchen furniture as I gave the rest of the children. 8th, I give unto my daughter Betsey Jane Mary her two youngest children as good a horse as the rest with a saddle and bridle a Cow and Child Calf, bed and furniture and bedstead, also the bed which her grand Mother give her and such house hold and kitchen furniture as I gave to the rest and if any of said property should die this season, my wish is that it be made up to the loser out of the property left to as to place them again on an equalty my part of Poke Root I give to Christopher C Hudson which is the fourth part I wish the residue of my stock cattle & etc. together with the tracts of land called the Bruce and Gray tracts sold and my debts paid with t this exception I wish as much stock of different kind kept as may serve as an ample support to the family for three years and I wish the balance of my land and negroes to remain undivided for three uears unless they Sally and Polly both marry sooner, then I want the balance of my land equally divided between my daughters should they be living and if they are not to be divided between their heirs and at which time I want my negroes together with the rest of my property equally divided amongst my living children or the heirs of the deceased. And if Abram at the time of said division should make choice of this place on which we now live in preference to the one designed for him I wish him to have it. Ans lastly I make and constitute and appoint my sons Morgan H. Hogins and Abram C. Hogins my Executors to this my last Will. In testimony whereof I have hereunto set my hand and seal this 16th day of September in the year of our Lord 1840.

                        W. Hogins

N.B. and should the heirs refuse to make a right to the minor child of Wm. W. Hogins deceased when he comes of age then for him to have it made up to him our of the rest of my estate.

D. Gray   M. Hogins
A.D. Hogins

I, Wm. Hightower, Clerk of the County Court do hereby certify that the foregoing is a true copy of the original Will of Wm. Hogins dec'd and recorded by order of the County Court and on file in my office Nov'r. the 5th 1840.

                       Wm. Hightower, Clerk.

(145) (JOHN NESBITT No.88)

In the name of God Amen. I, JOHN NESBITT, of the County of Dickson and State of Tennessee being weak in body but of sound mind and memory (blessed be Almighty God for the same) do this second day of August in the year of our Lord, eighteen hundred and thirty eight make and publish this my last Will and Testament in manner and form as follows that is to say, I give and bequeath my spirit to Almighty God and my body to be decently buried and after all my just debts being paid I give and bequeath to my youngest son, Allen Nesbitt the tract of land whereon I now live containing three hundred acres also one other tract which I lately bought of Jim B. Walker containing two hundred and fifteen acres. The said Allen Nesbitt paying to the rest of my heirs the sum of three hundred and twenty five dollars as hereinafter specified. Also one bed and furniture I give to my said son Allen Nesbitt. The rest of my children that is Thomas, John and Robert Nesbitt and Fanny Walker when they left me I gave my three sons each a bed and furniture and two cows and calves which I estimated at thirty dollars each, and my daughter Fanny Walker, in addition to the bed and furniture and Cows and Calves I gave one horse and saddle, the whole estimated at one hundred and five dollars. Now it is my will and desire that my three negroes should be valued by two disinterested men and that my children should take them among

(146) them at their valuation. It is my desire that my son Thomas Nesbitt take my boy Harry and if his valuation should exceed his equal part of my estate after the devise already made to my son Allen being taken out then he shall pay over the overplus to my Executors that an equal division be made so also with my negro woman. But if my children should not be willing to take them at their valuation then they shall be sold with all the rest of my perishable property and the proceeds together with the three hundred and twenty five dollars to be paid by my son Allen, to be divided between Thomas, John and Robert Nesbitt my sons and Fanny Walker, so as to make them equal taking into view what they have before received and I hereby make and ordain my sons Thomas and Allen Nesbitt my Executors of this my last Will and Testament. In witness whereof I the said John Nesbitt have to this my last Will and Testament set my hand and affixed my seal the day and year above written.

                        John Nesbitt (seal)

Signed, sealed, published and declared by the said John Nesbitt the Testator as his last Will and Testament in the presence of us who were present at the time of signing and sealing thereof.

                        A. Coldwell
                        Thos. McNeilly

State of Tennessee, Dickson County, I, William Hightower, Clerk of the County Court of said County do hereby certify that the within last Will and Testament of John Nesbitt dec'd is duly recorded in Book B. pages 25, 26, June 8th 1841.

                        Wm. Hightower, Clerk.
                        By his Deputy Tho. J. Kelly

(DANIEL TAYLOR No.89)

State of Tennessee, Dickson County, I, DANIEL TAYLOR being in a perfect and sound mind but in an infirm state of health do make and ordain this to be my last Will and Testament as follows, Viz:

1st-My will is that all my just debts be first paid.

(147) 2nd-I will and bequeath to my wife Mary Ann Taylor during her natural life or widowhood the House and land where I now reside and all the stock of Horses, Cows, Hogs & etc. together with my household and kitchen furniture-the said furniture I wish her to have as her own should she marry again I wish her to have all of my plantation tools and utensils.

I likewise will to my wife Mary Ann Taylor, my Grist Mill and the profits arrising therefrom during her natural life or widowhood.

Lastly-I do hereby nominate constitute and appoint my wife Mary Ann Taylor, and Claiborne Taylor, my true and lawful executors to t this my last Will and Testament to carry the same into execution hereby annulling and Revoking all other Wills heretofore made by me. In testimony hereof I have hereunto set my hand and affixed my seal, this the twenty-eight day of April Eighteen hundred and forty one.

Test-Benjah Gentry   Daniel Taylor   (seal)
  Mark Harris

State of Tennessee, Dickson County, I, William Hightower, Clerk of the County Court of said County do hereby certify that the within last Will and Testament of Daniel Taylor dec'd is duly recorded in Book B. Page 27, June 8th 1841.

                William Hightower, Clk.
               By his Deputy Tho. J. Kelly.

(HENRY LEEK No. 90)
In the name of God Amen. I, HENRY LEEK of the County of North Hampton and State of North Carolina being in sound and perfect mind and memory thanks be to God do this first day of November in the year of our Lord, one thousand eight hundred and thirty two, make and publish this my last Will and Testament.

(148) First-I give and bequeath unto Elizabeth Leek my land lying and situated on the North side of Ruban Swamp together with negro woman Lidia by Luke Anthony Daniel two feather beds and the dwelling house furniture.

Secondly-I give and bequeath unto Nancy Siles the wife of John Sikes, Yellow Lucy and her increase.

Thirdly-I give and bequeath unto Josiah Leek negro Isham and Anderson, and the Blacksmiths tools.

Fourthly- I give and bequeath unto grand children of my deceased sister Mary, each of them the sum of five hundred dollars.

Fifthly-I give and bequeath unto Benjamin Young the sum of five hundred dollars.

Sixthly-I give and bequeath unto the aforesaid Benjamin Young and the grand children of Mary Young deceased all the negroes left to me by the death of my brother Randolph Leek together with all their increase.

Seventhly-I give and bequeath unto my cousin Meriah Leek the sum of five hundred dollars and one feather bed together with the house yard and garden room during her single life.

Eightly-Provided that Levina Sikes daughter of John Sikes shall live to attain the age of eighteen years or sooner if she marries I give and bequeath to her all my land lying and being on the South side of Wrichan Swamp making the main run the line between her and Elizabeth Leek hereby giving unto her Father John Sikes the full privilege of to make use or rent out said tract of Land until the said Levina shall attain the age of eighteen years or marries as before mentioned.

Ninthly-It is my desire that all the remainder of my negroes not given away with the exception of old woman Tyna as hereinafter mentioned to be sold those not above the age of Ten years to be sold with their Mothers together with all the stock and other property of every description and the moneys arising from such sale after paying over to the several legatees or as above mentioned I hereby give and bequeath unto Elizabeth Leek all the remainder hereby giv and bequeath unto Elizabeth Leek all the remainder. It is my will and I do hereby ordain and allot to old woman Tyna her time during life and to be maintained by the aforesaid Elizabeth Leek out of the estate allotted to her in witness whereof the said Henry Leek have to this my last Will and Testament set my hand and seal the day and year above written.

Signed, sealed, published and declared by the said H. Leek the Testator as his last Will and Testament in the presence of us who was present at the time of signing and sealing thereof,
Davis Bryan
John Bryan
                      his
            Henry X Leek
              mark

(149)
CODICIL
I desire that all the negroes before mentioned that are to be sold instead of credit must be sold for cash down and as soon as the money that is raised out of my estate to be paid over to the Legatees as soon as collected, the tract of Land which I purchased of Edward Nally and other lying on Roanoake river containing one hundred and fifty seven acres and a half known as the Bell tract I desire to be sold to the best advantage and to be given to my deceased sister Marys children except Bennet Young for whom I make no provisions concerning said & etc. In witness whereof I have hereunto set my hand and seal and delivered in the presence of David Bryan.

        his
  Henry X Leek
      mark

State of North Carolina, North Hampton County, This last Will and Testament was exhibited on open Court and proved by the oaths of Davis and John Bryan and the codicil was proved by the oath of Davis Bryan whereupon the same was ordered to be certified and recorded.

Test-Richard H. Weaver, Clk.

State of North Carolina, I, Richard H. Weaver Clerk of the Court of Pleas and quarter sessions of the County of North Hampton hereby certify that the foregoing is a correct copy of a paper writing admitted to Probate as the last Will and Testament of Henry Leek deceased from the record and original in file in my office. Given under my hand at office in North Hampton with the seal of office the 22nd day June 1833.

Henry H. Weaver, Clk.

(150) State of North Carolina, North Hampton County, I, Samuel Calvert Chairman of the Court of Pleas and Quarter Sessions of said County do hereby certify that Richard H. Weaver whose name is affixed to the above certified is and was at the time of signing the same acting clerk of our said County Court duly elected and qualified that due faith and credit are due to his attestations as such and that the same is in due form of law. Given under my hand at the Court house in the town of Jackson this 22nd day of June 1833.
Samuel Calvert C.C.P.Q.R.S.

State of Tennessee, Stuart County, J.W. Cook, clerk of Stewart County Court do certify the foregoing to be a true copy as the same remains on record in my office. Given under my hand at office in the town of Dover this 13th day of October 1841.

Wm. Cook, clk.

State of Tennessee, Dickson County, I, William Hightower, Clk, of the foregoing is a true copy of an attested copy of Henry Leeks Will which was ordered by the County Court of said County to be recorded at the Nov. Term of said Court of said County to be recorded at the Nov. Term of said Court 1841.

Given under my hand at office this 2nd day of November 1841.

Wm. Hightower, Clk.
By his Deputy Tho. J. Kelly.

(JOSHUA WHITE No.91)

In the name of God Amen. I, JOSHUA WHITE do make and publish this as my last Will and Testament hereby revoking and making void all other Wills by me at any time made. First, I direct that all my debts be paid as soon after my death as possible out of any moneys that I may die possessed of or my first come into the hands of my Executor.

Secondly- I will and bequeath unto my beloved wife Martha White during her natural life or widowhood all my lands, negroes, crop stalk, household and kitchen furniture all the property of every description that I may die seized or possessed of except such as are otherwise bequeathed.

Thirdly- I will and bequeath unto my son David one two year old colt which I value at forty dollars.

Fourthly- I will and bequeath unto my son Benjamin a colt two years old which I also value at forty dollars.

Fifthly- I desire that all my other sons and daughters namely Elizabeth, James, Nancy, Jesse, Raney and Daniel when they arrive to or as near the age of 18 years as practable to be furnished with a colt about two years old and to be worth about forty dollars and if either of these childred should not be furnished with a colt of the value above directed it shall be made up to such child or children at a final division. I also desire that my negro woman by the name of Rachael should be sold by my Executor within the limits of two years after my death having regard to a suitable time for the sale of such property.

I wish to be understood that I desire an equal division among my children. Lastly, I do hereby nominate and appoint my wife Martha White and Owen Sullivan my Executors. In witness whereof I do this my will set my hand and seal this 5th day of October 1841.

Benajah Gentry
John Porter

Joshua White.

(151) State of Tennessee, Dickson County, I, William Hightower, Clerk of said County do hereby certify that the foregoing is a true copy of the last Will and Testament of Joshua White deceased which was ordered by the Court at December term 1841 to be recorded. Given under my hand of Office this 10th day of December 1841.

Wm. Highhtower, Clk.
By his Deputy Tho. J. Kelly.

(WILLIAM WILEY No. 92)

State of Tennessee, Dickson County, May the 21st day 1839. In the name of God Amen. I, WILLIAM WILEY of the state and County aforesaid being weak in body but sound in mind, memory blessed Almighty God for the same do make and ordain this my last Will and Testament in manner and form as follows, to wit:

First. I wish my just debts paid and then I bequeath and give unto my son Josiah Wiley the sum of one dollar, then I give and bequeath unto my son Jess Wileys heirs the sum of one dollar, then I give and bequeath the sum of one dollar, to my son in law Isaac Griffin then give and bequeath to my son Jonathan Wileys heirs the sum of one dollar, then I give and bequeath to my Daughter Elizabeth Myatt the sum of one dollar then I give and bequeath unto my son Ebenezer Wileys heirs the sum of one dollar, then I give and bequeath unto my grand son Jesse Wiley the sum of one dollar, then I give and bequeath to my grand son Eli Wiley the sum of one dollar, then I would wish the land whereon I now live to be sold at my death and the money put in the hands of my loving wife Ann Wiley for her maintainance then at my wifes death I give and bequeath to my two grand daughters Dose Ann Griffin Elisa Jean Griffin the sum of fifteen dollars a piece provided there that much left at my wifes death I would my Executor to pay it to them when they come of age. I also would wish all the balance of my property sold in like manner, and the money put in my wifes hands. I hereby appoint David Gray my Executor of this my last Will and Testament hereby revoking all former Wills by me made the year and day above written.

(152)

Signed, sealed and declared his last Will and Testament in the presents of us.
J. Thornton, Nancy X Landrith
                   mark (her mark)

William X Wiley (seal)
         mark (his mark)

State of Tennessee, Dickson County, I, William Hightower, clerk of the county court of said county do hereby certify that the foregoing is a true copy of the last Will and Testament of William Wiley dec'd which was ordered by the Court at February Term 1842 to be recorded. Given under my hand at office this 22nd day of February 1842.

Wm. Hightower, Clerk.
By his Deputy Tho. J. Kelly.

(153)

I, William Hightower, knowing the uncertainty of life and being desirous that my estate after my death should be distributed somewhat differently from the manner by which the laws of the State would direct the distribution do hereby make and ordain this my last Will and Testament revoking all others heretofore made. First, my just debts are to be paid out of what monies I may leave, of which my wish that my Mother have the use and services of my negro boy Nelson during her life for her support; but at her death it is my desire that the children of my Illigitimate daughter with all my other property except the sum of two hundred and fifty dollars which I hereby give to my sister Polly Kirk wife of William Kirk-If the sum of two hundred and fifty dollars should not appear to be left in money by me at my death it is my wish that said sum be raised out of my estate and given to my said sister-Now in case my daughter Mary aforesaid should die without leaving children it is my desire that the children of my said sister should have all the estate both real and personal which is hereby given to the children of my daughter. To recapitulate-My Mother is to have the use and services of of Nelson during her life. The sum of two hundred and fifty dollars to be given to my sister Polly. The remainder of my estate both real and personal to be given to the children of my daughter Mary wife of Willis Jackson, and in case she dies without leaving children the property that would have descended to them is to be given to the children of my sister aforesaid-Altho. the word "children" is employed in relation to my said daughter Mary yet the meaning is one child or more than mery one. In witness whereof I have hereunto set my hand and seal this 29th day of November 1840.

                                                  Wm. Hightower   (seal)

Signed and sealed in the presence of
J. Voorheis
Jacob A. Kames

    I appoint Willis Jackson and William Kirk to be Executors of the above Will.

(154) Test-   Wm. Hightower.
J. Voorheis
Jacob A. Kames

    State of Tennessee, Dickson County Court, August Term 1842. Then was the annexed last Will and Testament of William Hightower dec'd produced in open Court and proved to be such by the oaths of J. Voorheis and Jacob A. Kames subscribing witnesses thereto and the same was ordered to be recorded.

                                                  Test-Tho. J. Kelly, Clerk
                                                            of said Court.

    State of Tennesssee, Dickson County Court Clerks Office, August 8th 1842. Then was the annexed last Will and Testament of William Hightower dec'd recorded in Book B. Page 33,34,35.

                                                  Tho. J. Kelly, Clerk.

(HENDERSON ADCOCK No.94)
    In the name of God Amen. I, HENDERSON ADCOCK of the State of Tennessee, Dickson County, being weak in body but sound mind and memory and being mindful of my mortality do make and constitute this my last Will and Testament.
    1st-I resign my body to its Mother dust to be buried in a decent manner, at the discretion of my friends and relatives.
    2nd-I resign my soul to God who gave it.
    3rd-after all my just debts are paid I give and bequeath unto my beloved wife Dolly M. Adcock all singularly and every part of my property after my just debts and funeral expences are paid which is to be for her use and benefit during her widowhood and should she remain in that state its for her use her natural life should she intermarry my wish is that she have and possess a proportionate part with the rest of my heirs at that time. In testimony whereof I have hereunto set my hand and seal this twelfth day of September A.D. 1842.

                                                                  his
Signed in presence of   Henderson X Adcock (seal)
David Gray   mark
     his
Matthew X Myatt
    mark

    State of Tennessee, Dickson County Court, December Term 1842. Then was the within last Will and Testament of Henderson Adcock deceased produced in open Court and proven to be such by the oaths of

(155) David Gray and Matthew, subscribing witnesses thereto and the same was ordered by the Court to be recorded. Witness my hand at Office this 5th day of December 1842.

    Thos. J. Kelly, Clerk of said Court.

State of Tennessee, Dickson County, County Court Clerks office December 7th 1842. Then was the within last Will and Testament of Henderson Adcock deceased, recorded in Book B. Pages 35, 36.

    Tho. J. Kelly, Clerk of Dickson County Court.

156) JACOB EVANS No. 95)

This day being the fifteenth of March 1835 I proceed to make this my last Will and Testament now in my right mind and proper sences I first will my soul to God who gave it and my body to the Earth from whence it was taken.

2nd-I will all my just debts to be paid lastly I will all my estate to my beloved wife Mary Evans during her natural life or widowhood at the Expiration of either this will is declared null and void I further provide when at any time it is made appear to the satisfaction of a majority of all the justices of the Peace when settling in a Court capacity for the County that said Mary is waisting sd Estate willfully or unnessarily said Court or any Court may proceed to Grant Letters of Administration without any regard to this will provided it first appear that at least twenty days notice has been given to said Mary in writing setting forth to her the cause or causes why Letters of Administration is about to be applied for so I conclude leaving said Mary sole Executrix to this my last will and no security required of her.

    Subscribed in my own hand.
    Jacob Evans

Test-
    his
Allen X Hunter
    mark
C.A. Baker

State of Tennessee, Dickson County, County Court May Term 1843. Then was the foregoing last will and Testament of Jacob Evans dec'd which was proven to be such by the oaths of Allen Hunter and Charles A. Baker subscribing witnesses thereto and was ordered by the Court to be recorded.

Witness, Tho. J. Kelly, Clerk of said County Court at office this 1st Monday in Monday in May 1843.

    Thos. J. Kelly, Clerk.

State of Tennessee, Dickson County Court Clerks office, July 6th 1843. Then was the annexed last Will and Testament of Jacob Evans dec'd Recorded in Book A. pages 155, 156.

    Thos. McNeilly, Clerk.

(MOSES STREET No. 90)

Jan. 17th A.D. 1843. The last Will and Testament of Moses Street Sn'r. I, MOSES STREET Sen'r do now make my last will and testament being in my proper mind and natural senses.

1st-I bequeath my spirit to God who gave it & take it away amen. Wishing to be decently layed away and Buried, committing my Body to its Mother dust-Amen.

2nd-I bequeath to my beloved wife Ailsey for the true love and respect I have for her the house and farm we now live on and in

(157) with all the appertainances thereto annexed as follows, three head of horses & two thirds of my cows, hogs & sheep the other third to my son Jechonias during his attention to the same also the house hold and kitchen furniture two Beds and furniture Execepted also nine negroes, consisting of a woman and children to have and to hold during her natural lifetime or widowhood for her support at her decease or Marriage the above named property is to be divided as follows:

1st-To my son David one negro boy named Belfield.
2nd-To my son Jechonias one negro boy named Edmond.
3rd-To my son Abram one negro boy named Charles.
4th-To my son Moses one negro boy named Henry also one man negro at the death or marriage of my beloved wife Ailsy if there by an increase of negroes if not he is to have two hundred and fifty Dollars in proper valued by disinterested men.
5th-To my daughter Joanirah Willy one negro girl named Diahhah
6th-To my Daughter Susan Self one negro girl named Mary.
7th-To my Daughter Martha two negro girls named Kitty Ann & Mirah & as it respects the household and kitchen furniture and stock at the death or marriage of Beloved wife Ailsy if theres any left after my son Moses gets his two hundred and fifty dollars in property it is to be equally divided among my male and female children again 1st to my son Davis Street I bequeath the tract of land on which he now lives containing seventy two acres also one hundred acres of entered land lying north east of the seventy two acre tract, 2nd to my son Jechonias Street I bequeath all the land lying between David Street south line and the Creek also a piece off the East part of the tract where I now live running as follows, commencing at Crooked White Oak at or near the mouth of a hollow west of the apple orchard running near south to a dead chesnut in the field thence with that ridge to the south boundary line, 3rd to my son Abram Street, I bequeath the mill tract of Land and Mill also one Bed and Clothing for the same which was excepted in the fore part of my will, 4th To my daughter Martha one Bed and furniture including one of the two which was expepted aforementioned also one negro woman Diay, lastly, I nominate and appoint David Street & Jechonias Street my two oldest sons Executors to this my last Will and Testament, this signed and sealed in presence of C.C. Davidson

    Jeromiah X Thompson   Moses Street (seal)
      mark

(158) State of Tennessee, Dickson County, County Court March Term 1843 Then was the foregoing last Will and Testament of Moses Street dec'd which was proven to be such by the oaths of George C. Dodson & Jeromiah Thompson subscribing witnesses thereto and ordered by the Court to be recorded. Witness Tho. J. Kelly, Clerk of said Court at office the 1st Monday in March 1843.

                Tho. J. Kelly, Clerk.

State of Tennessee, Dickson County, County Court Clerks office the Dickson 8th 1843. Then was the annexed last Will and Testament of Moses Street dec'd recorded in Book A. Page 156, 157, 158.

                Tho. McNeilly, Clerk.

(MARY BALTHROP No. 97)
This is to certify that I have this day give and bequeath unto my son Willie Balthrop the Balance of five hundred & ninety nine Dollars and 84cent of the within note for the consideration of which the said Willie Balthrop agrees to maintain the balance of my time here so long as I should live given under my hand and seal this 11th day of February 1837.
                her
              Mary X Balthrop
                mark

Test-
James Daniel
H.M. Slayden

    State of Tennessee Dickson County, July 4th 1843. Then was the above will produced in open Court and proved by the oaths of James Daniel and H.M. Slayden subscribing witnesses and ordered by to be recorded.

                              Test-Tho. McNeilly, Clerk.

    State of Tennessee, Dickson County, County Court Clerks Office July 8th 1843. Then was the last Will and Testament of Mary Balthrop recorded in Book A. page 158.

                              Tho. McNeilly, Clerk.

159) (JAMES JOSLIN No. 98)

    I, JAMES JOSLIN, being in a low state of health but of sound mind and sisposing mind and knowing that it is the lot of all men once to die, do make this my last Will & Testament revoking all others heretofore made by me. In the first place I reccomend my soul to God who gave it & my body a decent Christian Burial and those things it has pleased God to give me I divide in the following manner (to wit)

    Item 1st-It is my will that all my debts and Burial expences be first paid out of the first money that comes to the hands of my Executor.

    Item 2nd-I will & bequeath to my Daughter Juretha Caroline Cochran & Children of her body one fourth of my Estate after her Husband Wm.H. Cochran pays up the amount of the Notes I hold on him.

    Item 3rd-I will & bequeath Matilda Ann Boyd and Children of her body, one fourth of my Estate after her husband James H. Boyd pays up the amount of the notes I hold on him.

    4th-I will and bequeath to my Daughter Elizabeth Jane Joslin one fourth of my Estate.

    5th-I will and bequeath to my Daughter Mary Morgan Joslin the other fourth of my Estate-In the event of either Daughters death without a living child of her womb then and in that case I wish the above mentioned property to be equally divided among my other daughters & their lawful children. It is my will & desire that a trustee be appointed in to whose hands the property be put & he have the entire control of that share of my Estate going to my two oldest Daughters & children of & manage it to best advantage possible to the promotion of their Interest & welfare I will and request that my lands be rented out and all my negroes be hired out annually & publickly to the highest Bidder till my youngest Daughter becomes of age then my Lands sold on a credit of 1-2 & 3 years and that money to be divided as the balance at the same time I wish all my Perishable & other property sold on similar credits and the money divided as above. It is my will and request that those notes which I hold be collected as soon as practicable and that the money be laid out in young negroes to be together with the others divided equally according to to valuation I have a plain note now in possession which was given to Wm. H. Cochran for $206 & some cents executed by Joseph Crockett & others said note should have been executed to me instead of Wm. H. Cochran contend for said note, I wish that amount deducted from the said note I wish that amount deducted from the due proportion which may be given to his family from Estate and it is my will that my Ex-

160) ecutors put my daughter Elizabeth Jane Joslin & Mary Margaret Joslin

in some respectible Industrious Family where they may be taken care of, educated and learn to work, and I do hereby appoint John R. Hudson & John W. Napier Executors to this my last Will and Testament. In testimony whereof I have hereunto set my name & affixed my seal July 23rd. 1843.

Test by James Joslin
J.W. Baxter
J.W. Napier

 State of Tennessee, Dickson County Court, September Term 1843. Then was the annexed last Will and Testament of James Joslin, deceased produced in open Court and proven to be such by the oaths of John W. Napier and Jess W. Baxter subscribing witnesses thereto and the same was ordered by the Court to be recorded.

        Test-Tho. McNeilly, Clerk

 State of Tennessee, Dickson County, I, Tho. McNeilly, Clerk of the County Court of said County do hereby certify that the foregoing is a true copy of the last Will and Testament of James Joslin which is this day recorded in Book A. pages 158,159,160. September 8th 1843.

        Tho. McNeilly, Clerk.

(JANE GOODRICH No. 99)

 I, JANE GOODRICH do make and publish this as my last Will and Testament hereby revoking and making void all others Wills by me at any time made.

(161) First-I direct that my funeral expences and all my debts be paid as soon after my death as possible out of any money that I may die possessed of or may first come into the hands of my Executors.

 Secondly-I give and bequeath to Norman F. Baker one tract of land whereon Armstrong Baker now lives containing fifty acres.

 Thirdly-I give and bequeath to Felix C. Baker one sorrel mare five years old.

Fourthly-I give and bequeath to Dave J. Baker one yellow mare three years old.

 Fifthly-I give and bequeath to Augusta Baker all my hogs consisting of about forty head.

Sixthly-I give and bequeath to Mary Ann Baker 6 head of Cows.

 Seventhly-I give and bequeath to Mary Ann Baker and Jane Timm ten head of cows to be equally divided between them.

 Eightly-I give and bequeath Again Baker two Feather Beds.

 Ninethly-I give and bequeath to Mary Ann Baker one feather Bed.

 Lastly-I do hereby nominate and appoint Armstrong Baker my Executor, and request of the County Court not to exact security in witnesses whereof I do to this my will set my hand and this 23 day of August 1843.

        her
       Jane X Goodrich
        mark

 Signed, sealed and published in our présence and we have subscribed our names hereto in the presence of the Testatrix.
Test-
G.W. Tatom
Samuel Bugg

 State of Tennessee, Dickson County Court, September Term 1843. Then was the annexed last Will and Testament of Jane Goodrich deceased produced in open court and proven to be such by the oaths of G.W. Tatom and Samuel Bugg subscribing witnesses thereto and the same was ordered by the Court to be recorded.

Test-Tho. McNeilly, Clerk

(162)   State of Tennessee, Dickson County, County Court Clerk office, September 9th 1843. Then was the last Will and Testament of Jane Goodrich recorded in Book A. pages 160,161.

Tho. McNeilly, Clerk.

(MINOR BIBB No. 100)

In the name of God Amen. I, MINOR BIBB of the County of Dickson & State of Tennessee being seriously and heavily afflicted by disease of body but of sound and legally disposing mind do make and ordain the following as my last Will and Testament hereby revoking and making null and void any & all Wills & Testaments heretofore made by me.

Imprmis-I wish my Body after my decease to be decently interred by my Executors and I commend my soul to my Maker and hope for acceptance by and through the merits of the Lord Jesus Christ.

Item-I wish my just debts all to be paid and my Executors hereafter named are fully authorized to sell a sufficing of my Estate either real or personal at their entire discretion either for cash or on a credit as the necesities of the case may require to pay and discharge all my debts.

Item-After the payment and discharge all my debts I leave to my wife all the residue of my Estate both real and personal, except what may be herein after otherwise disposed of, to my beloved wife during her natural life to be subject to her entire will and controll & not subject to the hindrance influence or control of any other person whatever during her life, and at her decease I wish the same to be equally divided among my four children Sarah M Jackson, Susan Stewart, John M. Bibb and Elizabeth Bibb and Minor B. Haynes in a distillery in Hickman County, Tennessee by a written article of copartnership which has expired by limitation & which has since been continued by verbal agreeament between said parties

163)   and each of said parties has an equal joint Interest in the personal stock belonging to sd. Distillery (not including the Land & Distillery Still tubs & etc which have heretofore been given by me to my son John M. Bibb) Now it is my will and desire that at my Decease the debts due from said Copartnership shall be paid out of the preceeds & stock belonging to said Establishment and the residue if any be which may belong to me I hereby give and bequeath to my son John M. Bibb his heirs and assigns for ever. My said Executors are hereby vested with the Power to continue said business untill it can be advantageously closed at their discretion.

Item-Whereas I purchased and am the Legal owner of three cantiguous tracts or parcels of Land lying in Hickman County Tenn purchased from Sam'l S. Porter on which is situated a Grist Mill the Qualities and Boundaries of which may be seen by Reference to the Deed from sd. Porter to me-It is my wish that my son John Bibb & Minor B. Hayns at my Decease shall have the privilege of paying to my Executors the consideration money and Interest thereon paid by me for said Lands in which event my Executors are hereby authorized to make a deed of conveyance to them for said Lands with gereral Warranty.

Item-And whereas I purchased of John Griffith a tract of Land containing 53 acres and of John Greer a tract of 50 acres adjoining the foregoing mill tract which two last mentioned tracts (to wit) the Griffith & Greer Tracts were paid for with the joint finances of sd copartnership afore mentioned, Now provided the sd John M. Bibb & M.

(164) M.B. Haynes shall elect to the mill tract or Porter Lands I wish then also to have the privilege of taking the whole of two Tracts (to wit) the Griffith and Breer Tracts on paying to my Executors the one third of the one third of the purchase money & Interest in which case my sd Executors are authorized to convey all my Interest in said Lands to them & their heirs.

Item-It is my wish that in the disposition or sale of my property to my Executors for the purpose of paying debts my beloved wife shall a controlling influence in the selections & that no sale shall be valid except with her express consent provided that shall be property sufficient for that purpose other than the property selected by her.

Lastly-I hereby constitute and appoint my beloved wife my Executrix and my son John M Bibb & my son in Law Vernon F. Bibb my Executors of this my last Will and Testament and I hereby wish and desire that it be distinctly understood & it is my will that my said Executrix and Executors shall not be required by the Court to give security for the performance of the duties hereby required of them. Hereby revoking any and all Wills by me heretofore made and confirming this my last Will and testament to which I the said Minor Bibb have hereunto set my hand and seal and declared and published this my last Will & Testament at Dwelling House in Dickson County and State of Tennessee on this sixteenth day of January in the year of our Lord one thousand eight hundred and forty four.

            Minor Bibb (seal)

Signed, sealed published and declared in presence of us and attested by us in the presence of & at the request of the Testator
John C. Collier
John Brown
Wiley Davis

State of Tennessee, Dickson County, Feb'y Term 1844. Then was the withis Will proven in open Court by the oaths of John C. Collier John Brown and Wiley Davis subscribing witness and ordered to be recorded by the court.
            Test-Tho. McNeilly, Clerk.

State of Tennessee, Dickson County, I, Tho. McNeilly, Clerk of the County Court do hereby certify that the annexed last will and Testament of Minor Bibb was duly Recorded in the Will Book on Pages, 162, 3,4,5, this 18th day of March 1844.
            Tho. McNeilly, Clerk.

(165)
(JOHN BREWER No.101)
Know all men by these presents that I, JOHN BREWER of the County of Dickson and State of Tennessee, being of infirm body but of sound and disposing mind & memory desire & ordain this to be my last Will and Testament.

First-I wish to commend my soul to the care of my heavenly Father with a full & abiding & perfect reliance upon his promise of infinite love & mercy to leave to my relatives & Friends the assurance of my most sincered desire for their future as well as present prosperity & happiness and also to offer to the Throne of the Almighty a most earnest heartfelt & merciful petition that my God in his suppossing goodness will vouchsafe to extend to my Family his Fatherly protection & mercy.

Secondly-I will and desire that all my just debts be paid to all my contracts corned through honerable & fairly in accordance with the spirits of the agreement I may have made.

Thirdly-I will that my Executor be permitted to sell all or any part of my Land Negroes, stock or other possessions up on such time & in such manner & the proceeds together with all other funds of mine which have or may hereafter come to his hands be vested & Aplied as he may deem most conducive to the Interest of my Family without Restriction as to town or place & I furthermore wish that my Executor be himself permitted to bid at my said of my property with the same condition & obligations as other Bidders I also will and bequeath to my betrothed wife Susan apart of all my possessions equal to the share of each of the children to have & to hold the same during her life. Finally I wish that Frank Hardeman Executor this my last Will & testament according th the intent and meaning thereof & as his is not a resident of this County I require no se-

(166) curity but furthermore desire to invest him with Discretionayy power to act in all cases in which no specific directions are herein given as he may deem best I also will that such property as may be set apart as hereby directed to each of the heirs namely my wife Susan My Daughter Sarah Elizabeth & my Daughter Mary Ann Brewer be divided to them upon Demans so soon as they or either of them are permitted by the Laws of the Land to dispose of peoperty or so soon as either of them may marry or as soon after as the delivery can with property be made I now establish this Instrument as my last Will and Testament as containing a fair expression of my wished concerning my worldly affairs in Testimony whereof I hereunto subscribe my name and affix my seal this the 7th day of June 1844.

    Acknowledged in the presence of)   John Brewer   (seal)
    J.R. Hudson   )
    John H. Stone   )

State of Tennessee, Dickson County, July Term 1844. Then was the foregoing last Will and Testament of John Brewer produced in open Court and proven to be such by the oaths of J.R. Hudson & John H. Stone subscribing witnesses and ordered to be recorded July 1st 1844.

                                                     Tho. McNeilly, Clerk.

State of Tennessee, Dickson County, I, Tho. McNeilly of the County Court of said County do hereby certify that the foregoing is a true Record from the original will of John Brewer dec'd as filed in my office witness my hand at office this 13th day of July 1844.

                                                     Tho. McNeilly, Clerk.

(167) (ROBERT DUKE No.102)

In the name of God Amen. I, Robert Duke of the County of Dickson and State of Tennessee being infirm in body but of sound mind and memory do make and publish this my last Will and Testament in manner and form following that is to say I commit my soul to God and my body to the dust from whence it came to be buried at the discretion of my friends.

Item 1st- I desire that all my just Debts be paid out of the property I now own after that is done I give and bequeath to my beloved wife Charlotte Duke the Houses and plantation whereon I now live during her natural life and at her death I do give and bequeath the same to my son Green W. Duke I also give and bequeath to my beloved wife all the Household and kitchen furniture together with all my stock of every kind consisting of Horses, Cattle, Hogs, Sheep & etc with all the farming utensils of every kind & descritption to be at her own disposal forever in any way she may think proper.

Item 2nd-I give and bequeath to my son Green W. Duke all my lands lying near the mouth of harpeth with the Exeception of that part reserved for my beloved wife during her lifetime and at her death to decend to my son Green W. Duke as named in Item 1st. also a certain portion of Land laid off and designed for the use of my Grand son William Baker commencing on the Bank of Harpeth River at a white oak and running through the old orchard by a Pear tree to a Popplin then to Hunders Line and with its several Boundaries to a Popplin then to Hunters Line and with its several Boundaries to a popplin then to the river so as to include all on the east side of said Line also one Ball faced Horse and one cow and calf and one Bed and furniture to him and his Heirs forever.

Item 3rd-I give and bequeath to my Grand son William L. Baker that portion of Land as named and described in Item 2nd to him and his heirs forever also one other Tract of Land containing seventy five acres lying on the road from the mouth of Harpeth to Charlotte to him and his heirs forever. It is to be understood that I have given to my Daughter Miry P. Duke who intermarried with William Baker her full part and portion of my Estate and further will that the said William Baker with whom she married it not to have any more of my Estate in any way whatever.

I also Nominate and appoint my wife Charlotte G. Duke & Green W. Duke my Executrix & Executor of this my last Will and Testament revoking all other wills or will heretofore made by me in the Eleventh day of September 1838.

                Robert Duke (seal)

Signed & sealed in)
presence of us)
Caleb Rooker   )
Joseph Marris   )

(168) Dickson County Tennessee, September 11th 1838; State of Tennessee Dickson County, March 3rd. 1845. Then was the annexed Will produced in open Court and proven by the o'aths of Caleb Rooker the other witness Joseph Morris being dead his hand writing was proven by the oaths of Washingto Hunter and Caleb Rooker whereupon the Court ordered the same to be put on Record.

                Tho. McNeilly, Clerk.

State of Tennessee, Dickson County, I, Tho. McNeilly, Clerk of said County do hereby certify that the foregoing is a true copy of the original Last Will and Testament of Robert Duke deceased as will appear on file in my office March 4th 1845.

                Tho. McNeilly, Clerk.

(169) SHADRICK BELL No. 103)

In the name of God Amen. I, SHADRICK BELL of Dickson County and State of Tennessee being in firm of body but of sound mind and memory do make and publish this as my last Will and Testamtne revoking and making void all other wills by me at any time made.

Firstly-I direct that I shall be decently buried and that my funeral expences and all my debts be paid as soon after my death as possible and of any moneys that I may die possessed of or that first come into the hands of my Executors.

Secondly-As to my worldly goods I dispose of them of them in the following manner:

Item 1st.- I lend to my daughter Mary T. Ross the following negroes (to wit) Nelson, Charity and Charlotte during her natural life and in the event she dies Childless it is my will that the three negroes above mentioned with their increase revert and be divided equally between my sons Shadrick and Elisha.

Item 2nd- I give and bequeath to my son Thomas Bell that part of a two hundred acre tract of Land lying on the East side of Bear branch which was entered by me also three negroes (to wit) Jim, Mary and Ned likewise a parcel of land containing by estimation fifty two acres and bounded as follows, to wit, Beginning, at a Beech the south west corner of the tract where on he the said Thomas Bell now lives running thence west 52 poles to a stake, thence North 142 poles to an Elm on the bank of Cumberland River then up said River to the mouth where said branch runs Eastwardly, then leaving said branch and running south to the beginning also my saw and Brist Mill and it is my will that one acre on the East and one acre on the west side of the Creek be reserved for the use of the said Mill.

Item 3rd- I give and bequeath to my son Shadrick Bell Junior the following negroes (to wit) Dency Wiley and Viney to him and his heirs forever.

(170) Item 4th- I give and bequeath to my son Thomas Bell and the remaining part of that tract of Land or parcel of Land purchased by me of Thomas Williams be the same more or less also three negroes Alston Daniel and Ben, in trust however for the following purposes which I desire to carry out according to my last wishes, to wit, That my Daughter Nancy Williams shall enjoy the rents profits and emoluments of said Land and retain possession thereof during her natural life and which life interest not to be liable for the contracts and debts of her husband Wesley A. Williams also that she shall retain the possession of and enjoy the hire labour and all other benefits arrising from the possession of said negroes Alton Daniel and Ben, during her natural life and which life interest in not to be liable for the contracts of and debts of her husband Wesley A. Williams and her sole and separate Recept from time to time for the possession of said Land and negroes shall be a sufficient voucher for the said Thomas Bell in the execution of this trust, and it is my further will that after the death of my daughter Nancy Williams the said Thomas Bell shall sell the aforesaid Land and divide the proceeds equally among her children and also divide the above named negroes and their increase among the children of my said Daughter Nancy Williams.

Item 5th- I give and bequeath to my Daughter Elizabeth W. Coldwell the following negroes, to wit, Alfred Wilson Paralee Vester & Hannah to her and her heirs forever.

Item 6th- I give and bequeath to my son Elisha Bell the following negroes to wit, Caroline and her four children, Rachel, Aggy, Vilet & Dilsy also Venis also two Beds and furniture to him and his heirs forever.

Item 7th- I give and bequeath to my son Elisha Bell all the residue of my Land after deducting the Land bequeathed in trust for my Daughter Nancy Williams as before mentioned and the lands bequeathed heretofore to Thomas Bell in this Testament I bequeathed all the residue to my son Elisha because he has paid eight hundred dollars to my son Shadrick for one portion of it I make this as an explanation of this Item.

Item 8th- I give and bequeath to my Grand son Joseph A. Dickson named one negro girl named Kitty or Catherine to him and his heirs forever.

Lastly I do hereby nominate and appoint my two sons Thomas & Elisha Bell my true and Lawful Executors to this my last Will and Testament. In Testimony whereof I have hereunto set my hand and seal this 9th day of June in the year of our Lord one thousand eight hundred and forty six.

```
Signed, sealed in presence)                          his
of us                      )        Shadrick  X  Bell   (seal)
J. Fenly                   )                  mark
J.P. Bell                  )
W.B. Smith                 )
```

State of Tennessee, Dickson County Court Nov'r Term 1846. Then was the last Will and Testament of Shadrick Bell dec'd produced in open Court and proven to be such by the oath of James Finly one of the subscribing witnesses and John P. Bell being dead his hand writing was also proven by the oath of James Finley where upon the Court ordered the same to be recorded Nov'r 2nd 1846.

Test-Tho McNeilly, Clk.

(171)   State of Tennessee, Dickson County, Then was the last Will and Testimony of Shadrick Bell sen'r recorded in Will Book pages 169,170 171. Nov'r 4th 1846.

Tho. McNeilly, Clk.

(ANN WILEY No.104)

In the name of God Amen. I, ANN WILEY of the County of Dickson and State of Tennessee being mindful of my mortality do make and constitute this my last Will and Testament.

1st-I wish to be buried decently at the discretion of my children and surviving friends.

2nd-I give and bequeath to my beloved daughter Elizabeth Myatt after my funeral Expences together with my other debts I owe are paid, one cupboard, one bed furniture and stead with all and singular every part of House hold Stuff that I now possess or may have after accumulate and thirdly after the will of my deceased husband Wm. Wiley is executed according to Law then should there any money remain
(172)   unexpended I also give that sum more or less to the above named Elizabeth Myatt. In Testimony whereof I have hereunto set my hand and seal this 14th day of August 1842.

```
Signed, sealed and delivered                         her
in presence of                           Ann  X  Wiley   (seal)
David Gray                                   mark
Fannin Yates
```

I hereby constitute supplement nominate and appoint David Gray my Executor to this my last Will and Testament.

```
                                                     her
David Gray                               Ann  X  Wiley   (seal)
Fannin Yates                                 mark
```

County Courts Clerks office, December Term 1846. This day was produced in open Court the last Will and Testament of Ann Wiley which was proven to be such by the oaths of David Gray and Fannin Yates subscribing witnesses and ordered to be recorded December the 7th 1846.

Tho. McNeilly, Clerk.

County Court Clerks office, January 28 1847. Then was the foregoing last Will and Testament of Ann Wiley dec'd Recorded in Will Book pages 171, 172.

Tho. McNeilly, Clk.

173 (THOMAS GENTRY No.105)

In the name of God Amen. I, THO. GENTRY do make and publish this as my last Will and Testament hereby revoking and making void all other Wills by me at any time made.

First-I direct that my funeral Expences and all my debts be paid as soon after my death as possible out of any moneys that I may die possessed of or may first come into the hands of my Executors.

Secondly-I give and bequeath to my beloved wife Anny during her natural life all of the tracts of Land on which I reside Household and kitchen furnature Farming utensils all of my stock of Horses, hogs and sheep and all of my crop, to wit, Corn, wheat, oats and tobacco.

Thirdly-Having given my beloved son Anderson Gentry one hundred and seventy one & one half acres of land on which he now resides I charge him three hundred dollars for it having given my beloved son Benjah a tract of Land lying on Piney River in 2nd District of Dickson County containing one hundred and nineteen acres I charge him five hundred five hundred dollars for it is my will that my beloved Daughter Jane, Consort of Thomas Brown, shall have all the Land lying 4th district of Dickson County within the following Boundries, to wit:

Beginning where the Road called Bells oar Road Crosses the Franklin Road running Eastwardly to where the Columbia Road intersects the Franklin Road thence along the Columbia Road to George Mitchels North Boundry line thence west with his line seventy two Poles to a Double Red Oak the said Mitchels north west corner thence south twenty poles to a double to a red oak on said Mitchels line thence west 73 poles to a hickory thence north to where the line crosses the said Bells oar Road thence north westwardly with said Road to the Beginning at one hundred and fifty dollars it is my will that my beloved Daughter Lucinda shall have after the death of her Mother all of the tracts of land on which I now reside excepting so myc as lies east of the following line, to wit, beginning where the Road called Bells Oar Road crosses the read leading from Charlotte to Franklin running north to my north boundry line now it is my will that she have this without its being considered any protion of her distributive share of my Estate it is my will that my beloved Daughter Lucinda have one horse saddle bridle and Blanket one cow and calf to be worth as much as the same king of property given to my Elder Children to have it any time she may call for it, now it is my will at the death of my beloved wife that all of my children that I have not given andy property to shall be made equal with those that I have given property to wit, Anderson Benjaah & Jame and if there should be any after they are all made equal it shall be equally divided amongst all of my children, it is my will that the Horse saddle bridle and Blanket that is named for Lucinda shall not be considered any portion of the distribution I have of my Estate going to her having given all of my children her equal with the others having given all of my children ten dollars in cash except Elizabeth & Lucinda now it is my will that they have ten dollars in cash and then come in for an equal share of the balance of my Estate.

Lastly-I do hereby nominate and appoint my son Anderson Gentry in witness whereof I do tb this my will set my hand and seal this 29th day of September 1846.

           Thomas Gentry (seal)

(174) Signed, sealed and published in our presence and we have subscribed our names hereto in thepresence of the Testator this 29th day of September 1846.

           V.F. Bibb
           Matthew L. Gentry

State of Tennessee, Dickson County Court, **March Term 1847.** Then was the within last Will and Testament of Tho. Gentry dec'd was the within last Will and Testament of Tho. Gentry Gentry dec'd produced in open court and proven to be such by the oaths of V.F. Bibb & Mathew L. Gentry subscribing witnesses thereto and the same was ordered to be Recorded, witness my hand at office this 1st day of March 1847.

Tho. McNeilly, Clerk.

State of Tennessee, Dickson County. Then was the last will and Testament of Tho. Gentry Recorded 25th July 1847.

Tho. McNeilly, Clerk.

(175) (ROBERT NESBITT No.106)

I, ROBERT NESBITT of the County of Dickson and State of Tennessee being far advanced in life and knowing that in the course of nature my frail body must shortly be consigned to the Grave, but still being of sound and perfect mind do make and publish this my last Will and Testament, herby revoking and making void all former wills by me at any time heretofore made.

First-I direct that my body be decently interred at Alen Nesbitts in the County of Dickson and state of Tennessee.

Second-as to such worldly estate as it hath pleased God to entrust me with, I desire that after my Death the same be disposed of as follows, to wit:

1st-I direct that all my debts and Funeral Expences be paid as soon after my Death and out of any money that I may die possessed of or may first come into the hands of my executors from any portion of my estate Real or personal.

2nd-I direct that all my property of every discription (except my two negro woman Lucy and Mary and any increase that Mary may have together with one good feather Bed and furniture) be sold by me my Executors as soon after my Death as possible on a Credit of twelve months, and that the money arising therefrom together with any money that may be due me or in my possession at my death after paying my Debts and Funeral Expences be put out at Interest, Except so much shall be herein after directed to be paid out and Expended.

3rd-I direct that the services of my two negro woman and the money that may be loaned out, go for the support of my son Robert, and I also authorize and direct my Executor to pay any Bills for medical aid that may be necessary for my son Robert, out of the money that may leave at my Death or that may be out at interest.

4th-I desire that my son Robert have the Bed and furniture above mentioned for his own use during his lifetime and at his death that be sold and the money disposed of as all the other effects that may remain.

5th-I desire that after my death my Nephew Allen Nesbitt (if he is willing) take my son Robert under his care and protection and if he finds it necessary that he build him a comfortable cabin or House, for which my Executors is authorized and requested to pay him a reasonable price, out of the money loaned out as aforesaid or that may come to his hands and I also desire that my Nephew Allen Nesbitt have the services of Lucy and Mary together with the interest that may accrue upon the money loaned out as aforesaid for his care and support of my son Robert during his (Roberts) lifetime.

6th-I desire that at the death of my son Robert, Mary with her increase (if any) be sold and that the proceeds of said sail together with andy money that may be in the hands or under the controol of my Executors after paying the funeral expences of my son Robert be equally divided among my children.

7th-I direct that after the death of my son Robert if Lucy is still living, then I desire my beloved son Samuel who I hereby constitute and appoint my Executor to this my last Will and Testament, to give Lucy a chance to select a person with whom she wished to live, and that if that person should be Allen Nesbitt or any of my children then if they are willing to buy her that the person so selected take her at valuation and the money arrising from her sale to be equally divided among my children. In witness whereof I do to this Will set my hand and seal this 2nd day of February A.D. 1844.

            Robert Nesbitt (seal)

Signed, sealed and published in our presence and we have subscribed our named hereto in presence of the Testator this 2nd day of February 1844.

            Robert McNeilly
            John M. Sanking

Dickson County Court, March Term 1847. Then was the foregoing last Will and Testament of Robert Nesbitt produced in open Court and (177) duly proven by the Oaths of Robert McNeilly and ordered to be Recorded March 1st 1847.

            Tho. McNeilly, Clerk.

(HARTWELL U. SLAYDEN No. 107)

I, HARTWELL U. SLAYDEN No. 107 of the County of Dickson and State of Tennessee do make and publish this my last Will and Testament.

1st-I direct that my body be decently interred and as to such Worldly Estate as it hath pleased Almighty God to intrust me with I dispose of the same as follows.

2nd-I direct that my Debts and funeral expences be paid as soon after my decease as possible out of any money I may die possessed of or may first come into the hands of my Executor from any portion of my Estate real or personal.

(178) 3rd-I direct that each of my children when grown or marry shall have a Horse saddle Briddly & etc. of good quality together with all necessarys for the house keeping commonals or a negro of Equal value not exceeding twenty years old.

4th-I direct that my Companion Jane shall have the balance of my Estate both real and personal for life or Widowhood but if she marries I direct all my Estate both real and personal be equally divided, Jane taking an equal share with my children shall equally have my Estate should Jane live a widow and there be an increase of the negroes or be more than she may need I direct them given to my children in all cases equal.

5th-I direct that economy be used in raising my children and family and that none of the negroes be sold to pay my debts that may be contracted in raising sd family all the above named property I give to my children and there heirs my daughters and their bodily heirs in all cases it is my desire that my negroes would not be put up and sold out of the family for a Division N.B. provided any of the negroes become contrary and ungovernable by my Companion Jane or by any of my Children (viz) Boys who are of age to govern and manage slaves such of the negroes shall be put up and sold to the highest bidder by giving public Notice on a Twelve Months Credit with good and sufficient security and when the money is collected put out on Interest by good and undoubted security till it may be needed on a Division among my children.

I do hereby make ordain and appoint Mr. May my Executor of this Will and Testament in witness whereof I, Hartwell M. Slayden the

179) said Testator have to this my will written on one sheet of paper set my hand and seal this 10th day of July in the year of our Lord one Thousand and Eight hundred and forty six in presence of John May Jr. Samuel Adams.

               Hartwell M. Slayden (seal)

  State of Tennessee, Dickson County Court March Term 1847. Then was the last Will and Testament of Hartwell M. Slayden produced in open Court and proven to be such by the oaths of John May Jr., and Samuel Adams subscribing witnesses thereto and ordered to be recorded witness my hand at office this 1st day of March 1847.

               Tho. McNeilly, Clerk.

  State of Tennessee, Dickson County. Then was the last Will and Testament of Hartwell W. Slayden dec'd recorded 26th day of July 1847.

               Tho. McNeilly, Clerk.

(MARY A. BELL No. 108)

  In the name of God Amen. I, MARY ANN BELL being weak in body but of sound mind do declare this as my last Will and Testament Viz:

  Item 1st- I give to my brother Montgomery Bell Senior my negro girl Harriet a slave for life.

  Item 2nd- I give to my sister Jane my negro girl Kate a slave for life the balance of my Estate both real and personal I wish to be equally divided among my other brothers and sisters, but the whole of my estate both real and personal is to be charged with the support of my Father John I. Bell during his natural life and I do farther nominate and appoint my brother Thomas Drew Bell the Executor of this my last Will and Testament, signed at the mouth of Harpeth this 5th day of February 1847.

               M.A. Bell

Witnesses
B.C. Duke
H.C. Larkins

  State of Tennessee, Dickson County Court, March Term 1847. Then was the within last Will and testament of Mary A. Bell produced in open Court and proven to be such by the oaths of B.C. Duke and H.C. Larkins subscribing thereto and the same was ordered to be Recorded. Witness my hand at office this 1st March 1847.

               Tho. McNeilly, Clerk

(180)   State of Tennessee, Dickson County. Then was the last Will and Testament of Mary A. Bell recorded 26 July 1847.

               Tho. McNeilly, Clk.

(ISIAH TIDWELL No. 109)

  I, ISIAH TIDWELL do make and publish this my last Will and Testament, hereby revoking and making void all other Wills by me at any time made.

  First- I direct that my funeral expences and all my debts be paid as soon after my death as possible out of any monies I may die possessed of or may first come into the hands of my Executors.

  Secondly- I give and bequeathed to my beloved wife Rebecker Tidwell, all and every of my Estate both real and personal including all dues and demands in any manner belonging to or decending to my from any and all sources what ever, to have and to use for her support and maintanance during her natural life and after her death I direct that my Executors shall sell to the highest bider upon the usual credits any and all of my said Estate that may be left at the death of my said wife Rebecker Tidwell after deducting all expences to pay over to each of my nine Daughters one equal ninth part of the same: Lastly I do nominate and appoint my son in law John Porter my Executor. In witness whereof I do to this my last Will set my hand seal this 12th day of March 1848.

                 his
              Isaiah X Tidwell (seal)
                 mark

Signed, sealed and published in our presence and we have subscribed our names hereto in the presence of the testator this 12th day of March 1848.
D.C. Chamberlain
William E. X Pendergrass
  mark

April Term 1848. Then was the last Will and Testament proven in open Court by the oaths of Daniel C. Chamberlain and Wm. E. Pendergrass subscribing witnesses to the same and ordered to be Recorded April 3rd. 1848.

                Tho. McNeilly, Clerk.

State of Tennessee, Dickson County, Then was the last Will and Testament of Isiah Tidwell, Recorded June 1st 1848.
                Tho. McNeilly, clk.

(181)

(J.W. DODSON No. 110)

I, JAMES W. DODSON make and publish this this my last Will and Testament hereby revoking and making void all other Wills by me made at any time.

First-I direct that my funeral Expences and all my debts be paid as soon after my death as possible out of any moneys that I may die possessed of, or may first come into the hands of my Executors.

Secondly-I give and bequeath to my beloved Wife Susan provided she remain a widow and should not marry again all my slaves namely

(182) Jack Manuel Adaline & Fillis with there increase also all of my stock of every discription which may be necessary for her to keep, also my waggon and gear and farming utensils my household and kitchen furniture of all kinds and all debts which may be due me at my death, but if she should mary equal with my children that may then be living of all my property both real and personal only.

Thirdly-My will is further that if my wife chose to remain on the place on which I now reside that with my children have the use and benefit of it Jointly, but if she should become dissatisfied to live on it, it is my will that she sell the land with the advice of my Executors and apply the proceeds of said sale to the purchase of other land or negroes for the use and benefit of my said wife and childred Jointly it is further my will that my wife keep my children all with her and give them as good an Education as she may be able.

Lastly-I do hereby nominate and appoint my Brothers in law Samuel Farmer and Nicholas P. Hardeman my Executors without being required to give security, in witness whereof I do to this my Will set my hand and seal this 14th day of February 1847.

                James W. Dodson (seal)

Test- Wm. Garrett
  Ezekiel Hickerson

State of Tennessee, Dickson County Court, April Term 1847. Then was the foregoing last will and testament of James W. Dodson produced in open Court and proven to be such by the oaths of Wm. Garrett Ezekiel Hickerson, subscribing witnesses thereto and ordered to be Re-

Recorded April 5th 1847.

Tho. McNeilly, clerk.

(183) State of Tennessee, Dickson County, Then was the last Will and Testament of James W. Dodson Recorded June 2, 1848 in Will Book A. pages 181, 2,3. June 2nd 1848.

Tho. McNeilly, Clerk.

(E.W. NAPIER No111)

Know all men by whom it may concern th at I, Elias W. Napier of the County of Dickson and State of Tennessee being weak and infirm in body and of advaned age but of sound and perfect mind and memory do make and publish this my last Will and Testament hereby revoking and making void all other Wills by me at any time heretofore made.

Item 1st- I will my body to the dust of the earth from whence it came to be decently interred after my death by my friends and my soul to God who gave it in hopes of a Glorius resurection beyond the Grave through the merits of the Lord Jesus Christ, and that my burial and funeral expences and all my just debts be paid out of any money that I may die possessed of or that may first come to the hands of my Executors as soon after my death as practicable.

2nd Item- I hereby Emancepate and set at liberty the following named slave to wit, Judy my seamstress and her five children to wit, Fanny, William Carroll, James Monroe, Tho. Benton and Andrew Jackson and also the children of Fanny to wit, Leroy Lott, Malena Lott, Margaret Arabella Lott, Judia Adonia Lott and Mary Jane Lott together with any increase that she the said Fanny may have, Lizza or Elizabeth my cook that she the said Fanny may have, Lizza or Elizabeth my cook (a yellow girl) Amanuel a Forgeman and his wife Creecy Jack a Mulatto man his Female children to wit, Evaline their youngest Tom Keys my waggoner and overlooker and his wife Eady, Charity Cha my old Female cook, Sam Dillahund my good and faithful old servant, and also my little house servant boy named Simon about nine years old. Daniel an old man who has been a teamster for a number of years, and his brother Jim Brown and Perry a man of advanced age a Coaling round hand. Many of these servants are advanced age and have with faithfulness aided me in makin g what property and money I have and those yellow Female servants have with vigilence and fidelity take care of my property both by day and night both in Alabama and in Tennessee particularly in Alabama watching and putting out fire placed in it to consume it by Incendarier, and I do also hereby Emancipate and set at liberty a Yellow boy named Solomon about six years old the son of a Mulatto Girl called Angelin this boy is to be put under the care and charge of Judy and Lizzy to be subject to their control under my Executors untillhe is twenty one years of age and in case of the death of Judy and Lizzie then he is to be under the care of one of Judy's children which ever he may choose. The Emancipation of these slaves (above named) has been the result of my deliberation for years passed which I this day bring to a close while I am in perfect and sound mind, an as this great Boon under the existing laws of the state of Tennessee cannot be bestowed only under a strict and minut compliance with the late of the said state I therefore request the earnest and direct attention of my friends Benjamine C. Robertson and Robert McNeilly who are to be my Executors to see that my will in this as in all other respects be faithfully and strictly carried out.

(184) 3rd Item- I will and bequeath to Charlotte Napier the widow of my deceased Brother Richard C. Napier one hundred dollars, and to her son Madison C. Napier one hundred dollars and to Leroy Napier his woungest son one hundred dollars and to the two Female children of

James R. Napier dec'd two hundred dollars each and to his youngest son Richardson C. Napier two hundred dollars and to his oldest son Blunt R. Napier Five dollars all of which said sums are to be are to be paid by my Executors after they shall have wound up all the business of my Estate by making sales and collections.

(185) 4th Item-I will and bequeath to Martha Gould wife of James Gould two hundred dollars and to Elizabeth Gilbert wife of Thomas Gilbert one hundred dollars and to the Heirs of the Body of Margaret Garrett wife of Phenias Garrett two hundred dollars all of which sum, are to be paid as above directed to be paid to Charlotte Napier and others in Item 3rd.

5th Item-I will and bequeath to Jesse Beck Jr. son of Jesse and Judy Beck two hundred dollars and to David C. Andrew J. and John T. Beck the three youngest sons of Jesse Beck & his wife Judy Beck to each two hundred dollars, and to Wm. J. Beck oldest son of Jesse Beck and his wife Judy Beck five dollars & to Martha Jane Johnson, Daughters of Jesse Beck and his wife Judy Beck, five dollars and to Jesse Beck Sr., and his wife Judy Beck five dollars each making in all eight hundred and twenty dollars all of which sums of money are to be paid as those directed to be paid in the 3rd Item of this will and I give and bequeath to Lucy Ann Edwards, Daughter of Judy and Jesse Beck a certain tract or parcel or peace of Land the same more or less known as the land which I conditionally contracted to David Record and on which he built a Cabin and lived a while this claim deed given to the same as soon after death as practicable.

6th Item-I will and bequeath to William J. Therman and his wife Elizabeth five dollars each and to their daughter Judy Ann three hundred dollars to Richardse John, William and James Therman sons of
(186) said Wm & Elizabeth Therman two hundred dollars each. And to Carter or Dock youngest son of the said W.J. & Elizabeth Therman fife dollars, these respective sums amounting in all to the sum of nine hundred and fifteen dollars are to be paid by my Executors as that directed to be paid in the 3rd of this my Will.

7th Item-I will and bequeath to Fountain Luster and his wife Sarah Ann, Five dollars each and to the surviving lawful heirs of their bodies two hundred dollars each to be paid over by my Executors out of the last money collected winding up my Estate.

8th Item-I will and bequeath to Richard Thompson & his wife Lucy Ann five dollars each and two hundred dollars to the surviving heirs of the said Richard Thompson and wife Lucy Ann if any there be of them yet living to be paid as above.

9th Item-I will and bequeath to Benjamin C. Robertson and his wife Ann G. five dollars each and to them present surviving five children (to wit) Martha D. Edward A. Christopher W. John H. & Benjamin J. Robertson, five hundred dollars each then seven respective sums in this Item mentioned amounting in all to the same of Twenty five hundred and ten dollars are to be paid by my Executors as those memtioned in the 3rd Item of this my will.

10th Item-I will and bequeath to Mary Elizabeth Wilson an orphan girl at this time living in the family of Wm. H. or John W. Napier on Bartons Creek three hundred dollars which send is to be paid by my Executors for her support and shhooling or so much thereof as shall be deemed necessary by my Executors and and the balance (if any) to be paid to her when she becomes of lawful age.

11th Item-I will and bequeath to James Theadford and his wife during their natural lives and at their death to decend to their lawful heirs that piece or tract of lnd on which same James Thedford now lives and a negro woman named Peggy late the wife of Bob dec'd h whose occupation at present is to caves in the Coaling. This property wish my Executors to give him the said Thedford woman and to hand him over notes which will be found amoung papers drawn by him in favour of my to the amount of some five or six hundred dollars more or less previous topaying said notes and negro woman into the possession of said James Thedford or making the quit claim title to said land by my Executors the said James Thedford and his wife and to come forward and make a title for four hundred acres of land adjoining Montgomery Bells Mathis Ore Bank said tract of land was and conveyed to my by said hands of William C. Napier for Regristration as the law requires and was lossed or mislaid by him so that it cannot now be found and consequently the Land was not registered and the said Thedford is to Execute a receipt in full for all claims he nay have against my Estate.

12th Item-For and in consideration of the esteem and regard I have and entertain for my friend Robert McNeilly I give and bequeath to his oldest son James Hugh McNeilly my negro infant child of my negro woman Clary said Child is a girl and is named Kitty and in now at the breast of Its Mother the said child Kitty is to be delivered to said Robert McNeilly as soon as it can be taken from the breast of its Mother with the title for the same.

13th Item-I give and bequeath to the two Female children of John and Eliza Zuthman whose names are -------- to each four hundred dollars to be paid over as those sums specified in the 3rd Item of this will and it is my will that My Executors hand over to thesaid John Zuthman a note which will be found in my papers drawed by J.& R. Zuthman for about Three thousand dollars and made payable to me dated about ten years since this my Executors and to do after the said John Zuthman Executes his receipt for all claims he has against if any he has.

14th Item-I give and bequeath to P.S. James my negro woman Lananna about 22 years old the daughter of Landono & Jane his wife dec'd and Eliza a woman about 32 years old whom I bought in Alabama of a man by the name of Only and a gay Horse at this time working in a team at Mt. Etna Furnace which bought of Dr. J.R. Hudson for which I am to give him one hundred dollars in castings. Said property is to be delivered with title to the same by my Executors after he shall have executed his receipts to my Executors after he shall have executed his receipts to my Executors for all demands against my Estate for sarvivors & etc.

15th Item-I give and bequeath to Tarlton F. Moore my negro man Hiat about 22 years of age and five dollars to be paid in money also several notes which I hold against said Moore and his Father the said negro man and the notes are to be handed over to said T.F. Moore by my Executors and a title to the negro after the said Tarlton T. Moore shall have remained in the servises of my Estate untill the same is settled up and after he and his Father shall have executed their receipts to my Executors in full of all claims that they have against my Estate for services & etc.

16th Item-I give and bequeath to James M. Holt my negro man Burwell and his wife Francis (a yellow woman) and their child, Jarrato negro man about 30 years old & his wife Esther Cephus and his wife Mima and their two children named Sam and Georga, together with four dollars in money to be paid as the the other donations in this will and a title to said slaves and woman thereof is to be given by my Executors to said James M. Holt shall have remarried in the services of my Estate untill the same is settled up and after the said James M. Holt shall have executed his receipt in full of all claims or de-

demands he may have against my estate for services & etc up to that date.

17th Item- I will and bequeath to my kind and affectionate Brother John W. Napier during his natural life and to decend from him th the Lawful heirs of his daughter Araminta who is intermarried into Dr. John R. Hudson the following property to wit, my negro woman Lucy the only daughter of Charity and Billy her Husband Patrick Shelton my Collier Angeling and her youngest Daughter called Judeanna and a coloured female child of Carolina called Judy, three negroes one to be passed into the possession of my said Brother with titles to the same or so many of them as may be then living or that may not before that time have been disposed of by myself at the time my Executors may make a general distribution of my negro property given to my other legacies.

(189) 18th Item- I give and bequeath to my kind and affectionate nephew William H. Napier my negro woman named Cloey and her oldest Daughter that is with her named Nancy and her son named Fred the boy is about nine years old and the girl is about seven years old and my negro man named Landon & his son Albert and my negro man (Mark Landon) & Mark are teamsters) and my negro man Edmond Lester a Wood Hauler.

19th Item- I will and bequeath to the lawful heirs of John B. Carpenter and his wife Mary , my neice and daughter of my deceased Brother Thomas Napier a negro woman named Drumica who they now have in their possession and one thousand dollars in money to be paid my Executor as the sums directed to be paid in the 3rd Item of this my Will to my other legatees.

20th Item- I will and bequeath to my kind faithful and worthy nephew William C. Napier one of my Brother Thomas, sons, Jim RoundTree & Sam McCray, the gift of James and her child exceed above I have caused to be erased at my executors are to give him my quit claim and to all the Iron property personal and Real Estate belonging to the same that I purchased of Napier & Catson and of Judge Catsons on Shoals Creek chief Creek and Bruch Creek and their tributary streams together with his note which I hold for about fifteen hundred dollars which is at this time due and unpaid, privious to any action by my Executors in this particular the said William C. Napier is to come forward and file his Receipt in the Clerks office in full payment and satisfaction of all debts due and demands that he may have against my Estate by note Book account or otherwise the adjustments of this Item will be foreclosed as in the settlement with the other Legatees.

21st Item- I will and bequeath to the lawful heirs of Benjamin Stones and his wife Mary a daughter of my deceased Brother Henry A.C. Napier five thousand dollars to be paid over by my Executors to a Trustee selected by a majority of them and in case they cannot agree they are to refer to the chairman of the County Court to give the casting vote, and said Trustee is to give good and sufficient security for the twenty and proper depositions of said Money and Interest arising thereon for the benefit of said heirs.

22nd Item- I will and bequeath to the Heirs of Samuel B. Lee and his wife Amanda the daughter of my Brother John W. Napier six thousand dollars to be paid over by my Executors by a trustee selected by a majority of them and if they cannot agree they are to refer the casting vote to the Chairman of the County Court and said Trustee is to give good and sufficient security for the proper and timely dispos-
(191) itions of said money and the Interest arising thereon for the Benefits of said Heirs.

23rd Item- It is my will and desire that all my real and personal property in the Counties of Davidson & Hickman and thereal Estate

lying in the adjoining counties to said Counties which was produced
for the Benefits of my different Iron Establishment be sold on a
credit of one two three four and five years to be paid in equal Installments and that notes be taken for the same with good security
and a lien retained in the property until the last payment is made
and out of the fund arising from said sale is to be paid the procddd-
ing Items of this my last will and the Balance which may be left on
hand I desire to be equally divided between the lawful heirs of my
Brothers H.A.C. Napier (Except Benja Stone and wife Mary for whom
I have provided in the 21st Item of this will) and the lawful Heirs
of Dr. JOhn R. Hudson and his wife Araminta the Daughter of my Brother John W. Napier each of the Heirs of Dr. John R. Hudson and wife
to receive equal shares with each of the Heirs of H.A.C. Napier my
Brother in said remaining fund after retaining the money neCessary
for the approprations that I have herein after directed to be retained for the Benefit of Solomon whom I in this will emancipated and
Dr. J.R. Hudson whom I in this will emancipated and Dr. J.R. Hudson
and wife Armainta are to have each five dollars out of said remaining fund that otherwise go to their Heirs.

    24th Item- I will and bequeath to several of the slaves that I
have Emancipated certain sums of money which may be found in their
possession at my death and I desire my Executors to protect them in
the possession and prudent use of the same and all my House hold and
kitchen furnature I give to Judy and her four sons and to Lizzy to be
divided between them as my Executors may think just and equitable
should there be any dissatisfaction in the division of said property
by themselves but if there is none then the division made by themselves is to stand and the yellow boy Solomon whom I have set free
in the second Item of this my will is to be furnished by my Executors with fifty dollars pr annum for his schooling & etc. untill he
is to be put to some trade which my Executors may select having due
Regard to his Genius and capacity and they are to pay into his hands
when he is twenty one years of age the sum of Five hundred dollars
to commence his trade on, which sums of money they are to retain in
their hands for said purposes this donation of five hundred dollars
is to be given to him provided he may be of sober and steady habits
otherwise I leave it with my Executors to furnish and treat him as
his conduct may deserve I alsowish the negroes which I have Emancipated to be furnished out of my smokehouse and other places with Bacon
corn or meal sugar coffee and salt sufficient to last them for provisions for twelve entire months after my death, now it is my will and
(192) desire that should any of those negroes that I have Emancipated chooSe
to live in davidson county or make that their general home then my
Executors are to send an officer and take possession of said Emancipated slave and put him or her on the Block in the Town of Charlotte
and have hire him out for month until he may quit Davison County and
Choose some other place for a home and the money arising from said
hire (if any) is to be equally divided among the other slaves that I
have Emancipated.

    24th Item- I wish it to be understood that the negro child that I
(193) gave to Robert McNeilly oldest son in the 12th Item of this will I
have this day Executed a Bill of sale of said negro child Kitty to
James H. Thomas, L. Felix, C & Robert A. McNeilly the four sons of
Robert and Margaret McNeilly which is in full sale faction of said donations made in the 12th Item of this my will.

    25th Item- And now if I should servive and dispose of any of the
property devised or donated in this will before it should be proven
in Court I wish it understood that the titles and transfers that I

may make shall be good both in Law and Equity against the Claims to said property so transferred which may be set up under any of the provisions of this my will.

    26th Item-My Executors are to have it to their choice whether they will give personal security for the faithful and vigilent performance of their duties that will devolve on them in the execution of this will or they may file an affidavit in the Clerks office that will faithfully timely and vigilently perform the duties incumbant on them in the execution of this will to the best interest of the Estate and those concerned in it to be the best of their ability and knowledge.

    27th Item-Now for and in consideration of the confidence I have in the Philanthropy and sterling integrity of my Executors and confidential friends Robert McNeilly, Benjamine C. Robertson and William H. Napier who reside in the immediate neighbourhood of my principal business I particularly injoin it upon them to have fully carried out all the requisits necessary to carry out my views and wishes in regard to the several slaves that I have Emancipated in or out of the County of Dickson or state of Tennessee as the circumstances of their cases may require.

    28th Item-No it is my will an I do hereby constitute and appoint William C. Napier of Hickman County and Robert McNeilly and Benjamine C. Robertson and William H. Napier all three of Dickson County and all four are citizens of the state of Tennessee my Executors of this my last Will and Testament, and it is my will that all my notes not otherwise herein disposed of and all my Book account and debts or every kind due my Estate be considered a partof my personal Estate and is to be disposed of as directed in the 23rd Item of this will and now before the signing of this will, I will here explain that on the first page of this will at the end of the 24th line the words and his wife Caroline are erased and in the 25th line from the top the word two and ren at the end of the word child and the word Judy and the word and, are erased and at the end of said line the words their youngest is enterlined and on the 5th page of this will at the end of Item 11th between the 14th and 15th lines of on said page the following words are enterlimed (to wit) Recept in full for all claims he may have against my estate and on the 6th page of this will and in the 14th line from the top of said page between the words Money and in said line the following is enterlined to wit. Also several notes which I hold againsg said Moore and his Father and in the 15th line on said 6th page the words and thenotes, are enterlined and on the 7th page in the 5th and 6th lined from the top mark my House Carpenter is erased, and on the 12th page in the 12th line "the words, to be are enterlined, and now having had this will written out and having carefully Examined and digested each and all of its items I do hereby establish and constitute this to be my last will and Testament. In witness whereof I have hereunto set my hand and deal this 12th day of June 1848, in presence of Thomas Overton and Thomas McNeilly witnesses by the request of the Testator.

                                                           E.W. Napier   (seal)

Tho. McNeilly
Thos. Overton

    I, Eliaa W. Napier having heretofore made and published my last Will and Testament do make and declare this as a codicil thereto to wit.

    I do hereby Emancipate and set at liberty after my death my negro man Ephragin who has one eye out and it is my will that he be treated in the same manner and be subject to the same Restrictions as those

(194)

(195) Emancipated in the 2nd Item of the foregoing will I Emancipate Ephragn in consequence of his faithfulness honesty and industry in attending to my business as a teamster. I hereby give to my Faithful seamstress Judy and her five children the use and possession of my Farm on Richland Creek in Davidson County together with the crop now growing on the same and all the stock of every kind at sd Farm, the stock and crop are to be subject to their entire controll and dispesition, and they are to enjoy the possession of said Farms until the 1st day of March next unless they choose to quit the possession of the same sooner and on their leaving said Farm my Executors are to take possession of the same and rent it out or dispose of it as they may think proper untill it is sold and at my death Tom Keys and Ephragm are to select my best waggon and eight of my best mules and Gear which my Executors are to place in the possession of those slaves that I have Emancipated for their own use and benefit all of which are to be and remain their property.

Immediately after my death my Executors are to take all my property into their possession and they are to proceed on the 6th day of March next at the upper end of the Markett House in the City of Nashville to sell my farm on Richland Creek in Davidson County on the terms sp specified in the 23rd Item in the Body of will first having advertized the same for two months in the Louisville Journal and in some popular News paper in the city of Cincinatti and in the Nashville Whig and they are to have all my Iron Works carried on untill the first day of May next when they are immediately thereafter to proceed to sell to the highest bidder at the "hite Bluff Forge first the White Bluff Forge first the White Bluff Forge and next the old Turnbull Forge and the Lands attached to them Respectively and the next they are to sell the negroes belonging to said Forges and then they are to sell the other Perishable property at the Forges, then they are to proceed to Piney Furnace and first sell the Furnace and the lands belonging to the same and next the negroes at said Furnace and then the other Perishable property at the Furnace. Then they are to proceed to Mt. Etna Furnace and first sell the Furnace & Lands thereto belonging then the negroes at said Furnace and then the other Perishable property at said Furnace first having advertized the sale of said property for two months in the Louisville Journal and in the most popular News paper in the City of Cincinatti and in the Nashville Whig all of which property is to be sold on the terms presented in the 23rd Item of my Will, and the profits after paying the necessary Expences and charges incident on carrying on the workd are to constitute a part of my Estate and be disposed of as directed in my will, and now having had this Codicil written out and having duly considered its provisions, I do hereby Establish and constitute the same as a part of my Will and I desire that the same be so considered and carried out by my Executors. In witness whereof I have hereunto set my hand and seal this 22nd day of July 1848 in presence of Robert McNeilly and Farlton F. Moore witnesses by the request of the Testator.

Robert McNeilly)
Farlton F. Moore)   E.W. Napier   (seal)

(197) I hereby Renew the above Codicil and Emancipate and set at liberty Caroline and her child Judy who are to go with Judy and other emancipated slaves and are to be subject to the controll of Carroll and James and if her conduct deserves it they are to expel her from the Company and send her back to this Country with her youngest child and should Caroline the Emancipated slave indulge exeessively and notor-

notorously in draulness and debauchery she is to be expelled and sent back to this County by Carroll and James two of my Emancipated slaves in witness whereof I have hereunto set my hand seal. This the 4th day of August 1848 in the presence of Farlton F. Moore and Joseph Groves at the request of the Testator.

                                                          E.W. Napier   (seal)

Test
T.F. Moore   )
Joseph Groves)

    Know all men whom it may concern that I,E.W. Napier having heretofore made my will and being now very weak and infirm do make this as a Codicil thereto I Hereby request authorise and empower my Executors to set at liberty my negro boy Smith after he shall have remained in the services of my Estate until after the sale of the same and I wish it understood that I do hereby Emancipate subject to the above condition and he is then to stand the same footing with the others that I have Emancipated, In witness my hand and seal this 6th day of August 1848.

                                                          E.W. Napier   (seal)

Test
Robert McNeilly
Jesse Beck

    State of Tennessee, Dickson County Court, August Term 1848. Then was the foregoing last Will and Testament with all its Codicils of E.W. Napier dec'd produced in open Court and proved to be such by the oaths of Tho. McNeilly, Tarlton F. Moore, Joseph Groves and Jesse Beck subscribing witnesses thereto and the same was ordered to be recorded.

                                                    Test-Tho. McNeilly, Clk.
                                                         of said Court.

    State of Tennessee, Dickson County Court office, August the 22nd 1848, then was the last will and Testament of E.W. Napier dec'd Recorded in Will Book pages 183,4,5,6,7, & etc.

                                                              Tho. McNeilly, clerk.

(198)   (B. HARRIS No.112)
    I, BUCKNER HARRIS of the County of Dickson and State of Tennessee do make this my last will and Testament. I commit my soul to God who gave it and my body to be burried in a Christian manner as touching my temperal Estate what it has pleased God to endow me with.
    I will that my wife Lucy keep all the property together on the farm for the Education and support of my children. I will that my wife Lucy to sell my Hogs & Chattle and enough to pay my debts if my wife Lucy should marry I wish all of the Personally property sold Except my negroes I wish them to be hired out until my youngest child becomes of age, I will them to be hired out until my youngest child becomes of age, I will that my lands then should be sold on the Farm & on a credit of twelve months.
    I will that the money the land brings &Personally property brings to be equally divided between my wife & children I will that the negroes & the hire should be equally divided between my wife & children when my youngest child becomes of age I appoint my wife Lucy administrator to this my last Will and Testament this 28th August 1847.

                                                                 Buckner Harris   (seal)
Witness-
Warren Jorden
Burrell Jackson

State of Tennessee, Dickson County Court, Oct'r Term 1847, then was the foregoing last Will and Testament of Buckner Harris dec'd produced in open Court and proven to be such by the oaths of Warren Jourden & Burrell Jackson, subscribing witnesses therto and ordered to be Recorded.

Tho. McNeilly, Clk.

State of Tennessee, Dickson County, then was the foregoing last Will and Testament of Buckner Harris dec'd Recorded in Will Book A. Page 198, 99, this 23rd August 1848.

Thomas McNeilly, Clk.

(199) (A. PULLEN No. 113)

In the name of the Lord Amen. I, ARCHIBALD PULLEN Of Dickson and State of Tennessee knowing the certainty of death and the uncertainty of life, being now in a perfect sound state of mind, do make and establish this my last Will and Testament hereby revoking all former wills made by me:

First- It is my will and desire that all my just debts be paid as speadily as the nature of the case will admit after my death.

Secondly- I will and bequeath to my beloved wife Polly Pullin if she should outlive me my tract of land on which I now reside together with all my household and kitchen furniture, farming utensils and stock of all description or so much thereof as she may choose to keep and also two of my slaves that is to say any two that she may make chose of, all of which I wish her to have during her natural life or widowhood.

Thirdly- I will and bequeath to my son James C. Pullin the tract of land on Nails Creek that I purchased from E. Bishop together with the money that I have paid for him which is to make his land equal to the other lands herein given to my other sons.

Fourthly- I will and bequeath to my son Nelson B. Pullen the one half of my tract of land lying on the waters of Tumblin Creek in Humphreys County state of Tennessee.

Fifthly- I will and bequeath to son William C. Pullin the other half of my tract of land in Humphreys County the line to be made between my sons Nelson & William equally or in any way they may agree upon.

Sixthly- I will and bequeath to my Daughter Sophia B. McNeilly, two slaves, to wit, Peter and Adline which I consider to make her equal to my sons I give her these slaves instead of land.

Seventy- I will and bequeath to my son John A. Pullin my tract of land I now live on to take possession at the death of his Mother.

Eight- It is my desire that my slaves be equally divided amongst my children and kept by them I do not want them sold or put out of the family. I wish my tract of land lying on Nails Creek deeded to me by David Passmore to be sold together with all the property (to wit) Stock, household and kitchenfurniture, farming utensils & etc, should there be more than my wife wants to keep and the money equally, divided amongst my children.

Ninth- If either of the slaves I have given to Sophia B. McNeilly should die before the division I want my Executors to pay to her four hundred dollars in money in lien of said slave.

Tenth- At the death of my wife Polly Pullin I wish the two slaves that she leaves to be valued and kept by some of my children they paying the other their part thereof and all other property that she may have to be sold and the money equally divided amongst my children.

Eleventh- I hereby constitute and appoint my son James C. Pullin & my son-in-law William Y McNeilly my true and lawful Executors to carry out this my Last Will and Testament, in witness whereof I have hereunto set my hand and affixed my seal this the 9th day of July 1842.

Test- A. Pullin (seal)
Isaac Hill)
William Thompson)

(201) State of Tennessee, Dickson County Court Oct'r Term 1848, then was the Last Will and Testament of A. Pullin dec'd produced in open Court and proved to be such by the oaths of W. Thompson one of the subscribing witnesses and the Hand writing of the other witness I Isaac Hill was proven by the oath of Reubin White and ordered to be Recorded.

Tho. McNeilly, Clerk.

State of Tennessee, Dickson County, then was the foregoing last Will and Testament of A. Pullin dec'd Recorded in Will Book A. pages 199, 200, 291, this 24th November 1848.

Tho. McNeilly, Clerk.

(J. SANDERS No. 114)

State of Tennessee) I, JOHN SANDERS do make and publish this my
Dickson County   ) last will and Testament hereby revoking all and making void wills by me at any time made.

First-I direct that my funeral expences and all my debts be paid after my death as soon as possible out of any monies that I may die possessed of or may first come into the hands of my executors or Executrix.

Secondly-I will and bequeath to Susan J. Choat, Samel W. Sanders Marshall Larkins and James McCollum my negro woman Mary and her child John and also fifty acres of land including the place where James McCullum lives lying at my Northwest corner running East to Colman's line thence South & etc for compliment the said fifty acres of Land I value at one hundred dollars which James McCullum can take said Land at the price I have valued it I give it to Samuel Sanders at the above price of one hundred dollars the above named property to be divided between the above named heirs and should they not agree in the valuation of said negroes they are to be sold by my executor and the money equally divided between the above named heirs including the above described Land at one hundred Dollars.

Thirdly-I will and bequeath to my beloved wife Susan the use and benefit of all my land that I possess except the fifty acres I have disposed of and also all my household and kitchen furniture all of my stock of Horses, hogs, cattle and sheep and all of my farming utensils and every thing else purtaining to said premases during her natural lifetime or widowhood for the purpose of shhooling and raising of the minor children and also my present crop on hand and at her death or marriage all the property then on hand, and also all my Land except the fifty acres I have disposed of to be sold and equally divided between my heirs then living except those I have already provided for in Item Second and my wife Susan should marry she is to come in as one of the heirs for a childs part.

Signed, sealed and published in our presence and we have subscribed our names hereto in the presence of the testator this 26th day of November 1848.

his
John X Sanders (seal)
mark

(203) Test-
W.S. Colman
D.C. Chamberlain

And I do hereby appoint my wife Susan Sanders and Marshall Larkins executrix and Executor to this my last Will and Testament.
Signed, sealed and published in our presence and we have subscribed our names hereto in the presence of the Testator this 26th day of November 1848.

                his
              John X Sanders (seal)
               mark

Test-
W.S. Colman
D.C. Chamberlain

  Dickson County Court Jan'y Term 1849. Then was the last Will and Testament of John Sanders dec'd produced in open Court and proven to be such by the oaths of W.S. Colman and D.C. Chamberlain and the same was ordered to be recorded.
                Tho. McNeilly, Clerk.

  State of Tennessee, Dickson County. Then was the foregoing last Will and Testament of John Sanders Dec'd Recorded in Will Book A. pages 201, 2&3 this 4th day Feby 1849.
                Tho. McNeilly, Clerk.

(204) A. WORK No. 115)
  I, ANDREW WORK being old and infirm but of sound & disposing mind do make this my last will & Testament Revoking all others heretofore made by me.
  Item 1st- It is my will that all my just debts & Burriel Expences be paid out of the first money that comes to the hands of my Executor
  Item 2nd- It is my will I do give and bequeath to my beloved wife Cathering Work the following property (to wit) the following Described part of the tract of Land on which I live, beginning at a poplar standing a little North of the Spring, running thence East to the Charlotte Road thence South with said Road to Piney River thence down said river its meanders to the fork thence up the west fork of Piney with its meanders far enough to include the Bottom Field nearest A.C. Hogan, thence a North course so as to include twelve acres of timbered land outside of the Hantalion thence to the beginning, also my Bay mare side saddle & Bridly, one cow & calf & all the part of my stock of hogs known by the name of the Brown stock, one half my stock of sheep all the fowels of every description which I own, one feather bed, Bedstead & Furniture all the cooling utensils kitchen ware of every kind, water pailm washing tub, all my cupboard or Table ware one Table six setting chairs, which property she is to have and hold during her natural life or widowhood, but if she marry again or dies then said property is to be sold by my Executor to the highest bidder & the Proceeds of said sale be equally divided amongst my following named children named, Samuel Work, Andrew Work, Robert John F. Work Mary Dudley, Nancy Phipps, Jane Ezell & Rebecca Goulding. Its my

(205) will that all the Ballance of my tract of Land together with all the Ballance of my Property not allready disposed of be sold to the highest bidder by my Executor and the proceeds of said sale together with all the debts due me, after paying all my just debts, be equally divided among my children before named, & I do hereby nominate & appoint A.C. Hogans my Executor to this my last Will and Testament, in Testamony whereof I have set my hand & seal 9th January 1850.

              Andrew Work (seal)

Witnesses-
Tho. Hulme
William Green

  State of Tennessee, Dickson County June Term 1850. Then was the

Then was the foregoing last Will and Testament of Andrew Work dec'd produced in open Court and proven to be such by the oaths of Thomas Hulme and Wm. Green and the same was ordered to be recorded.

Tho. McNeilly, Clerk.

State of Tennessee, Dickson County, then was the foregoing last Will and Testament of Andrew Work dec'd Recorded in "ill Book A. Pages 204 & 5, this 5th July 1850.

Tho. McNeilly, Clerk.

(R. PRICHARD No.116)

I, RICHARD PRICHARD of the County of Dickson and State of Tennessee being in bad health but sound mind do make this my last Will and Testament. I will that my Brother Cary Prichars is to pay all of my just debts and to have all the property I possess both personally and Real Estate. I also give my interest in my Uncle John Prichard Estate of Montgomery County I also appoint by brother Cary Prichard my administrator without giving security to this my last Will and testament this 18th December 1847.

Richard Prichard (seal)

Witness-
Warren Jourdan
Susan Prichard

(206) State of Tennessee, Dickson County Court, March 4th, 1848 Term. This day was produced in open Court the foregoing last will & Testament of Richard Prichard dec'd which was proven to be such by the oaths of Warren Jorden and Susan Prichard subscribing witnesses to the same and ordered to be Recorded March 6th 1848.

Tho. McNeilly, Clk.

(R. F. BIBB No.117)

In the name of God Amen, this twenty third day of February one thousand Eight hundred and forty six. I, ROBERT F. BIBB of Dickson County and State of Tennessee, being of sound mind and memory do make this my last will and Testament at the same time utterly revoking all former will made by me declaring this to be my last Will and Testament.

First- I give and bequeath to my loving wife Nancy Bibb all the property I am possedsed of every description whatsoever and wheresoever to her proper and discressionary use and benefit during her death all my property to be sold and the proceeds of the sale equally divided with or among all my children with this proviso or condition (to wit) one hundred dollars to be charged or deducted from my son James Bibbs interest or dividend, the above drawback as above named on James Bibbs is to fall to my other children in away to make them all equal or their intrest or legacys all equal as I have given the above named legateed, to wit, James Miner and John G. Bibb. At the same time I do appoint my wife Nancy Bibb my my Executrix with full and ample power to sell any of the personal property to satisfy the debts that my Estate may be owing if any and also to sell any of my personal peoperty for her own use and benefit when and as she may please and I do further appoint my son James Bibb to be an asistant Executor with his Mother, and I further ppovide for my son John G. Bibb that in the event that I should be paid by the Government for the Horse that my son John G

Bibb lost in the Florida War in my life or in the life of my wife Nancy Bibb then and that case my son John G. Bibb is to be charged with in this my last Will and Testament to which I have hereunto set my hand and seal this Twenty third day of February one thousand Eight hundred and forty six. Signed and delivered in presence of us

Jesse Beck
Oliver Spicer   Robert F. Bibb   (seal)
Joseph T. White

Dickson County Court, August Term 1850. Then was the last Will and Testament of Robert F. Bibb dec'd produced in open Court and proven to be such by the oaths of Jesse Beck and
(208) Joseph F. White and there was ordered to be recorded.
Tho. McNeilly, Clerk.

(T. D. BELL No. 118)

Memorandum of the Will and Wishes of Mr. THOMAS D. BELL in Referance to such Desposition of his worldly effects as he desires to be made in the event of Death which his present condition indicates, Viz;

1st-Bequeath, I give to my beloved sister Marcinna, my negro boy William.

2nd-I Bequeath to my Brother Montgomery my negro woman Patsy.

3rdly-I Bequeath to Thomas Finley my Nephew, my negro boy, Vergil.

4thly-I bequeath to my neice Rebecca Finley, my negro girl Tempy.

5thly-I bequeath and injoin it upon my Executor to divide my landed Estate equally between my sister Marcinna, my Brother
(209) Montgomery Bell and my sister Elizabeth. I do hereby appoint Silvester Finley of Dickson County Tennessee my Executor in order to the fulfilment of the above request. In testimony whereof, being at present of sound mind and memory but of weak body infirmity, I hereunto subscribed my name in presence of these witnesses,
W. T. Graves   Thomas D. Bell
C C. Cobb

Commonwelth of Kentucky Crittenden County Court, October Term 1850, I, Robt. L. Bingham, Clerk of said Court hereby certify that at said Term of said Court this writing was produced into Court and proven to be the last Will and Testament of Thomas D. Bell by the oaths of C. C. Cobb & W. S. Graves, subscribing witnesses thereto & ordered to be Recorded, whereupon I have duly Recorded the same and this certificate in my Office. Given under my hand this 4th day of October 1850.

R.L. Bigham
A copy atest in witness of which I have hereunto set my hand and the seal of the Crittenden County Court this 5th December 1850.

R.L. Bigham, Clerk of
the Crittenden County Court.

Commonwelth of Kentuckey, Crittenden County set. I, Samuel L. Phillips Eldest and prediding Magestrate in and of the Crittenden County Court, hereby certify that R. L. Bigham whose

(210) name appears subscribed to the above and foregoing certificate is now and was at its date the Clerk of the Crittenden County Court and that his certificate and attestation is in due form. Given under my hand this 1st day of January 1851.

                                          Sameul L. Phillips

Crittenden County Set. I, R.L. Bigham Clerk of the Crittenden County Court certify that Samuel L. Phillips whose name is subscribed to above and foregoing Certificate is the Oldest and presiding Magistrate of the Crittenden County Court and that his signature is given.

                                          R.L. Bigham, Clerk.

(E. JACKSON No.119)

My last Will and wishes is I appoint Thomas Overton, James Jackson and Samuel D. Bowen my lawful Executors to this my Will I wish a Inventory taken forthwith of all my Effects anywhere both at the Home place and at Hurican Humphrey County and anywhere else that I may have any property. I wish all kept together till the crop is made so as to admit a sale of all my effects by the 1st of November next, sell all my Slaves, All my effects by the 1st of November next, sell all my Salves, all my real Estate all my household and kitchen furniture except three beds and furniture given to my wife Sarah and the three youngest children which is by her. Pay all my debts (I_nt), and the remainder equally divided into Eleven parts equal such as has had to have nothing till those that has had nothing is broght up even then equal after, I think this is the Best way to dispose of my property with my kneedy family to keep Isaac all the sums under 10 dollars Cash, all sums over 10 & 100 Dollars 4 months all sums over 100 and under 6 months all sums over 500 are 12-24 & 36 months. My Executors to be paid for their trouble is my cost as witness my hand May 6th 1850.

                                          Epps Jackson

N.B. The name of the children interested is as follows, Adalenen Oliphant, James G. Jackson, Wm. M. Jackson, Mary Ann Bowen, EpseyAnn Richard P. Van of the first set my Present wife Sarah and her children Robert Jackson & Sarah, Infintes all to be equal in what may be left after all my Just debts is paid as Witness my hand seal the 6th May 1850.

                                          Epps Jackson

(211)   Give to James G. Jackson Edmond at $360, out of his interest. All the purchases to give good security and a Lein Retained on Real Estate.

                                          E. Jackson.

State of Tennessee, Dickson County Court Sept Term 1850. This day was produced in open Court a paper writing purporting to be the last Will and Testament of Epps Jackson dec'd which was found carefully laid away among the valuable papers of the said Epps Jackson where upon Jesse Beck N. M. Hale & Thomas McNeilly came into open Court and after being duly qualified depose and say they are well aquainted with the hand writing

(212) of the said Epps Jackson and that they are fully satisfied that the said Will is in the hand writing of the said Epps Jackson and whereupon the Court ordered that the same be Recorded Sept'r 2nd 1850.

Tho. McNeilly, Clerk.

State of Tennessee, Dickson County. Then was the foregoing last Will and Testament of Epps Jackson Recorded in Will Book A. pages 210, 11 & 12 this the 5th day of Oct'r 1850.

Tho. McNeilly, Clerk.

(J. BROWN No. 120)

I, JOHN BROWN do make and publish this as my last Will and Testament hereby Revoking and making void all other wills by me at any time made.

First- I direct that my funeral expence and all my debts be paid as soon after my death as probable out of any moneys that I may die possessed of or may first or may come into thehands of my Executor.

2nd- I give and bequeath to my wife Martha Brown the plantation whereon I now live Encluding 100 acres be the ssame more or less during her natural life time also my Brown mare Jin also one Milch Cow also a sufficient support for one year.

3rd- I bequeath to my son James Brown the aforesaid plantation after the death of my wife during his natural life time.

4th- I bequeath to my son James Brown the aforesaid plantation after the death of my wife during his natural life time.

4th- I bequeath to my wife all my household furnature during her natural lifetime.

5th- It is my will that all the Rest of my Property be sold and after all my just debts is paid equally divided between my Children my son Solomon heirs to have a childs part.

6th- It is my will that at the death of my wife that my household property be sold and equally divided as aforesaid.

7th- It is my will that at the death of my son James Brown the aforesaid land be sold and Equally divided as aforesaid.

Lastly- I do hereby nominate and appoint my sons John Brown and James Brown my Executors in witness whereof I do to this my (213) last Will, set my hand and seal March 25th A.D. 1845.

his
John X Brown (seal)
mark

Signed, sealed and published in our presents we have subscribed our names hereunto in the presence of the testator.
Wiley David
Henry Garton

I, John Brown sen'r having heretofore made and published my last Will and Testament do make and declare this as a Codicil thereto, to wit, that part of my Will which directs that my land which I bequeathed to my son James to be sold at his death is hereby revoked, It is my will that at the death of my beloved wife that my son James Brown have my land and convert it to his own use as he may see proper forever, Lastly it is my desire that this Codicil be attached to and constitute a part of my Will to all intents and purposes this 4th day of Feby 1849.

his
John X Brown
mark

Signed, sealed and published in our presents we have subscribed our name hereto in the presence of the Testator this 4th day of February 1849.
H.R. Brown
Gideon Davis

State of Tennessee, Dickson County Court August Term 1850. This day was broght into open court a paper writing purporting to be the last Will and Testament of John Brown dec'd with a Codicil annexed which was proven to be such by the oath of Wiley Davis and Henry Garton witnesses to the will and H.R. Johnston and Gideon Davis witnesses to tthe Codicil and ordered to be Recorded.
Tho, McNeilly, Clerk.

State of Tennessee, Dickson County, then was the foregoing last Will and Testament Recorded in Will Book A. pages 213 & 214 October 5th 1850.
Tho. McNeilly, Clerk.

(214) (C. STRONG No.121)

In the name of God Amen. Know all men by these presents that I, CHRISTOPHER STRONG of the Court of Dickson and State of Tennessee being far advanced in age and weak in body, But of sound and perfect mind and memory, and calling to mind my mortality that I with all other men must die, and having by the blessing of God been permitted to have and enjoy & poasess a liberal portion of this worlds goods, I do hereby make and publish this my last Will and Testament.

And first of all I do give and bequeath my soul to God who gave it to me, and my body to the dust from whence it came, to be decently Burried in my Family Grave Yard, In hopes of a Glourious Resurrection through the merits of Lord and Savior Jesus Christ.

Item 2nd-I give and bequeath to my beloved wife Rosannah
(215) Strong three thousand Dollars in money, Fifteen hundred of which is to be her own and not subject to any divisions. The other fifteen hundred dollars is given her during her widowhood or her natural life and at her marriage or Death it is to be Equally divided between my heirs and hers (or so much of it as may then be remaining) that is she is to have three fourths of the whold three thousand to be disposed of as she may think proper, and this sum of three thousand dollars is to be paid to my wife out of the first monies that may come to the hands of my Executors and I give her five good Feather Beds, five Good bed steads, with all the furniture and clothing thereto belonging, and six cows and calves (her choosing) six head of young cattle from one to three years old, & one fourth part of my stock of hogs & sheep, and as much of the household and kitchen furniture as she may choose to keep and two mules & one horse or mare as she may choose & she to have liberty of choosing the mules, and my Buggie & Harness & two plows & four hoes, & two axes and one mattock, one Log chain and one waggon and all the Gear thereto belonging, she to have choice of the waggon & gear, and all my carpenters tools, and her own saddle and bridle and Blanket, and all the fowles & Poultry on the place, and one fourth part of all my Books Except those herein after given to Charles Betts those that were her own before marriage with me

(216) as a part thereof, and my Rifle Gun, and she is to have one years provision laid off for her by three dienterested men and I give to her the Farm I now live on with its appurtenances (the corn crusher to remain on the farm) during her natural lifetime or widowhood and she is to have all the above mentionedproperty life time or widowhood. But should she marry she will forfeit her rights to all the property Except three fonrths of the money, and the beds and bedsteads and furniture and one Horse or mare as the case may be the Buggie & Harness and her own before marriage with me, now should she marry then marry then she will forfeit the whole of the fifteen hundred dollars which was above last mentioned which I entend for her support (instead of the Negroes which I herein Emancipate) But should she have Expanded any part thereof then she will forfeit what soever may remain, the Residue not Excepted after my wifes marriage or Death is to be sold on a credit of one year, and the proceeds is to be divided as I direct in a subsequent Item of this my Will for the Resedory portion of my Estate and the property above Expepted is to be her own and subject to her Disposition.

2nd-Item I give to the Heirs of my Daughter Martha Dickson the negroes named in a deed of Loan from me to Molton Dickson and his wife made and Recorded many years since and their increase to be divided among them according to law.

(217) 3rd-Item, I give and bequeath to John and Reas Bowen the Farm on which I now live which included two Hundred acres Entered by me South of and adjoining the old Tracts and also the land I Bought at the sale of their Fathers lands under a a Decree of the circuit court of Dickson County which lies west of Jones Creek, and which is the land that I have herein given to my wife during her natural life, all of which they are to have possession of immediatly after her Death, and when they get possession of said land they are to pay into the hands of my Executor or those who may then Represent my Estate, five hundred Dollars each, which sum of one thousand dollars is to constitute a part of my Estate and is to be divided as tthe Residuary portion is herein after directed to be divided.

4th Item-I give and bequeath to Priscilla Dickson B. and Egbert Raworth, Five hundred and twelve acres of land lying on Hagwood County in the State of Tennessee in Range one and Section nine to be equally divided between them.

5th. Item-I do hereby give and bequeath to Charles Betts and Joseph Dickson (My Great Grand sons) six hundred and forty acres of land lying in Henry County in the State of Tennessee on the Walnut Fork of Obion River entered in my name adjoining Jesse Goodwin on the north and also two hundred and Eighty acres adjoining the same on the west to be equally divided between them and I give them the following Books, to wit, Henrys Commonstories on the Bible in six Volumes the calvinestic Library 5 Vols., Marshums Church History 12 Vol, Newton on the prophesis 2 Vols, Browns Bible Dictionary 2 Vols B. Keaths Metophare to be equally divided between them and if either of them should die before they complete their course of Education then their this other is to have the Books, or if either of them should not become a minister of the Gospel in the oposiate Reformed Church then the books to belong to the other, and if neither of them should become a minister of the Gospel in the Aposiate Reformed church then the books to belong to the other, and if neither of them should become a minister of the Gospel in the Aposiate Reformed Church then the Book to be sold and the proceeds divided among my Grand Children as the other effects of my Estate's and I do hereby direct my Executors to Reserve in their hands and pay out for the Education of Charles Betts and Joseph Dickson, and for their boarding and for Necessary Books, and for their traveling Expences in their Education a sufficient sum of money to give them a Liberal Education such as will qualify them for the Gospel Ministry in the Aposiate Reformed Church, It being my intention under God to Educate them for the Ministry, But my Executors are not to allow more out of my Estate than at the Rates of one Dollar and fifty cents pr week for their Board, Charles Betts is to be kept at the college where he now is or at some other college under the care of the Aposiate Church, until he Graduates, then he is to be kept at the study of Theology under the Direction of the Aposiate Reformed Church until he is deemed to be qualified to enter the Gospel Ministery in the Aposiate Reformed Church and Joseph Dickson is to be kept at the preparatory schools and colleges under the controll of the Aposiate Reformed Church in like manner until he is qualified for the Gospel Ministry in said A.R. Church, their Expences (as above) to be paid by my Executors out of funds retained by the for that purpose and my Executors are to see that they are prudent and Exonomical in their Expences & etc.

(218)

I do hereby give donate and bequeath to the Treasurer of Clark and Erskin College situated at Due West Corner Abbeville District South Carolina an sd to his suceessors in office in Trust forever. The sum of Seventy four hundred Dollars, two thousand dollars of said sum is to be held in trust by said Treasurer and his successors in office, for the endowment of said Clark & Erskin College, to be paid over by said Treasurer so soon after the same may come to his hands, as it may be required for the endowment of said College and Twenty two hundred Dollars of said sum is to be held in Trust by said Treasurer, and his successors in office, for the benefit of Home Missions, which is to remain a purpetual fund, the interest of which is to be annually applied under the direction of the Aposiate Reformed synod of the South for the benefit of Home Missions, and twenty two hundred dollars of said fund is to be held in like manner and the interest thereon is to be applied in like manner by sia Aposiate Reforme d Synod of the South for the bendfit of the Foreign Missions, and the remaining one thousand Dollars is to be held by said Treasurer and his successors in office in like manner and is to constitute a perpetual fund and the interest arising thereon is to be annually applied under the Direction of the Aposiate Reformed Synod of the South for the Education of Indigent young men who are preparing for the Gospel Ministry in the Assosiate Reformed Church said Synod is to have the Discretion of applying said Interest annually or adding it to the principal as they may deem best but it is to be applied for the above and no other purpose the above Missionary funds may be applied to Missionary Labors or for the publication purchase or Distribution of Books or in any other way that said Synod may direct for Missionary purposes and I desire that discretionary powers given to the Aposiate Reformed Synod of the

(219)

(220) South, in applying the Interest arrising on said sum of money shall not be so constructed either in law or Equity so as to defeat my object, and that no want of form or technicality shall effect the donation of Seventy four hundred Dollars, (But that the same be applied according to my meaning and Intention.

7th Item- I do hereby Emancipate all the slaves that I may possess of and my Executors are as soon after my Death as practicable to take the necessary means out of my Estate and send them all to Siberia except John Westly and Tennessee but if they or any of them refuse to go after they have been fully informed of the benefits of being in Siberia and being free then they who Refuse to go to Siberia are to be sold to the highest Bidder, and the money arrising from their sale is to be a part of my Estate and to be distributed as other monies of sd Estate and to be distributed as other monies of sd Estate and my wife is to keep John Westly and Tennessee, during her life or until they are twenty one years of age then they are to choose whether they will go to Siberia or not, and if they refuse to go then they are to be sold as the others and the money applied in like manner But should they or any of t them be willing to go to Siberia, then the funds are to be taken from my Estate and they are to be sent there and I desire if they or any of them should choose to be free and go to Siberia, that my Executors place them under the care and

(221) proctection of the American Colonezation Society and it is my will that my wife havethose three Children, John Westly and Tennessee taught to Reas the Bible if Practicable.

8th Item- I give and bequeath all the ballance of my Books not hereing disposed of, to the heirs of my three Daughters Jane Farrar, Sarah Bowen and Martha Dickson to be divided in three equal shares among them.

9th Item- And now it is my will and desire that all my lands that I have not disposed of in this my will or that may not have been disposed of before my Death, shall be sold to the highest Bidder on a credit of one two and three years, the purchasers to give Bond with good security, and a Lien to be retained until upon the land untilthe last payment is made and immediately after my Death my Executors are to sell all my property of every description not herein otherwise disposed of to the highest Bidder on a credit of Twelve months, taking notes with good security from the purchasers and they are also to put all my notes and accounts that I may have or may be entitled to at my death in a train of collection as soon as practicable and they are then as soon as collections can be made first to pay my wife and three thousand dollars, and they are to pay over the Donation, that I have made in trust, to the Treasurer of Clark & Erskin College and they are to retain the means necessary to carry out all the Items of my will and all the Ballance after defraying the Expences of Executing this will as well that arrising from the sale after my wifes Marriage or death, as all other sums of money is to be equally divided

(222) between all my Grand Children Except Christopher Bowen and his children is to have one share and I do hereby constitute and appoint him Trustee to take into his possession and under his controll all that I have given to his children, and he is not to be required and the three Raworth children are to have one

share jointly, and if either of them should die without Heirs of their body then the others are to be their Heirs and if all of them should die without heirs of their body, then the brothers of their Mother are to be their heirs, so far as both the land and money given them in this will is concerned and Charles Betts and Joseph Dickson are neither of them to receive any share in said Distribution.

10th Item- I do hereby constitute and appoint my beloved wife Rosahhah Strong my Executrix and John Montgomery Christopher S. Bowen, Christppher W. Dickson and Robt. McNeilly my Executors to this my last Will and Testament and they are not to be required to give security for the performance of the duties devolving upon them in the Execution of this Will, but they are to make affidavit that they will faithfully, Honestly and Vagilently Execute this will, to the best of their knowledge and ability.

And last of all I do hereby establish this to be my last Will and Testament hereby revoking and making void all other Wills or parts of will by me at anytime heretofore made. In testamoney whereof I havehereunto set my hand and seal in presence of Robt. McNeilly witnesses at my request, to this my (223) last Will, this 16th day of November 1849.

                 (seal)
               Christopher Strong

Test-
Robert McNeilly
John McNeilly

 State of Tennessee, Dickson County Court, Dec'r Term 1850. Then was the foregoing last Will and Testament of Christopher Strong dec'd produced in open Court and proven to be such by the oaths of Robert McNeilly and John McNeilly subscribing witnesses thereto and the same then ordered by the Court to be Recorded. Then came into op en Court Rosannah Strong, John Montgomery & Robert McNeilly three of the Executors mentioned in said Will and qualified as directed in said Will.

             Test-Thomas McNeilly, Clk.

 State of Tennessee, Dickson County, then was the foregoing last Will and Testament of Christopher Strong Dec'd Recorded in Will Book A. pages 214 to 223, this December 20th 1850.

              Tho. McNeilly, Clerk.

(E. GLEAVES No.222)
 I, ELIZABETH GLEAVES of Dickson County, State of Tennessee being of sound mind and memory do publish this as my last Will and Testament.

 Item 1st- I do bequeath to my Daughter Isabella Weakley my Eldest negro Girl Mary, to her during her natural life and her bodily heirs forever.

 Item 2nd- I do bequeath to my son Ezekiel S. Gleaves my negro woman and her children as follows, Martin, Violet, Emily, Joseph and Calib also all the increase of said negroes if there be any to him and his Heirs forever.

(224) I do bequeath to my Grand children as follows, to wit, the Heirs of my daughter Emaline Binkley, Parile Elisa and Araminta

Morris also my Grand son William D. Gleave the sum of fifty dollars to each to be paid so soon as the amount convenently be made by the Heirs of the above named Negroes, which I have bequeathed in Item 2nd to my son Ezekiel S. Gleaves. I do also bequeath to my Daughter Isabella Weakley my Gray mare Beck, bridly and saddle.

Item 4th- I do appoint my son Ezekiel S. Gleaves, Executor of this my last Will and Testament, signed this 28th January A.D. 1851.

                                             Elizabeth Gleaves (seal)

Signed and acknowledged on this 28th January A.D. 1851.
Gardner Green
P.W. Simpkins

So much of the within will altered I give Emely to Isabella instead of E.S. Gleaves the ballance of said Will to remain in full force and virtue May 20th 1851.

Test-   her
J. W. Simpkins   Elizabeth X Gleaves
W. D. Gleaves   mark

State of Tennessee, Dickson County Court July Term 1851. This day was Broght into open Court a paper writing purporting to be the last Will and Testament of Elizabeth Gleaves which was proven to be such by the oaths of Gardner Green and J. W. Simpkins & W. D. Gleaves whereupon said Will was ordered to be recorded, whereupon E. S. Gleaves who was appointed Executor by said Will came into open Court and Executed and acknowledged his Bond as Executor in the sum of four thousand dollars with W. D. Speight and B. W. Bell as his securities and qualified according to laws and the Court ordered that letters Testamentary Issue to him.

                                                     Thomas McNeilly, Clerk.

(225)   State of Tennessee, Dickson County, then was the foregoing last Will and Testament of Elizabeth Gleaves dec'd Recorded in Will Book A. pages 223,4 & 5, this 24th July 1851.

                                                     Tho. McNeilly, Clerk.

(J. GROVES, Will, No.223)

I, JOSEPH GROVES do make and publish this as my last Will and Testament hereby revoking and making void allothers Wills by me at any time made.

First- I direct that my funeral expences and all my debts be paid as soon after my Death as possible out of any moneys that I may die possessed of or may first come into the Hands of my Executor.

Secondly- I give and bequeath unto my step Daughter Lydia Ann Williams, one third of all the land that I now possess, also one mare horse, one bed & bedstead, one Cow.

Thirdly- I give and bequeath to my son John, one third of my land, one mare colt, a Gun and Saddle.

Fourthly- I give and bequeath to my daughter Mary Francis

(226) one third of my land, one Horse, one Bed and Bedstead,,two H Heifers, I also give and bequeath to the said Lydia Ann and Mary Francis, my waggon & Harness to be equally divided between them, all the Household furniture to be Equally divided between the said Lydia Ann, John & Mary Francis.

Lastly- I nominate and appoint Lydia Ann Williams my Executrix In witness whereof I do to this my will set my hand and seal this 30th of April 1851.

                                Joseph Groves

Signed, sealed & published in our presence & we have subscribed our names in presence of the Testator.
   W. T. Sturat
   W. Caldwell.

State of Tennessee, Dickson County Court, July Term, 1851. This day was Returned into open Court a paper writing purporting to be the last Will & Testament of Joseph Groves which was proven to be such by the oath of William Coldwell, whereupon Court ordered the same to be Recorded.

                                Tho. McNeilly, Clk.

State of Tennessee, Dickson County, then was the foregoing last Will and Testament of Joseph Groves dec'd., Recorded in Will Book A. Pages 225, 86 or 8, & 6, this 24th July 1851.

                                Tho. McNeilly, Clk.

(W. GARRETT, Will, No. 224)

State of Tennessee, Dickson County, July 3rd 1851. I, WILLIAM GARRETT of the County & State of Tennessee being in feeble health, but of sound mind, do make this my last Will and Testament, I give and bequeath unto my affectionate wife Sarah Garrett the following slaves (Viz) Ben and his wife Pheriba & (227) children and also boy Jerry to have & to hold for her own use and benefit during her life & at her death to dispose of them among the children as she may think proper or should she think proper she can dispose of them among the children at any time previous to her death, I also give to my wife, the tract of land on which I reside to have and to hold during her life & at her death to be sold on a credit of one two and three years & the proceeds to be Equally divided among the children.

It is my desire that my wife should have & I hereby give unto her whatever articles of household furniture she may want or think proper to reserve. I do desire for her to have her choice in selecting Four cows & calves as many of the farming tools as she may want also I give unto her the entire stock of sheep two of the choice mules and the sorrell Horse a choice Yoke of Oxen & as many of the stock Hogs as she may think proper to keep & I wish her to have a support for Twelve months out of the present growing crop & stock also to have a light ore cart such as she may desire, purchase and paid for out of the means of the Estates. I think it is right & I desire that my affectionate daughter Martha Ann Garrett should be charged the sum of one hundred dollars to be deducted out of her distributive share, the same having been paid for her Board & Witt Tuition as I am desirous of granting my slaves the privilege of

(228) selecting their Masters I wish my Executors to allow them that privilege and to sell them at private sale provided they can be sold at full valuation, otherwise to be sold together with all the remainder of my property not herein before given to my wife at public sale to the highest Bidder on a credit of Twelve months and the proceeds after paying my just debts to be equally divided among the children. I hereby appoint as my Executors my friend B. A. Collier, and in the event that anything should occur to prevent his acting then appoint my friend Tho. McNeilly as my Executor. In testimony whereof I hereunto set my hand and affixed my seal the day and date above written. Signed in the presence of

William H. Sensing
J. M. Larkins

William Garrett (seal)

State of Tennessee, Dickson County Court Aug. Term 1851. This day was produced in open Court a paper writing purporting to be the last Will and Testament of Wm. Garrett dec'd which was proven to be such by the oaths of W. H. Sensing and J. M. Larkins subscribing witnesses thereto & the Will was ordered to be Recorded whereupon Benjamin A. Collier the Executor of sd Will came into open Court and Executed and acknowledge his Bond as Exe'r in the sum of twelve thousand dollars, with B. C. Robertson and Wiliam H. Napier as his securities and quallified according to law, whereupon the Court ordered that letters Testamentary Issue to him.

Tho. McNeilly, Clk.

(229) State of Tennessee, Dickson County, then was the foregoing last Will and Testament of Wm. Garrett dec'd Recorded in Will Book A. pages 226, 7,8 & 9, this 12th day August 1851.

Tho. McNeilly, Clk.

(R. B. HINTON, Will, No. 225)

I, RICHARD B. HINTON do make and publish this as my last Will and Testament hereby revoking and making void all other Wills by me at any time made.

First-I direct that my Funeral Expences and all my just Debts be paid as soon after my death as possible out of any moneys that I may possess of or may first come into the hands of my Executor.

Secondly-I wish my Executor to carry on and continue business in my name for five years after which time, I wish all my property both personal and real to be equally divided between my two beloved Sisters, Elizabeth Boyd Hinton and Rachael Adaline Hinton.

Lastly-I do hepeby nominate and appoint my Father John J. Hinton my sole Executor to qualify and act as such without giving security. In witness thereof I do to this my will set my hand and seal this the 20th day of October in the year of our Lord one thousand Eight hundred and fifty one (1851)

Richard B. Hinton (seal)

Signed, sealed and published in our presence, and we have subscribed our names hereto in the presence of the Testator this 20th day of Oct'r 1851.

R. C. Robertson
Wash Hunter

Signed, sealed and published in our presence, and we have subscribed our names hereto in the presnece of the Testator this 20th day of Oct8r 1851.

R. C. Robertson
Wash Hunter

(230) State of Tennessee, Dickson County Court, Nov'r Term 1851. This day was brot into court a paper writing purporting to be the last Will and Testament of Richard B. Hinton which was proven to be such by the oaths of B. C. Robertson and Washington Hunter and ordered that the same be Recorded whereupon John J. Minton came into open and qualified as Executor and the Court ordered that Letters Testamentary Issue to him.

Thomas McNeilly, Clk.

State of Tennessee, Dickson County, then was the foregoigg last Will and Testament of Richard B. Hinton dec'd Recorded in Will Book A. Pages 229 & 30 this 15th day Nov'r 1851.

Tho. McNeilly, Clerk.

(R. WEST, Will, No.226)

In the name of God Amen. I, ROBERT WEST of Dickson County and state of Tennessee being of sound mind and memory but of infirm and delicate health do on this 18th day of July in the year of our Lord 1850, make and publish this my last Will and Testament hereby revoking all other Wills by me made.

Imprivisio, I will and desire that all my just debts be paid by my Executors hereinafter named out of any monies which may come to their hands belonging to my estate.

2nd- It is my will and desire that my wife Nancy West have & retain my family Residence together with all the lands & appurtenances thereunto belonging embracing the following Tracts of land (to wit) one Tract containing three hundred and twenty acres lying on Yellow Creek in Dickson County and state of Tennessee which was Granted by the state of North Carolina to Robert Heaten by Grant No. 105, one other Tract containing Eighty acres described in a Deed of conveyance from my Brother George West to my in said County, one other tract conveyed to me by Wm. Morrison for twenty five acres, one other tract granted to me by the state of Tennessee for three hundred and eighty six acres No. Grant 12666, one other tract for four hundred and ninty acres conveyed to me by Elizabeth Hays and others one other tract conveyed to me by E. Hays & others for one hundred and fifty acres, one other tract granted to mm by the State of Tennessee for six acres No. of Grant 1475; in all making Fourteen hundred and fifty seven acres all which lands are in said County of Dickson and constitute the Home Tract the boundaries of which may be seen on Record as contained in the title papers for the same and my said wife is to have natural life, and at her death I will and desire the same to my two sons Robert J. West and Isaac D. West and at the death of either to the survivior to him and his heirs forever.

(231)

I further give and bequeath to my wife during her life the following negroes, to wit, Bill, Sylvia, Penny, Nancy, Hetty, Sarah Lydia & all her children, Jack (Dortch) Peter Nelson & Tom; and at her death the same bo be equally divided among my five children, to wit, Louisa McClure, Robert J. West, Isaac D. West, Martha J. Stacker and Sally C. West, and in the event that any of my said children above named shall at the time departed this life leaving children or child, the shear of sd. deceased parent to go to said child or children, I also give to my said wife for her use and support during life as much of my (232) stock of every as she may want also as much Household and kitchen furnature & of farming utensils as she may desire. I also give to her five hundred dollars to be paid to her by my Executors as she may need or call for the same. I also give bequeath & desire to her my said wife & her heirs forever all my right & title to the Estate both Real and personal which was devised to her by the last Will and Testament of her Father Isaac Dortch dec'd including what has heretofore been received & what may hereafter be coming to her at the death of her Mother Mrs, Martha Dortch.

I hereby give and desire to my sons Robt. J. West and Isaac D. West to them and their heirs forever my tract of land on Cumberland River below the mouth of Yellow Creek containing one thousand and fifty seven acres more or less which was purchased of the Trustee of the University of North Carolina and case of death of either without children surviving then to the survivor of my said two sons.

4th- I give and bequeath to my two Grand children John Minor and Charles Minor, fifteen hundred Dollars each not taking unto consideration what was given to their Mother to be paid over to their Guardian or Trustee in two years after the qualification of my Executors to this my will and if either of them should die before arriving at full age, and without any child or children surviving then the survivor to take the whole this is all that I give to the said John & Charles Minor.

(233) 5th- I hereby give and descend to my Daughter Louisa McClure & her children now born and hereafter to be born, one negro woman named Zal & one negro Girl named Flora heretofore delivered, also the Tract of land on which Robert W. McClure now resided lying in Montgomery County near Clarksville purchased by me from Willie B. Johnson, containing Two hundred & seven and 1/4 acres in two tracts purchased by him from H and M. Clayton and part of a tract purchased by him from Vance & Dix also a tract of seventy acres more or less purchased by me of W. B. Johnson known as the Big spring tract and being the Balance of said tract purchased by him of said Vance and Bix, which said lands are estimated by me to be of the value of three thousand Dollars, & to be accordingly in the division of my Estate, the above described property both real & personal is hereby given to my said Daughter & her children as above for their use and benefit & the said Robt. McClure, for & during the life of my said daughter and not to be subject to the debts or contracts of the said Robert McClure, & at the death of my daid daughter the same to go to her said children have heretofore advanced to Robert McClure the sum of seven hundred Dollars and have taken up two Notes given by him to Isaac Dortch and which are now in my possession which money and Notes are to be accounted for, together with the other property in this Item contained.

7th- It is my will that all the perishable property belonging to my estate of every description at the home place and at the

(234) Furnace Forge, except what is given to my wife during her life
& excepting also my slaves, be sold by me Executors on a credit
of Twelve months taking notes with good and approved security
for the same & the proceeds divided as directed in the sixth
Item of this my will. It is my will that five hundred dollars
be appropriated to procuring Grave Stones for such of my Family
as have none & in fincing in and other wise improving the Grave
Yard at Sailors Rest so far as the above sum will go which I request shall be attended to by my Executors as soon as practicable.

(235) 9th-I give to my son Robt. J. West my new family Bible & my
Rifle Gun and to my son Isaac D. West I give my Horse Bridle
and saddle my old family Bible and my old farming Bible and my
watch and to give my Library of Books to my said two sons to be
divided between them as they may think proper. It is my meaning and intention that none of the property either Real or personal which is specifically bequeathed or divised to my said
two sons Robert J, and Isaac D. West is to be taken in to the
estimate on the division of my property as contained and directed in the sixth item of this my will.

    Kindly and affectionatly have my beloved wife and myself lived
and labored together and cheerfully do I bequeath my property
the result of our joint exertions to her and our children together with the love and blessing of a husband and wife and lastly I hereby nominate and appoint Qunties C. Adkinson of Memphis
Jesse C. Ingrum of Dover, Burrell B. Corbun of Sailors Rest,
and my sons Robert J. West and Isaac D. West and John C. Collier
of Charlotte Executors of this my last Will and Testament, and
they are not required by me to give security for the performance
of their duties as Executors, and the same is expressly dispersed with by me. In testimony whereof I have on the day and
year mentioned published and declare this to be my last will and
Testament and signed the same in the presence of the witnesses
called on by me to attest the same.

A .A. Brown
Nathan Nesbitt   Robert West (seal)
Lewis T. Hughes
N. C. Parrish
O. Nesbitt

    The following interlineations in this will were made before
the same was executed (to wit) on the third page the words,
"The Trustees of the University of North Carolina" and on the
fifth and on the bottom line the word here was inserted.
A. A. Brown
Nathan Nesbitt   Robert West   (seal)
Lewis T. Hughes
N. C. Parrish
O. Nesbitt

(237 State of Tennessee, Dickson County Court, November Term 1851.
This day was produced in open Court a paper writing purporting
to be the last Will and Testament of Robert West dec'd which
was proven to be such by the oaths of Nathan Nesbitt and Lewis
T. Hughes and the same was ordered to be reforded whereupon
Robert J. West, Isaac D. West, Burrell B. Corban and John C. Col-

Collier came into open Court and were qualified as Executors to said will and ordered that letters Testamentory Issue to them.

Tho. McNeilly, Clerk.

State of Tennessee, Dickson County, then was the foregoing last Will and Testament of Robert West dec'd recorded in the Will Book A. pages 231,232,33,34,35,36, this 20th November.

Tho. McNeilly, Clerk.

(W. PORTER, Will, No. 227)

I, WILLIAM PORTER do make and publish this my last Will & Testament hereby revoking and making void all other wills by me at any time made.

1st- I desire that my funeral expences & all my just debts be paid as soon after my death as possible out of any money that I may die possessed of or may first come into the hands of my Executors.

2nd- I give and bequeath unto my wife Mattilda Porter the tract of land on which I now live in all three Tracts containing two hundred and 27 acres be the same more or less together with my negro man Lewis & negro woman Nancy with all my stock of cattle horses sheep & hogs with all my household furniture during her life or widowhood at which time all are to be sold & equally divided between my four youngest children (to wit) Mary E. Porter, William M. Porter, Samuel M. Porter & Matilda I. Porter or to be divided between what of them that may remain living at the time of the death of my wife.

3rd- I give and bequeath unto my son J. W. Porter the tract of land on which he now lives and one dollar in cash.

4th- I give and bequeath unto my daughter Elizabeth Harvy, five dollars in cash.

5th- I give and bequeath unto my daughter Harvey five dollars in cash.

6th- I give and bequeath unto my daughter Nancy Sullivan five dollars in cash. This amount being as I believe their full shear as they have had all the Property that come by my first wife or their Mother.

7th- I give and bequeath unto my wife Matilda Porter all of my crop of corn, Oats & Wheat and every article that I may die possessed of, to be sold at her death & divided as directed in bequeath second.

8th- And lastly I do nominate and appoint B. B. Hall and Matilda Porter my Executor & Executrix, in witness whereof I do to this will set my hand and seal this 14th day of September 1849.

William Porter (seal)

(238) Signed, sealed & published in our presence and we have subscribed our names hereto in the presence of the Testator this 14th day of September 1849.

A. V. Hicks
N. M. Hall
James C. Pullen

State of Tennessee, Dickson County Court, May Term 1851,

(239) this day was produced in open Court a paper writing purporting to be the last Will & Testament of Wm. Porter dec'd which was proven to be such by the oaths of N. W. Hale & A. V. Hicks which ordered by the Court to be Recorded whereupon B. B. Hale & Tilan Porter Executor & Executrix of said Will came into open Court and Executed their Bond as Executors in the sum of two thousand dollars with James Bibb, B. T. Gentry & R. White as their securities and qualified as the law directs. Whereupon the Court ordered that letters Testamentary Issue to them.

                                                          Tho. McNeilly, Clerk.

State of Tennessee, Dickson County, Then was the foregoing last will and Testament of William Porter, Recorded in Will Book A. Pages 237, 8,9, this 20th Nov'r 1851.

                                                     Thomas McNeilly, Clk.

(G. RAPE, Will No. 228)

The last Will and Testament of Gustavus Rape of the County of Dickson, State of Tennessee.

I, GUSTAVUS RAPE, considering the uncertainty of the mortal life, and being of sound mind and memory do make and publish this my last Will and Testament in manner and form following, (that is to say).

First- I give and bequeath unto my beloved wife Barbra Rape the Tract of land which I purchased with all of the appurtenances also I give to my wife Barbra my negro boy John, Two beds and furniture, one horse, Saddle & bridle worth($70..00) seventy Dollars, one cow and calf, Sugar chest, one Table, one Trunk Brass Kettle, fifteen head of stock, hogs, also one year provisions (Item) I give and bequeath to William Johnson the sum of one hundred Dollars, And lastly as to all the rest residue and remainder of my real and personal Estate, Goods & chattles of what kind and nature soever I wish sold upon twelve months credit, and to be equally divided between my ten children (to wit) Henry Rape, Jacob Rape, Peter Rape, John Rape and the children of Daniel Rape, and the children of my daughter Mary Funderbuss my daughter Elizabeth Nowles, my daughter, Milly Hanks, my daughter, Franky Evins, and to my daughter, Nancy Thomas, two grand children (to wit) Daniel and Evaline Brums, I hereby appoint Executors of this my last Will and Testament, (240) William Johnson and Benjamin C. Robertson, hereby revoking all former Wills by me made. In witness whereof I have hereunto set my hand and seal this 3rd day July in the year of our Lord one thousand Eight hundred and forty eight (1848).

Test-
William D. Speight
G. W. Scott

                                        his
                               Gustavus X Rape (seal)
                                    mark

State of Tennessee, Dickson County Court, March Term 1852. This day was broght into court a paper writing purporting to be the last Will and Testament of Gustavus Rape Dec'd which was proven to be such by the oaths of William D. Speight and G. W. Scott, subscribing witnesses thereto whereupon the Court ordered the same to be Recorded. Whereupon William Johnson and B. C. Robertson the Executors appointed by the Testator came into open Court and Entered into Bond as Executors in the sum of ten thousand dollars with W. J. Mathis, W. D. Speight & Wm. H. Napier as their securities and they quallified as the law directs, and the Court ordered that Letters Testamentary Issue to them.

Tho. McNeilly, Clk.

State of Tennessee, Dickson County, Then was the foregoing last Will and Testament of Gistavus Rape dec'd Recorded in Will Book A. pages 239 & 240 april 24th 1852.

Thomas McNeilly, Clk.

(W. WILLEY, Will No.229)

In the name of God Amen. I, WILLIS WILLY of the State of Tennessee and County of Dickson, do hereby make and publish this my last Will and Testament and in the first place place it is my Will that after my Death my Body be decently Buried and I commit my soul to a Kind and MercifullGod in hope of a Glorious Resurection and Reanution of soul and body on the morning of the Resurection through the Merits the Lord Jesus Christ.

2nd- Immediately after my Death I wish my Executors to pay all my just debts, out of the first money that come into their hands, after paying my Funeral Expences.

And after all my just debtd are paid it is my will that my beloved wife shall have and retain all my Property of every Description and the use of all my land during her natural life or widowhood, Except at my Death she is to give to Martha Larkins our Daughter a Horse mare or mule at its valuation & saddle & Bridle, so as to make her equal with the rest, and she is to give John W. Willy our oldest son a Bed and furniture & cow & calf (he having rec'd a Horse, saddle & Bridly worth $50 when called for and she is to give to Michael B. Willy our 2nd son a Bed and furniture & calf & cow when called for (he having
(241)Rec'd a Horse, Saddle & Bridle worth 75 dollars, and she is to give to Willis Carroll Willy our youngest son a Horse and Saddle and Bridle & cow & calf and Bed and furniture at valuation when ea he calls for them, My two Daughters Martha and Mary have rec'd each a Bed & furniture and a cow and calf & some other small articles, and Mary Walker has rec'd a Mare Saddle & Bridle worth thirty dollars, and she has also rec'd Fifty dollars in Land, now to make my will easy of comprehension I here explain that it is my desire that all my children be made equal including what they have Received.

And at the death of my wife My Executors is to sell all my property of every description including my Land to the Higest Bidder on a credit of twelve months and to take Notes with good security from the purchasers & to retain Lein upon the land untill paid for, and after collections are made he is to equally divide the proceeds among my five children including the amounts that each have Received. Now should any of my children die before said Distribution, and leave an heir or heirs then said Heirs are to stand in the place of their parent (I mean a child or children) and not a Husband or wife.

I hereby constitute and appoint my beloved wife Polly Willy and my son John W. Willey my Executrix & Executor to this my last

my son John W. Willey my Executrix & Executor to this my last
Will and Testament, and having made this will (which is the
only one I ever have had written out) I do hereby establish it
to be my last Will and Testament, In testimony whereof I have
hereunto set my hand and seal in presence of Robert McNeilly
and Thomas K. Grigsby witnesses at my request this 6th day of
October 1850.

Robert McNeilly   Willis Willy (seal)
Tho. K. Grigsby

    Dickson County Court, June Term 1852. This day was produced
in open Court a paper writing purporting to be the last Will
and Testament of Willis Willy and which was proven to be such
by the oaths of Robert McNeilly & Thomas K. Grigisby and the
same was ordered to be Recorded.

                                            Thomas McNeilly, Clk.
    State of Tennessee, Dickson County. Then was the foregoing
last Will and Testament of Willis Willy dec'd Recorded in Will
Book A. pages 241,2, this 14th day of June 1852.

                                            Thomas McNeilly, Clk.

(243)(M. PARKER, Will No.250)
    I, MOSES PARKER of the State of Tennessee and Dickson County
being far advanced in years but in perfect mind and memory do
make ordain constitute and appoint this to be my last Will and
Testament, Viz:
    1st-I wish all my just debts to be paid.
    2nd-I wish at the death of my self and my wife Hannah Parker
that my servant girl Evaline be set free as the law directs in
such cases.
    3rd-I wish that my beloved wife should she survive me to be
put in possession of all things that the Law provided for her,
in such cases, where the above shall have be done.
    4th-My wish is that all my slaves(with the execption above)
be sold at public sale, together with all my stock & etc., at
twelve months credit and my wish is that my children agree among
themselves and make a division of my lands equally among themselves and when the money shall fall due for the property sold
my wish is that an equal division be made among my children
with the following variation, viz, My son John Parker having already had twenty one dollars and twenty five cents and my daughter Hulda May having had sixty two dollars, and my daughter Kiz-
zeah Garton having had seven dollars and also my son William
Parker having had one hundred and two dollars. Now my wish is
that the above deductions be made, and accounted for in the division, so that there may be equallity among them, and the rest
of my children. I hereby nominate and appoint my son Daniel Parker my Executor to this my Will and further I annul all other
Wills (should therehave been any) by me made null and void.
    In testimony whereof I have hereunto set my hand and affixed
my seal this 11th day of July in the year of our Lord one thous-
and eight hundred and fifty two.
Test-   his
David Gray   Moses X Parker (seal)
Francis Vanlandinghand   mark

Dickson County Court, September Term 1852. This day was produced in open Court a paper writing purporting to be the last Will and Testament of Moses Parker dec'd which was proven to be such by the oaths of David Gray & Francis Vanlandingham subscribing witnesses to said Will, which was ordered to be Recorded.

                Tho. McNeilly, Clk.

State of Tennessee, Dickson County. Then was the foregoing last Will and Testament of Moses Parker dec'd Recorded in Will Book A. pages 243 & 244, this 11th day of September 1852.

                Tho. McNeilly, Clk.

(245) (M. G. SENSING, Will No. 231)

  L, MCKENDRIE GARDNER SENSING of the County of Dickson and State of Tennessee former being in good health of body and of sound mind and memory do make and publish this my last Will and Testament at the same time utterly revoking all former Wills made by me declaring this to be my last Will and Testament.

  1st-Item- I desire all my just debts to be paid at the expence of my Estate and I further desire that my body be buried in a christian like manner on the farm where I now live by the side of my beloved daughter Margaret Ann Sensing.

  Item Second- I give and bequeath to my beloved wife Drewsillah B. Sensing, my negro boy Richman & Lovey my Land slao stock of all kinds, Household and kitchen furniture also what money I have, notes & accounts all the named Items to be hers during her life time or widowhood at her death or marriage all to be equally divided between my three children, John, Henry, Sensing Polly Welding Sensing, Wiley Powel Sensing except one horse bridle and saddle, one cow and calf, one bed and bedstead and furniture.

  Item the last I appoint my worthy friends Allen Nesbitt and William B. Bell my sole and joint Executors to this my last Will and Testament.

  Given under my hand and seal, in the year of our Lord and Savior one thousand eight hundred and forty seven. Signed, sealed & etc. in presence of

Test-
E. Hickerson   M. G. Sensing (seal)
Gilford Mills

State of Tennessee, Dickson County Court October Term 1852. This day was produced in open Court a paper writing purporting to be the Last Will and Testament of M. G. Sensing dec'd which was proven to be such by the oaths of Gilford Mills one of the subscribing witnesses and ordered to be Recorded.

                Tho McNeilly, Clk.

State of Tennessee, Dickson County. Then was the foregoing Last Will and Testament of M. G. Sensing Recorded in Will Book A. pages 245 & 246, October 7th 1852.

                Tho McNeilly, Clk.

(246) (W. E. PENDERGRASS no. 232)

  I, WILLIAM E. PENDERGRASS do make and publish this as my last Will and Testament hereby revoking and making void all other

Wills by me at any time made.

First- I direct that my funeral expences and all my debts be paid as soon after my death as possible out of any moneys that I may die possessed of or may first come into the hands of my Executors.

Secondly- I give and bequeath to my beloved Wife Rilly my farm on which I reside including my tow Canen fields, My negro woman Lucy, my gray and yellow mare, fonr cows and calves, my oxen and cart, my stock or Hogs and sheep, my household and Kitchen furniture with all of farming tools during her natural life or widowhood at the experation of either it is my will the property bequeathed to her sold and the proceeds equally divided between several children, First deducting out of the shares all ready and to be given in this Will (viz) I will to my son Van Buran the colt now sucking my gray mare and my afflicted son William E. to have my negro man Smith when he becomes of age I wish said negro hired out till that time, and the proceeds of said hire kept at interest with whatever of monies I now have on hand and due me til my youngest child and Daughter Sarah Elizabeth becomes of age or my wife dies, then to be equally divided among all of my living Children William E, excepted who I have heretofore provided for. My son Van Buran to account for the value pf the colt given him and my son John Harvey to account for what I have given & paid for him, say one hundred and fifty dollars- Then to come in equally with my other living children if he should be alive. It is further my will that my son Van Buran have my farm known as and called the Nunley Place, and my sons Cave and William C. to have at the death of my wife the farm and lands all ready divided to her or when my said Daughter Sarah Elizabeth becomes of age these last beque sts to William E. and Cave to constitute their entire interest with that heretofore given in this Will. It is my will and wish that my farm known as the Walker Place be sold and the proceeds put to Interest as all the other means I have and as heretofore directed I do hereby and in addition to all I have willed, Will and direct that the wants and necessities of my said Wife Rilly is to be duly respected and relieved out of any of my Estate so as to enable her to live above want and raise and take care of her self and children now living with her. I appoint my true and trusty friend William S White as my Executor given under my hand and seal this the 21st Aug. 1852.

Witnesses
W. Dunagan
John X P. Jordan
  mark

                                          his
                                William X E. Pendergrass
                                       mark

State of Tennessee, Dickson County Court, October Term 1852. (248) This day was produced in open Court a paper writing purporting to be the last Will and Testament of W. E. Pendergrass dec'd which was proven to be such by the oaths of W. Dunagan & John P. Jordan subscribing witnesses thereto and ordered to be Recorded.

                                               Tho. McNeilly, Clk.

State of Tennessee, Dickson County. Then was the foregoing last Will and Testament of W. E. Pendergrass dec'd Recorded in Will Book A. pages 246 & 248, October 8th 1852.

                                               Tho McNeilly, Clk.

(R. WHITE, Will No.233)

I, RUBEN WHITE of the County of Dickson and State of Tennessee being in sound mind and disposing memory but in an infirm state of health. Do make and publish this as my last Will and Testament hereby revoking and making void all other Wills by me at any time made.

First- I direct that my funeral expences and all my just debbs be paid as soon after my death as possible out of any monies that I may die possessed of or may first come into the hands of my Executor.

Secondly- I will and bequeath to my beloved wife Mary B. White during her natural life or widowhood, all my real Estate to support her family on provided she remains a widow and at her death for ti to be advertised twenty day & sold to the hightest bidder and the proceeds to be equally divided between by Lawful heirs. But if she should again marry then I wish for her to have one horse and saddle one cow & calf and one bed and furnitnew and the land to be disposed of as above directed at the time of her marriage.

Thirdly-I will and bequeath that my negro property remain with my wife, to have the full use of it during her natural life or widowhood. But if she should marry I wish for my negroes to be hired out until my youngest child shall become of age and if there should be any increase in my negro property so that they could be divided, I wish then for the to be equally divided among my lawful heirs if no increase to be equally divided among my lawful heirs if no increase to be sold and the proceeds divided equally among my lawful h eirs, and if they should be divided I wish them (the negroes to belong exclusively to my children and their increase as entailed property.

Fourthly-I will and bequeath to my niece Elizabeth Garton (Provided she remains with my wife until she (Elizabeth) marries, one colt and money to buy her a saddle, one cow and calf one bed and furniture, also I will to each one of my own children as they grow up and leave my wife the same articles bequeathed above to Elizabeth Garton. The ballance of all my stock and perishable property of every description. I will to my wife to have the full use of it for to support her family on provided she remains a widow if not then for it to be disposed of as is directed in the second Item, if she and my Executor should consider there a surplus of stock or other propertyfor them to dispose of such as they think she can spare and at her death for it all to be sold and equally divided among my lawful heirs, I further will and wish that as far as my means will allow for my Executor to see that my children have a liberal Country English Education for to be paid out of the proceeds of my property.

(249)

Firstly- I wish the note that I hold against Mother of $195.45cts for her not to be disturbed about it during her natural life but wish for her to renew it every five years and for it to stand good for my children at her death and then to be equally divided among them all.

Lastly- I do hereby nominate and appoint my brother my brother W. L. White my Executor, in witness whereof I do to this my Will set my hand and seal this 8th day of August 1852.

Signed, Sealed and published in our presence and we have subscribed our names in the presence of the Testator, day and date as above written.

John D. Mitchell   R. White   (seal)
N. R. Emery

State of Tennessee, Dickson County Court October Term 1852. This day was produced in open Court a paper writing purporting to be the last Will and Testament of Reuben White dec'd which was proven to be such by the oaths of N. R. Emory and John D. Mitchell, subscribing witnesses to the same, which was ordered to be recorded.

Tho. McNeilly, Clerk.

State of Tennessee, Dickson County. Then was the foregoing last Will and Testament of Reuben White dec'd Recorded in Will Book A. Pages 248,249,250, October 8th 1852.

Tho. McNeilly, Clerk.

(251) (A. J. AUSTIN, Will No.234)

I, ABRAHAM J. AUSTIN, do make and publish this my last Will and Testament hereby revoking all other Wills heretofore made.

Item the first-I will that all of my just debts and funeral expenses be paid.

2nd- I will that the heirs of my daughter Elizabeth Jane Seal have a certain parcel of my land, Beginning at the South west corner of a fifty five acre tract running East to a point, so as to run North seventy yards West of my tobacco Barn, to the North boundary of said Tract, thence West and South to the Beginning.

3rd-I will that my wife Martha Austin have all the Ballance of my land, together with all my personal property, during her natural life or widowhood, and at her death or marriage to my son Jacob J. Austin. This the 19th day of September 1852.

Executed in our presence,
O. L. V. Schmittou
Sellman Edwards

                    his
A. J. X Austin (seal)
                    mark

N. B. I appoint my wife, Marhta Austin, Executrix of my will withour security.

Dickson County November Term 1852. This day was produced in open Court a paper writing purporting to be the last Will and Testament of A. J. Austin dec'd., which was proven to be such by the oaths of O. L. V. Shhmittou, Sellman Edwards, subscribing witnesses thereto, which was ordered to be recorded.

Tho. McNeilly, Clk.

State of Tennessee, Dickson County. Then was the foregoing last Will and Testament of A. J. Austin dec'd,, Recorded in Will Book A. Page 251.

Tho. McNeilly, Clk.

(252) (W. D. Speight, Will No.235)

The last Will and Testament of WILLIAM D. SPEIGHT, of the County of Dickson and State of Tennessee.

I, WILLIAM D. SPEIGHT, considering the uncertainty of this Mortal life, Being weak and infirm but of sound mind and memory, do make and publish this, my last Will and Testament in manner and form following, (that is to say):

First- I give and bequeath unto my beloved wife Emily C. Speight all my household and kitchen furniture with the Exeception of the beds & furniture which are for my three children I also give to my wife Emily C. two good plows & two sets of Geer compleat, and my fan Mill, one oxccart, one yoke of oxen, two head of stock, hogs, two hoes and one sythe & cradle I also give and bequeath unto mywife Emily C. during her natural life, and at her death to be divided between our three children, Allis V. Pardise, and William D. the following property (to wit) Land & three negroes my negro man Jordan, my woman Martha, with her increase, if any, and my boy Daniel-A Tract or parcel of land Beginning at the mouth of a branch near an old Brick Kiln, on the River Bank, and running with the meanders of said Branch to a Beach Tree, that is a line tree in my sough boundary at or near what is known & called Lucas old coal Pit, thence with said line to the East corner thence with the line of a fifty acre survey to Harpeth River thence with the line of a fifty acre survey to Harpeth River thence up said River, with its meanders to the Beginning-Including all the improvements and Buildings of every kind, within the above described boundary. I also will to my wife Emily C. one years provisions-(Item) I give and bequeath unto my Daughter Allis V. my negro boy Virgil and my Girl Ann, which I value at $1200, Twelve hundred Dollars. (Item) I give and bequeath unto my Daughter Paradise my negro boy Alfred and my Girl Sarah Ann, which I value at $1200. Twelve hundred Dollars.(Item) I give and bequeath unto my son William D. my negro man Calebs, and my boy Joe, which I value at $1100. Eleven hundred Dollars, also the sum of $100 one hundred Dollars in cash to make his two negroes Equal in value, to those given to my two Daughters- (Item) I give and bequeath unto my three children, Allis V. Paradise and William D. all the rest and remainder of my real Estate, to be equally divided between them and Lastly, as to all the rest, residue and remainder of my personal Estate, goods, chattels of what kind and nature soever, I wish sold on a twelve months credit and after all of my debts are paid by Executors I wish the proceeds arising from said sale, with all the moneys left by me, to be equally divided between my wife, Emily C. and my three children, Allice V. Paradise and William D. Speight.

I hereby appoint B. C. Robertson, sole Executor of this, my last Will and Testament-In witness whereof, I have hereunto Set my hand and seal; this the 9th June in the year of our Lord one thousand Eighty hundred and fifty two (1852).

William D. Speight (seal)

The above instrument, consisting of one sheet was now here subscribed by Wm. D. Speight, the Testator, in the presence of each of us, and was at the same time declared by him to be his last Will and Testament, and we, at his request, sign our names hereto, as attesting witnesses.

Washington Hunter
William Johnson

(254) Dickson County Court, November Term 1852. This day was produced in open Court a paper writing purporting to be the last

Will and Testament of Wm. D. Speight dec'd which was proven to be such to be such by the oaths of Washington Hunter & Wm. Johnson, which was ordered to be recorded.

Tho. McNeilly, Clk.

State of Tennessee, Dickson County. Then was the foregoing last Will and Testament of William D. Speight dec'd recorded in Will Book A. in pages 252,3,4, November 5th 1852.

Tho. McNeilly, Clk.

(G. MITCHELL'S Will, No.236)

In the name of God Amen. I, GEORGE MITCHELL do make and publish this as my last Will and Testament hereby revoking and making void all other Wills, by me at any time made.

First- I direct that my funeral expences and all my debts be paid as soon after my death as possible out of any moneys that I may die possessed of, or may come into the hands of my Executor.

Secondly- It is my Will that my beloved wife Martha, shall have my entire Estate during her natural life or widowhood but if she should marry then it is my will that my Estate be wound up, and that she have only a childs part of my Estate, I have given to my beloved daughter Mary B. White property which I estimate to be worth ninety dollars, to Sarah fifteen to Josephus fifty, to Minor one hundred to Adelin fifteen, to John D. sixty to Asenatha ninety. It is my will that my beloved wife Martha sand my two sons Benjamin Franklin and Ballard to School, seven months, and if they should not be sent to School said Term of time that they shall in the final distribution of my Estate have forty dollars each in Lien thereon, Now if any of my children shall marry during the lifetime of their Mather, that is she can spare it, she give them together with what I have already give them to the to the amount of ninety dollars, and if any should marry to whom I have given nothing and she can spare it, that she give them ninty dollars wobhh of property. I have leased to my beloved son Minor a parcel of land, where he has cleared a field, the said lease to continue to the first of January A. D. 1861. And that he is allowed to clear what land he may think proper in said Term so that he does clear it all joining, and that he be allowed to build if he should see fit, at a spring down the branch where he now lives, provided that he shall not be allowed to sell said leas, and lease to any body elde to reside on it. It is my will that of my beloved Daughter Sarah Mead

(255) should live single till after the death of her Mother then she have one hundred Dollars more than the rest of my children but if she should marry it is my will that she have only one equal part I give her this on account of her being afflicted, it is my will after my death, that my Executor give public notice and seal all the property that I die possessed of that my wife may not have a use for, to the decent support of her self and family except what stock he and remain in the Laryard but to have that finished of and sold at public sale, and after collecting and paying of all debts to put the balance out on Interest except so much thereof as may be necessary for her decent support and at her death all property belonging to my Extate to be sold, and equal division to be made amongst all of my heirs, but if one of my heirs should not receive as much before her death as the others

at the distribution of my Estat it to be made up to them. Except the hundred Dollars, I have given to my daughter Sarah Mead on condition of her living single till after the death of her Mother.

Lastly- I will that my beloved wife be and Ihereby appoint her my Executor with the privalege of choosing one of my sons, to assist her, but no other person, in witness whereof I do to this my Will set my hand and seal this 30th day of May A. D. 1852.

George Mitchell (seal)

Codicil and subscribed to this the 17th day of October 1852. It is my will that if my beloved wife should die before the 17th of October 1862, that the final sale of my land and Property take place on the 17th of October 1862 and that my son D. Mitchell be appointed to Execute that part of my will relate to my Land and property-to live with his Mother and Sisters, until the date of 1852, if my survivors that is left at home and him can agree and that my Joseph be employed to work all of the stock in the yard and sell the same at private sald, collect the same and that he post up my Books. Collect the same made and subscribed to this day and date above written.

George Mitchell

Dickson County Court Nov'r Term 1852. This day was produced in open Court a paper writing purporting to be the last Will and Testament of George Mitchell, which was proven to have been found among his valuable papers, and that it was in the hand writting of the dec'd by the oaths of M. B. Stewart, W. S. White & B. Garton and ordered to be recorded.

Tho. McNeilly, Clk.

(256)   State of Tennessee, Dickson County. Then was the foregoing last Will & Testament of George Mitchell dec'd Recorded in Will Book A. pages 254,5,6, Nov'r 6th 1852.

Tho. McNeilly, Clk.

(257) (J. HARDIN, Will No.237)

I, JOAB HARDIN of the Town of Charlotte County of Dickson and State of Tennessee do make and ordain this my Latt Will and Testament hereby revoking all others by me heretofore made.

Item 1st- I charge my whold Estate both real and personal with the payment of my just debts and funeral expences and do to the rest and Residue thereof I will and devise the same as follows, to wit:

Item 2nd- I will and bequeath to Henry Guerin of the County of the County of Dickson one hundred and fifty Dollars, in trust to the users and purposes herein after diredted, that is to say, Seventy five dollars to be expended in my funeral cermonies, as may be directed by the Charlotte Lodge of free and accepted Masons No.97 and seventy five dollars to be expended in such manner in my burial and funeral expences as may be directed by the Buena Vista division the the sons of Temperance in the County of Dickson.

Item 3rd- I give and devise my dwelling House, store House and ware house in the Town of Charlotte, together with the lot on which they are situated in the Town of Charlotte to my beloved wife Genieva J. Hardin, during her natural life and at her death the same to go to my daughter Sarah Ann Harding and her heirs forever.

Item 4th- I give and devise my town lot in the town of Charlotte, on which the saddlers shop is situated being the lot bought by me of Tho's J. Kelly, to my daughter Lorena W. Hardin also one half of my Claylick Tract of Land, lying in the County of Dickson, and perhaps a small portion of it in Davidson County said tract containing about six hundred and forty acres to her heirs forever, the other half of said Claylick tract of Land I give and devise to my daughter Faustina B. Hardin to her and her heirs forever. I also give and devise to my daughter Faustina B. Hardin one hundred acres of Land lying in Dickson County near Cumberland River below the mouth of Johnson Creek to her and her heirs forever, Item

Item 5th- I give and bequeath to my daughter Sarah Ann the following slaves, to wit, Sawney a man aged about fifty years, John aged about nineteen, Stephen aged about sixteen years, Mary a woman aged about twenty years, and her infant child named Core to her and her heirs forever.

(258) Item 6th- I hereby nominate and appoint my friend E. E. Larkins of the Town of Charlotte Guardian of my said daughter Sarah Ann and desire and direct said Guardian of my said daughter not to hire out the slaves already given to her, nor those that may fall to her and the division of the remainder of my slaves at public auction, but I desire and do so direct that my friend the said E. E. Larkins, shall as far as may be in his power hire them out at private living to humane and just persons, although in doing so he may receive a smaller amount of hire and I also desire that in making contracts for hireing said slaves out he
(259) reserve the right to resume the possession in case he should think them badly treated, I also desire and direct that the said Guardian of my said Daughter shall annually pay to my old man Sawney, seven dollars and fifty cents, out of his hire and said Guardian shall pay five dollars annually to each of the other slaves, already given to my said daughter Sarah Ann, and to those slaves she may draw upon a division which money shall be paid out of their respective hires, and I will and desire that my said said daughter after her arrival at age to continue to give Sawney seven dollars and fifty cents yearly and to her other slaves five dollars each, yearly during their natural lives.

Item 7th- I desire my Executors herein after mentioned to sell my negro man Coleman and my negro woman Judy Neville at Public Auction and dispose of the proceeds of the sale as herein after directed, and I desire my executors to give each five dollars each of them, all the day they are sold.

Item 8th- All the rest and residue of my slaves, I will and bequeath to my wife Minerva my daughter Sarah Ann, my daughter Lorena and my Daughter Faustina equally to be divided amoung them, share and share alike to them and their heirs forever.

Item 9th- I hereby nominate and appoint my Father in Law Daniel Leech, Guardian of my two youngest daughters Lorena and Faustina, and I desire that he be governed in hiring their slaves out, by the direction given to E. E. Larkins, Guardian of my daughter Sarah Ann, and I desire him the said Leech to give each of said slaves five dollars annually out of their respective hire and I make the like request of my daughters after t their arrivals at age to continue said gift, to be annually made during the lives of said slaves, and I also request of my said wife to give to each of the slaves peoperty the sum of five dollars a year during their natural lives.

Item 10th- I give and bequeath my silver watch to my daughter Sarah Ann, Also I desire her to keep any note, that may be found in her hands made payable to her she is to have and not to be charged in the general division with said notes, nor for any money she may have claiming as her own, nor do I wish her Guardian to take any charge or control of any such notes or money so found and claimed by her.

(260) Item 11th- I give and bequeath to Delia Porch wife of Henry L. Porch, twenty dollars a year for ten years and I charge the the same on the portion give to my wife and children that is to say that each of my children and wife shall pay her out of the property they receive under my will five dollars a year each for the space of two years after my death.

Item 12th- I give to my wife my household and kitchen furniture, my horse, cow, calves and any and every loose article about the premises not heretofore named, and I desire that my wife shall not be charged with the value of the articles named in this Item in the Settlement of my Estate.

Item 13th- I will and bequeath to my daughter Sarah Ann, all my books, maps and charts of every kind, on hand at the time of my death.

Item 14th- I give and devise to my friend E. E. Larkins & his heirs forever, my town lot lying in the town of Charlotte known as lot No. 35 in the place of said town of Charlotte, and further known as the Nesbitt lot.

Item 15th- As to all the rest and residue of my Estate, Personal, real and mixed, I give bequeath and devise the same to my wife and my three children heretofore named equally to be divided among them.

Item 16th- I nominate and appoint my friend E. E. Larkins and Thomas McNeilly, Executors of this my last Will and Testament and I desire them in hiring out my slaves while in their hands to be governed by the directions given to the Guardians (261) of my Daughters and also pay them five dollars annually each out of their respective hires, while in their possession. In testimony whereof I have hereunto set my hand and seal this 26th day of June A. D. 1851. Signed, sealed and acknowledged in presence of J. W. Dickson, V. W. Fussell, Allen Nesbitt.

J. Hardin (S. S.)

Dickson County Court, December Term 1852. This day was produced in open Court a paper writing purporting to be the last Will and Testament of Joab Hardin dec'd which was proven to be such by the oaths of Allen Nesbitt and James W. Dickson, subscribing witnesses thereto, whereupon the Court ordered that the same be certified and Recorded.

Tho. McNeilly, Clerk.

State of Tennessee, Dickson County. Then was the foregoing last Will and Testament of Joab Hardin dec'd recorded in Will Book A. pages 257,8,9,60,61, December 13th 1852.

Tho. McNeilly, Clerk.
By Tho. C. Morris D. Clk.

(262) (A. SKELTON, Will No. 239)

In the name of God Amen. I, ARCHIBALL SKELTON of the County of Dickson and the State of Tennessee, being of perfect mind and memory do hereby make and publish this my last Will and Testament revoking all other wills made by me heretofore.

(263) First- I direct my funeral Expences and all my debts be paid as soon as possible after my death out of any monies that I may die possessed of or may come into the hands of my Execubor.

Second- I give and bequeath to my wife Sarah Skelton during her natural life the tract of Land on which I now live containing two hundred and thirty three acres, also one negro woman named Martha and her five children with her future increase also all my stock of Horses, Hogs, cattle, sheep, household and kitchen furniture, crop of whatever amount of Corn and Oats, Bacon and Pork, that be on hand at the time of my death, and to have use and profits arrising from the above named property to dispose of as she pleases andfurther she shall have power to sell so much of the stock furniture and corn, Bacon, Pork, oats & etc. as she may think proper.

Third- I five and bequeath to my son Abner Skelton at the death of his Mother two negro boys William and Henry.

Fourthly- I give and bequeath to my Daughter Mariah Allen at the death of her Mother my negro woman named Martha and her increase, to have and use until her death and if she should die without a bodily heir to return back to the Estate.

Fifthly- I give and bequeath to my Grand Daughter Sarah Elizabeth, Alford Skelton at the death of her Grand Mother Skelton one negro girl Ellen, together with her increase to the use and benefit of said Sarah E. A. Skelton, together with one tract of Land containing thirteen acres which is to be sold and the money arising therefrom to be paid to said Sarah E. A. Skelton the whole of which, Viz, the negro Girl named Ellen and the Thirteen acres of Land is to go to the use and benefit of said Sarah E.A. Skelton during her life and at her death to her Bodily heirs if any, if not the said property to Revert to my other heirs.

Sixth- I give and bequeath to my Daughter Malisko T. Cunningham at the death of her Mother, two hundred and twenty acres of Land known as the two Walker Tracts for her use and benefit during her life, and after her death to her children if she have any, if not the said Land to revert back to my other heirs, and in no event is the said Land to be either directly or indirectly at the disposal of her Husband Nathaniel Cunningham, neither shall the Land or any rents thereof be subject to any debt due by said M. Cunningham and I hereby appoint my Grand son John M. Skelton a trustee for the purpose of carring this clause of my Will into effect.

Seventh- I give and bequeath to my Grand son John H. Bartee at the death of his Grand Mother Skelton, the negro Boy named
(264) Patson for his use and benefits and at his death to his children if any, if not, to revert back to his brother Jasper B. Bartee.

Eight- I give and bequeath to my Grand son Jasper B. Bartee at the death of his Grand Mother Skelton one negro Boy named George for his use and subject to his Disposal, and at his death to his children if any, if not to return to his Brother John H. Bartee.

Ninth- It is my will and desire that at the death of my wife Sarah, all of the undivided portion of my property be sold and

and the monies arising from said sald shall be equally divided between my heirs according to Law except that portion which may fall to Malissa T. Cunningham which portion I leave to my Grand son John M. Skelton, all trust for the use of said Malissa T. and her children as specified in the sixth clause of this will.

    Tenth-Lastly- I do hereby nominate and appoint my son Abmr. B. Skelton my Executor to this my last Will and Testament in Testimony whereof I have hereunto set my hand and affixed my seal, this August 12th 1850.

Signed, Sealed and acknowledged)
in presence of   )   A. Skelton   (seal)
Jasper B. Bartee   )
C. Grymes   )
Andrew Jackson Brino   )

    State of Tennessee, Dickson County Court, June Term 1853. This day was produced in open Court a paper writing pupporting to be the last Will and Testament of Archiball Skelton dec'd which was proven to be such by the oath of C. Gryms, one of the subscribing witnesses thereto, and ordered to be Recorded.

                                               Thomas McNeilly, Clk.

    State of Tennessee, Dickson County Court Clerks Office, June 18th 1853. Then was the foregoing last Will and Testament of Archabald Skelton dec'd Recorded in Will Book A. pages 262, 263 264.

                                               Thomas McNeilly, Clk.
                              By Thom. C. Morris, D. C.

(265.) (A. WILKINS, Will No. 240)

    The last Will and Testament of Alexander Wilkins of Dickson County Tennessee.

    I, ALEXANDER WILKINS, considering the uncertainty of this mortal life, and being of sound mind and memory do make and publish this my last Will and Testament in manner and form following (that is to say)

    First Item- I give and bequeath unto my Eldest Son N. F. Wilkins the piece of land where on he now lives, supposed to be about thirty acres be the same more or less, beginning at a large Honey Locust at or near the Junction of N. F. Wilkins & Elizabeth Walkers spring branches, running in an Easterly Direction to a Double Sugartree in or about the East boundry line of the old Kirk tract, with said line South to the corner thence west and north to the beginning, so as to include all my Land south and west of the Lines specifie d which will be hisportion in all the Lands I am possessed of,

    Item 2nd-and lastly- as to all the Lands I am possessed of, as to all the rest, residue and remainder of my personal and Real Estate gooda and Chattles of what kind and nature soever, I give and bequeath the sum to my beloved wife, Sarah M. Wilkins full authority to sell any part or parcel of Land or perishable property she may think desirable whom I hereby appoint sole Executor of this my Last Will and Testament hereby revoking all other former wills by me made, the said Executors no to be had to give security, In witness whereof I have hereunto set my hand

and seal this 26th day of May A. D. one thousand Eight hundred and fifty three.

           A. Wilkens (seal)

 This Instrument consisting of a half sheet of paper, and written on both sides, was here subscribed by Alex'r Wilkins the Testator in the presence of us and was at the same time declared by him to be his last Will and Testament and we at his request sign our names hereto as attesting witnesses.

           Robert A. Reaves
           James M. Kirk.

 State of Tennessee, Dickson County Court, July Term 1853. This day was produced in open Court a paper writing purporting to be the last Will and Testament of Alexander Wilkins Dec'd which was proven to be such by the oaths of James M. Kirk one of the subscribing witnesses thereto, whereupon the Court ordered the same to be recorded.

           Tho. McNeilly, Clerk.
        By Tho. C. Morris, D. C.

 State of Tennessee, Dickson County Court Clerks Office July 5th 1853. Then was the foregoing last Will and Testament of Alexander Wilkins dec'd Recorded in Will Book A. pages 265 & 266.

           Tho. McNeilly, Clerk.

(267) (E. VICKS, Will No. 241)

 I, ELIZABETH VICK, being of sound and perfect mind and memory do make and publish this my last Will and Testament in manner and form following.

First- I give and bequeath unto Daniel Leech two negroes Sylvy a woman Isham a boy I do also give and bequeath unto Henry Hickerson, Violet a woman and her two youngest children. I also give and bequeath unto abner Skelton, two boys Andrew and John. I hereby appoint Abner Skelton, sole Executor of this my last Will and Testament hereby revoking all former wills by me made, In witness whereof I have hereunto set my hand and affixed my seal this 22nd day of September 1840.

 Signed, sealed, published and declared by the above named Elizabeth to be her last Will and Testament in the presence of us who have hereunto subscribed our names as witnesses in the presence of the Testator.

              her
Test-   Elizabeth X Vicks (seal)
George T. Cooksey   mark
William Rook.

 State of Tennessee, Dickson County Court, July Term 1853. This day was produced in open Court a paper writing purporting to be the last Will and Testament of Elizabeth Bick dec'd which was proven to be such by the oaths of George T. Cooksey one of the subscribing witnesses said Will, whereupon the Court ordered the same to be recorded.

           Tho. McNeilly, Clerk.
        By Tho. C. Morris, D. C.

State of Tennessee, Dickson County court Clerks, Office July Term 5th 1853, Then was the foregoing last Will and Testament of Elizabeth Vick dec'd Recorded in Will Book A. pages 267.

          Tho. McNeilly, Clerk
       By Thom C. Morris D. C.

(268) (B. TIDWELL, No.242)

I, BENJAMINE TIDWELL, being of sound mind and memory, but diseased in body, do make and publish this as my last Will and Testament hereby revoking and making void all other Wills by me, at any time made.

Firstly- I direct that my funeral expences and all my other just debts be paid as soon as possible out of any money that I may die possessed of or out of the first money that may come into the hands of my Executor.

Secondly- I give and bequeath to my beloved wife Lucinda, the whole of my real estate and personal property, for her use and and benefit during the term of her natural life or widowhood and at her death, or in the event of her marriage for a second time such real and personal estate to be equally divided between my children, share and share alike.

Thirdly- I will that my eldest son, Moses Harvey shall if he wishes it take my black filly, saddle and bridle at a fair valuation, the price to be decided by two disinterested parties.

Fourthly- I will that such surplus property as may be decided on by my wife Lucinda and my executor be sold on a credit of twelve months. And I furthermore leave it to my executor to decide as to what further property, real or personal it may be proper and necessary to sell, to defray my just debts said property also to be sold on a credit of twelve months.

Lastly- I do hereby nominate and appoint my brother, Silas Tidwell, of the County of Dickson State of Tennessee as the sole executor of this my will, In witness whereof I do, to this my Will set my hand and seal this 16th day of May one thousand eight hundred and fifty three.

          Bn. Tidwell, (seal)

Signed, sealed and published in our presence and we have subscribed our names hereto in the presence of the Testator, this 16th May 1853.

          Moses Tidwell
          John Brown

State of Tennessee, Dickson County Court, August Term 1853. This day was produced in open court a paper writing purporting to be the last Will and Testament of Benjamine Tidwell dec'd which was proven to be such by the oaths of Moses Tidwell and John Brown, the subscribing witnesses thereto whereupon the court ordered that the same be recorded.

          Tho. McNeilly, Clerk.

State of Tennessee, Dickson County Clerks office, August 18th 1853. Then was the foregoing last Will and Testament of Benjamin
(269) Tidwell dec'd recorded in Will Book A. pages 268,9.

          Tho. McNeilly, Clerk.

(SAM'L ADAMS, Will No. 243)

I, SAMUEL ADAMS do make and publish this as my last Will and Testament hereby revoking and making void all other Wills by me at any time made.

First- I direct that my funeral expences and all my debts be paid as soon after my Death as possible out of any moneys that I may die possessed of or may first come into the hand of my Executrix.

Secondly-I give and bequeath to my wife Sarah H. Adams all of my property that I am possessed of to have and to hold as her own to dispose of as she may think proper.

Lastly- I do hereby nominate and appoint Sarah H. Adams my Executrix, In witness whereof I do to this my will, set my hand and seal this 18th day of September 1852.

S. Adam (seal)

Signed, sealed and published in our presents and we have subscribed our named hereto in the presence of the Testator this 18th day of September 1852.
Test-
W. A. Moody
Hugh McClurkin

Dickson County Court, May Term 1852. This day was brot into open Court a paper writing purporting to be the last Will and Testament of Sam'l Adams dec'd which was proven to be such by the oaths of W. A. Moody and Hugh McClurkin subscribing witneses thereto, and ordered to be Recorded.

Tho. McNeilly, Clerk.
By Tho. C. Morris, D. C.

State of Tennessee, Dickson County Court Clerks office 13th May 1854. Then was the foregoing last Will and Testament of Sam'l Adams dec'd Recorded in Will Book A. pages 269,70.

Tho. McNeilly, Clerk.
By tho. C. Morris, D. C.

(271) (B. SMITH, Will No. 244)

Know all whom these presents may concern that I, BARTHALOMEW SMITH, of the County of Dickson and State of Tennessee, being of advanced age, and having become of infirm in body but of sound and disposing mind and perfect memory do make and publish this my last Will and Testament, hereby revoking and making void all other Wills by me at any time hereto fore made.

Item First- It is my will and desire that all my just debts and funeral expences are paid as soon after my death as convenient out of any moneys I may die possessed of or that may first come into the hands of my Executors or Executrix having after named and appointed.

Item 2- I give and bequeath to the Heirs of my Daughter Comfort T. Hudson dec'd one negro woman named Chancey and her increase, which they have in possession to them and their Heirs forever.

Item 3rd-I give and bequeath to my son William B. Smith, one negro woman named Nancy and her increase which he has in possession to him and his heirs forever.

Item 4th- I give and bequeath to my son Gray W. Smith three hundred dollars which I have paid for him, as follows, one hundred and fifty Dollars to John H. Marable, one hundred Dollars to Comfert T. Hudson and fifty Dollars to William Morrison.

Item 5th- I give and bequeath to my son Jackson Smith, one negro woman named Martha and her increase, which ever heretofore delivered to him & his family.

Item-6th- I give and bequeath to my daughter Nancy A. Everett one negrowoman named Viney and her four children namely Ellis, Peter, Mary and Blunt and their future increase for the Maintance and support of my said Daughters & her children during her natural life and after her death to her said children and their heirs forever.

Item 7th- I give and bequeath to my Daughter Tennessee Elliott one negro woman named Casandra and her increase for the maintanence and support of my said Daughter and her children during her natural life, and after her death to her said children and their heirs forever-These negroes were heretofore conveyed by me to my said Daughters and her children.

Item 8th- I give and bequeath to my son Madison H. Smith one negro man named Calvin to him and his heirs forever which negro has been heretofore delivered up to him.

Item 9th- I give and bequeath to my son Williason E. Smith and his heirs foerver one negro man named Bluunt heretofore delivered over to him.

All the foregoing negroes have heretofore been delivered over to my children respectively and were estimated by me at about the same value when received by them the same value when received by them.

Item 10th-I give and bequeath to my beloved wife Dorthy Smith during her lifetime or widowhood my farm and tract of land on which I live, together with all my other property of every kind and description whatever including my negroes namely North Raleigh Rachael, Nancy, Jimmy, Belfield and Mariah & her five children and their future increase, to have and to hold during her natural life or widowhood, and at her death or marriage the said property to be equally divided among all my children who may be then living and the children respresenting their deceased parents and the shares that shall or may fall to my said Daughters Nancy A. Everett and Tennessee Elliott are hereby given and intended for their support during their natural lives respectively and for the support of their said shares to go to their children respectively and theirs heirs forever, the said shares intended by me not to be subject to the debts or contracts of either of the Husbands of my said Daughters but for the uses and purposes above mentioned.

And my said wife shall have   , and is hereby authorized if she shall if she shall think proper to sell and dispose of any part of the stock or other perishable property, not including any of the negroes and to use the money or proceeds arising from such sales towards her support if necessary, and whatever of the said that may be remainint at her death, to be divided among my said children as above mentioned and limited and I hereby nominate and appoint my wife Dorthy Smith, my Executrix and my son Jackson Smith and my Friend Thomas Murrell, Executrix of this my last Will and Testament and shall not be required to give Bond and security as is registered by Law. In Testimony whereof I have hereunto set my hand and seal and published and declared this to be my Last Will and Testament on this 23rd day of December A. D. 1849, in the presence of Witnesses called on by me to attest the same.

(274)

Witness
Thomas Murrell
Thomas Flannery

Bartholmew Smith (seal)

Dickson County Court October Term 1854. This day was brought into open court a paper writing purporting to be the Last Will and Testament of Bartholmew Smith dec'd which was proven to be such by the oaths of Thomas Murrell Jr. and Tho. Flannery subscribing witnesses thereto, and ordered to be Recorded.

Test-Tho. McNeilly, Clk.

State of Tennessee, Dickson County, Then was the foregoing Last Will and Testament of B. Smith Dec'd Recorded in Will Book A. pages 271, 2, 3, 4, this 11th day of June A. D. 1855.

Tho. McNeilly, Clk.
By T. Morris D. C.

State of Tennessee.

(275) (WM. MATLOCK, Last Will and Testament No. 245)

I, WILLIAM MATLOCK of the County of Dickson and State of Tennessee, being in a low state of health but of a sound mind and a disposing memory do make and publish this as my last Will and Testament hereby revoking and making void all other wills by me at any time made.

First- I direct that my funeral Expences and all my just debts be paid as soon after my death as possible out of any monies that I may die possessed or or may first come into the hands of my Executrix and Executor herein after named.

Secondly- I give and bequeath to my beloved wife Miriah, during her natural life or widowhood all my property of every description which shall enbrace the four acres tract Deeded to me by Elizabeth A. Coff on which I now live and also the interest which is a third part of the Hundred acre tract lying adjoining the town of Charlotte that I purchased of F. M. Binkley and Nancy Coffee the boundarys of said tracts can be had by reference to the Deeds made to me by the said Elizabeth A. Coff, F.M. Binkley and Nancy Coffee which are Registered in the Registers office of Dickson County. It is my will and desire that my said wife have the said property to enable her to raise and school my younger children who have but little Education and for her Ann support and comfort, but should my said Wife marry then in that case my Land and what of the personal property may be left or remain is to be sold and divided equally among my wife and all my children, my wife taking a childs part. Should any of my children marry off my wife can give them any article of personal property that she may feel able and willing to spare and at the death of my said wife should she remain a widow all my property shall be sold and equally divided among all my children.

Lastly- I hereby appoint my trust friend Thomas McNeilly and my beoved wife my Executor and Executrix of this my last Will and Testament.

In witness whereof I do to this my last Will set my hand and seal this 1st day of September 1854.

Wm. Matlock (seal)

Signed, sealed and published in our presence & we have subscribed our names hereto in the presence of the Testator and at his request this 1st day of September 1854.
Robert McNeilly
Benjamine Corlew

State of Tennessee, Dickson County Court November Term 1854. This day was produced in open Court a paper writing purporting to be the last Will and Testament of William Matlock Dec'd which was proven to be such by the oaths of Robert McNeilly and Benjamin Corlew subscribing witnesses thereto whereupon the court (276) ordered said Will to be Recorded.

Test- Tho. McNeilly, Clerk.
By E. C. Morris, D. C.

(277) (T. ARMSTRONG, Will and Testament, No.246)

In the name of God Amen. I, THOMAS ARMSTRONG of the County of Dickson and State of Tennessee being much afflicted in body but of sound mind and memory and wishing to dispose of the property with which is a Kind Providence I have   , I do hereby and by these presents make and publish this my last Will and Testament, hereby revoking any and all Wills by me made committing my body to the earth and my soul into the hands of my maker hoping for acceptance through the merits of the Redeemer.

In the first place I will that all my just debts shall be paid out of the first monies which may come into their hands, belonging to my Estate.

Secondly- I wish my Executors to dispose of a sufficiency of my Estate to pay the several amounts in my hands as guardian of my three minor sons, Samuel, Geo W. and Joseph M. which I received & which descended to them from the Estate of my son John Armstrong Decd the property to be sold on a credit of Twelve months for the purpose of raising said several sums.

Thirdly- I give and bequeath to my Daughter Susan Ann Forehand, and her children now and hereafter to be born, the tract of Land formerly belonging to Benjamin Clark, which was sold by order of the Court and purchased by me, excepting that part of said tract of Land which lies on the North side of Bells metal or Iron works Road likewise excepting the spring and spring lot is now inclosed which spring is now used by me the value of said Land is now estimated by me at three hundred & fifty dollars which is to be accounted for & deducted out of their share of my Estate and the final division of the same as herein after directed.

Fourthly- I give and bequeath to my Daughter Jane Clark wife of George W. Clark and to her children now and hereafter to be born one negrowoman named Mariah her future increase estimated by me to be of the value of three hundred and fifty Dollars which sum to be deducted and accounted for out of their share of my Estate and the final division of the same as hereinafter directed.

Fifthly-I will and desire that all the balance of my Estate

(278) both real and Personal shall remain and be kept together for the benefit & support of my wife and thhee sons Samuel G.W.W.J. Joseph M. until the death of my wife or her intermarriage, and at the happening of either of these events then I wish the whole of my Estate both real and personal to be sold by my Executors on Twelve months credit, for the personal property, and on and two years for the Real Estate the proceeds thereof to be equally divided between my said wife in case she marry & all my children and the children of my Daughter Lucy Ballard they representing

(279) their Mother & taking one share deducting out of their share one hundred and sixty five dollars bearing interest from January 1853 until said final division shall be made which said sum was advanced by me to their Father Heophulers Ballars, also deducting the sum of one hundred and seventy five Dollars out of the share of William Armstrong which I paid to him to bear Interest from January 1853 till final division, also deducting the sum of threehundred and fifty Dollars out of the share of my Daughter Susan & her children on account of the Tract of Land give to them by the third Item of this my will. Also deducting the sum of three hundred and fifty Dollars out of the share of my Daughters Jane Clark & her children on account of the negro woman Mariah given to them by the 4th Item of this Will. It is my wish and intention that on the final division of my Estate the balance which may make all the shares equal and which may be giving to my said Daughters Susan A. & Jane be and the same is hereby given to them and their Heirs respectively.

Lastly- I hereby nominate and appoint my good friends Joel D. Everett, Whitson J. Mathis, Executors of this my last Will and Testament and they are not required by me to give security for the performance of their duty as Executors, of this my Estate, In Testimony whereof I do hereby publish and declare this ho be my Last Will and Testament to which I have hereunto set my hand and seal and acknowledge the same in the presence of the subscribing witnesses this 17th January 1855.

Signed, sealed and acknowledged
in our presence
John C. Collier   Tho. Armstrong (seal)
John F. Gafford

Codicil to this my Will. It is my will & desire that the children of my Son James Armstrong dec'd shall jointly have the share of my Estate to which he would have been entitled if living at the final division of my Estate given under my hand and seal 19th day of Jan'y 1855.

Tho. Armstrong, (seal)

Witnesses
(280) J. C. Collier
Matilda Porter

State of Tennessee, Dickson County Court March Term A.D. 1855. this day was brot into open Court a paper writing purporting to be the Last Will and Testament of Thos. Armstrong dec'd which was proven to be such by the oaths of John C. Collier and of the subscribing witnesses thereto, ant the Court ordered the same to be Recorded.

Tho. McNeilly, Clerk.

State of Tennessee, Dickson County 11th June 1835. Then was the foregoing last Will and Testament of Tho. Armstrong dec'd Recorded in Will Book A. pages 277,8,9,80.

Tho. McNeilly, Clk.
By E. C. Morris, D. C.

(281) (A. COLDWELL, Will & Testament No. 247)

In the name of God Amen. I, ABRAM COLDWELL BEing of sound mind and disposing memory do make and publish this my last Will and Testament hereby revoking all other Wills by me made.

Item 1st- I give to my beloved wife Nancy Coldwell during her natural lifethat part of land including the old tract of Two hundred acres also the tract I bought of Lebius Richardson also the tract I bought of Levis Tycer, also the following slaves to wit: March, Benjamin, Sela and Jeana, with all my household and kitchen furniture, farming utensils, Blacksmith tools, also including Horses, Hogs, sheep and all my stock of cattle & etc., to be at her disposal at her death.

Item 2nd- I give and bequeath to my daughter Polly Coldwell a negro girl named Flora and a negro woman named Jeana, and a negro man named March, and a bed and furniture the two last named negroes is not to be given up until her Mothers death.

Item 3rd- I give to my daughter Emaline a negro girl named Amanda, and after my wifes death Benjamin & Selia also a bed and furniture.

Item-3th-I give to my daughter Emaline a negro girl named Amanda, and after my wifes death Benjamin & Selia also a bed and furniture.

Item 4th- I give and bequeath to my daughter Delphia Jane Larkins a negro woman named Violet, and also a girl named Levena.

Item 5th- I give to my daughter Eliza Guthery a negro girl named Ellen.

Item 6th- My sons Thomas Montgomery, Orville Bradly, Abriam Ballard and John Campbell Coldwell the three negroes named John
(282) Roda, Ann child William to be divided or sold (or I would rather they would remain in the family the proceeds of said Negroes to be equally divided between my four sons, also the tract of Land I bought of Ellis Tycer and the tract known as the Meeting house tract also the tract of one hundred actes at the head of Rockey Creek, and that Orville & Abriam should account to Montgomery & John for a tract of six hundred acres lying in the B ----- South of the Stage Road which I have Deeded to them some time since, the above land is to be divided or sold at my death, The Lands as above mentioned as given to my wife at her death, is to be sold or divided between my above named four sons, Thomas Montgomery Orville Bradley, Abrian Ballard and John Campbell Coldwell.

I do hereby appoint my sons Thomas Montgomery and Oriville Bradley my Executors to this my Last Will and Testament. In testimony whereof I set my hand and seal this 19th day November 1853.

Alexander Coldwell, Clk.

Signed, sealed in the presence of
Allen Nesbitt , M. T. Berry.

State of Tennessee, Dickson County Court, March Term 1855. This day was produced in open Court a paper writing purporting to be the Last Will and Testament of A. Coldwell dec'd which was proven to be such by Allen Nesbitt and M. Berry and ordered to be recorded.

Test-Tho. McNeilly, Clk.

State of Tennessee, County of Dickson, County Court Clerks office, 12th June 1855. Then was the foregoing last Will and Testament of A. Coldwell, Dec'd, Recorded in Will Book A. pages 281, 282.

Tho. McNeilly, Clk.

(283) (W. RICHARDSON'S Will & Testament, No.248)

Know all whom those presents may concern that I Winnifred Richardson of the County of Dickson and State of Tennessee being of sound mind and disposing memory and being desirous of making a disposition by will of the Worldly Estate of which I am possessed or may be possessed do make publish and constitute this my Last Will and Testament in manner & form following, to wit:

First- I bequeath my Soul to God who gave it, and my body to my friends to be buried in a decent and christian like manner.

Item 2nd- It is my will and desire that after my death my executors herein after named pay all my just debts and funeral expences and of the first money that may come into his hands belonging to my Estate.

Item 3rd- I give and bequeath to my daughter Sally Walker one feather bed and furniture and one Bureau and having provided for her amply heretofore by Deed of Gift and otherwise this is all that I give her in this Item of my Will.

Item 4th- I give and bequeath to my Grand Daughter Elizabeth Jane Walker, one good feather bed, stead and furniture, and fifty Dollars in money which bequest I have made in consequence of her misfortune, to her and her heirs forever.

Item 5th- I give and bequeath to Emily Hulissis and Sarah Berry the children of my Grand Daughter Nancy Berry, twenty dollars each and if either of them should die before they arrive at maturity those of them who survive shall heir the same.

(284) Item 6th- I give and bequeath to Erbin H. & Rufus C. Lain, fifty acres of Land adjoining the Lands of John F. Willey on the Head Waters of Bartons Creek and should either of them die without a child or children before they arrive at the age of 21 years then the said fifty acres of Land shall belong to the surviving and should they belong both die before they arrive at age, whare a child or children then the said Land shall defend to their half Brother and sisters, to them and their heirs forever.

Item 7th- I give and bequeath to my Grand daughter Vinna my Sugar chest to her and her Heirs forever.

Item 8th- I give and bequeath to my Grandson Tho. J. R. Coleman my negro woman, Milly and one bed and furniture to him and his heirs forever.

Item 9th- It is my will that all the rest and residue of my property to be sold on a credit of 12 months and after paying the foregoing special legacies, my Executors will pay my daughter Sally Walker twenty Dollars, and the balance is to be paid over to my said Grandson Thos. R. Coleman.

Lastly- I do hereby nominate and appoint my trust friend tho. McNeilly my Executor of this my Last Will and Testament, hereby

hereby revoking and making void all other Wills by me at any time heretofore made. In testimony whereof I hereunto set my hand and affix my seal this 23rd day of June 1855.

              her
            Winnifred X Richardson
              mark (seal)

(285) Signed, sealed and delivered in our presence and at the request of the Testatrix the day and date above written.
 Mary McNeilly
 Tho. C. Morris
 Tho. McNeilly

 State of Tennessee, Dickson County Court, May Term 1855. This day was produced in open Court a paper writing, purporting to be the Last Will and Testament of Winnifred Richardson, which was proven to be such by the oaths of Tho. McNeilly and Thomas C. Morris, subscribing witnesses thereto which was ordered to be Recorded.

            Tho. McNeilly, Clk.

 State of Tennessee, Dickson County Court, Clerks office. 12th June A. D. 1855. Then was the foregoing Last Will and Testament of Winnifred Richardson, Recorded in Will Book A. pages 283,4,5.

            Tho. McNeilly, Clk.
        By T. W. Morris, D. C.

(286) (JOHN L. MARTIN'S Will & Testament No.249)
 In the name of God Amen. I, JOHN L. MARTIN of Dickson County Tennessee being in feeble health, but of sound and disposing mind and remembering the uncertainty of life and the uncertainty of death, do hereby make and publish this my last Will and Testament, and first it is my will & I hereby bequeath my soul to God who give it and my body to be decently burried in our family Grave Yard. And to my temporal effects, it is my will that all my just debts be paid out of the first money that may come into the hands of my Executors & for this purpose I wish the three one hundred Dollar Notes I hold on Joseph R. Oakley & my Turnpike Road (if it can be sold for a fair price, if not to be rented out) to be used, and if the Road cannot be sold for a fair price then I wish my Executors to sell my Mill including a Mill yard, aand such of my crop & stock as can be spared & I wish my Executors to have discretion as to the sale of the property to sell privately or in any way they may deem best for the interest of my Estate. And after the payment of all my Debts & the expences of clearing up my Estate, be handed over to my beloved wife, for the sole use of herself and my children, for the purpose of Educating & raising them, my said wife is to have possession of my said Farm and the enjoyment thereof during her natural life, and at her death my said Farm and all other property that may be left is to be equally divided among my children, and if said Farm cannot be divided, then that it be sold by my Executors, as they think best for the interest of my children. Now if my wife Minerva I. should live until any or all of our children should become grown and marry, then my beloved wife may give off to them such articles as she may think proper and prudent, which

which should be accounted for as advancements.

And for the purpose of carrying out & Executing this Will, I do hereby constitute and appoint my relatives and friends Robert McNeilly & Thomas McNeilly my Executors to this my last Will and Testament and I hereby revoke and make void all other Will or Wills by me heretofore made. In witness whereof I have hereunto set my hand and seal in presence of G.N. Larkins I Joseph Larkins, subscribing witnesses at my request. This 15th of July A.D. 1855.

G. N. Larkins　　　　　　　　　　　　　　　　John L. Martin (seal)
Joseph Larkins

State of Tennessee Dickson County Court August Term 1855. This day was produced in open Court a paper writing purporting to be the last Will and Testament of John L. Martin dec'd which was proven to be such by the oaths of G. N. Larkins & Joseph Larkins subscribing witnesses, which was ordered to be Recorded.

　　　　　　　　　　　　　　　　　　　　　　Tho McNeilly, Clk.
State of Tennessee, County of Dickson, County Court Clerk's office September 5th 1855. Then was the foregoing last Will and Testament of John L Martin dec'd Recorded in Will and Book A. pages 286 & 287.
　　　　　　　　　　　　　　　　　　　　　　Tho McNeilly, Clk.
　　　　　　　　　　　　　　By Tho. C. Morris D. C.

(288) (E. WALKERS, Will No. 250)

In the name of God Amen. I, ELIZABETH WALKER being in a low state of health, but of sound mind and disposing memory, do make and publish this my last Will and Testament hereby revoking and making void all other Wills by me at any time heretofore made.

First- It is my will and that all my just debts and funeral expences be paid out of the first money that may come into the hands of my Executor hereinafter named.

2nd- I give and bequeath to my son-in-law James James, fifty acres of land where he now lives on the South end of my 284¼ acre tract, granted to me by the State of Tennessee on the 1st day of May 1847, but the said James James is to pay to my Executor fifty dollars and if my title to said Land should not prove to be a good one, and the said James should be legally disposed of said Land, then my said Executors shall refund the said fifty dollars.

3rd- It is my will that Martin Harbard shall have at the time he arrives of age my Horse Colt called Ball, and a good saddle and bridle, provided he continues to live with my son John V. Walker and behave himself properly till he arrives of age.

4th- It is my Will and desire that my Daughter Martha T. Walker have my mare Luck and her saddle & bridle also her bed and furniture.

5th- All the rest and residue of my property both real and personal I wish to be sold on a credit of twelve months, and after paying all the Debts and Expences all endout on widing up my Estate should there be any remaining. It is is my will that Martha C. Reynolds my grand daughter have ten dollars, and the balance to be equally divided between my following named child-

children to Wit: Branetta J. Work, Cyntha A. Cook, J. V. Walker Martha Walker & P. N. James they having helped to make what little property I now own, the rest of my children all having left me many years ago.

Lastly- I do hereby nominate and appoint my kind and affectionate son John V. Walker my Executor to this my last Will and Testament. In Testimony whereof I have hereunto set my hand and affixed my seal this 2nd day of August 1855.

            her
          Elizabeth X Walker (seal)
            mark

Signed, sealed and published in our presence, and at the request of the Testatrix the day and date above written.
            Tho. McNeilly
           her
         Mary X James
           mark

State of Tennessee, Dickson County Court September Term 1855. This day was returned into ppen Court a paper writing purporting to be the last Will and Testament of Elizabeth Walker dec'd which was proven to be such by the oaths of Tho. McNeilly & Mary James subscribing witnesses, and which was ordered to be Recorded.

            Tho. McNeilly, Clerk.

(289) State of Tennessee, County of Dickson, County Court Clerk's office, 5th September 1855. Then was the foregoing last Will and Testament of E. Walker Dec'd Recorded in Will Book A. pages 288 & 289.

            Tho. McNeilly, Clk.
         By Tho. C. Morris D. C.

(290) (J. NESBITT'S, Will & Testament No.251)

I, JERMIAH NESBITT, do make and publish this my last Will and Testament hereby revoking and making void all other Wills by me at any time made.

First- I direct that my body be decently burried and all my just debts be paid as soon after my death as possible out of any moneys that I may die possessed of or may come into the hands of my Executor.

Secondly- I give and bequeath to my beloved wife during her natural life, the half of the tract of Land whereon I now live including the Home and Spring, known by the name of the Dickson Tract, together with all the Household furniture and farming utensils and all the stock, except what is hereinafter bequeathed to my children, also all my negro prpperty is to remain in her possession during her life time.

Thirdly- I give and bequeath to my sons, to wit: Joseph Nesbitt, William A. Nesbitt, Robert S. Nesbitt and Andrew F. Nesbitt all the two other tracts of land to wit, the Burns tract, and the Balthrop tract to be equally divided between them four by three disinterested men and valued by said three men, also I wish the land run out and marked by the county surveyor agreeable to the division of said men.

Fourthly- I give and bequeath to my son John C. Nesbitt the other half of the Home tract where I now live, to be divided in the same way, and by the same three men, and at the death of my wife, my wish is that my son John C. Nesbitt have all the the Home tratt, by paying the difference to the other children.

Fifthly- I give and bequeath to all my sons that has not had the same, one feather bed and furniture, and cow and calf, one Sow and pigs, and two head of sheep.

Sixth- I give and bequeath to all my Daughters to wit: Nancy W. Nesbitt, Margaret Nesbitt, Catherine M. Nesbitt, Betsy Ann, Nesbitt, and Martha Nesbitt, all one horse bridle and saddle to be worth one hundred and twenty five dollars each, also one feather bed and furniture, one cow and calf and Sow and pigs, and two head of sheep to make them up equal with my two daughters by my first wife, to wit, Sally & Betsey for what they have had.

(291) Seventh- At the death of my wife all my negroes are to be equally divided among all my daughters, my two grand children to wit, John Nesbitt and Betsey Nesbitt is to come in for one share to wit: their Mother's portion all to be valued, and if the valuation of the negroes overcomes the valuation of the land heretofore bequeathed to my sons, the girls is to make up to the boys and if the land overcomes the negroes in valuation the boys is to make up to the girls the difference, so as to make them all equal in value.

Eight- At the death of my wife all the property that is left in her possession is to be sold and equally divided among all my children.

Ninth & Lastly- I nominate my son Andrew F. Nesbitt my Executor, In testimony whereof I hereunto set my hand and seal this 9th day of August 1841.

Signed, sealed in presence of)   Jermiah Nesbitt (seal)
James Daniel   )
William R. Blount   )

State of Tennessee, Dickson County Court, September Term 1855. This day was produced in open Court a paper writing, purporting to be the last Will and Testament of Jermiah Nesbitt dec'd which was proven to be such by the oaths of James Daniel a subscribing witness came and being satisfied that W. R. Blount the other subscribing witness is beyond the Jurisdiction of this Court, his hand writing was proven in open Court, by the oaths of James Daniel, whereupon the court ordered that the same be recorded.

Tho. McNeilly, Clerk.

State of Tennessee) County Court Clerk's office 5th September
County of Dickson) 1855. Then was the foregoing last Will and Testament of Jermiah Nesbitt dec'd Recorded in Book A. pages 290 & 291.

Tho. McNeilly, Clerk.
By Tho. Morris D. C.

(293) (J. LAMPLEY, Will & Testament No.252)

I, JACOB LAMPLEY of the above named State and County being in a perfect and sound mind but in an infirm state of health, so make and ordain this to be my last Will and Testament as followeth, Viz:

First- My will is that all my just debts be first paid, I will and bequeath to my wife Rebecca Lampley, during her natural life or widowhood the Home and Land whereon I now reside, I will to my wife all my household and kitchen furniture together with all my stock of every description, likewise all my plantation tools of every description, I wish her to have all the above named property for the pupposes of raising my children, and I wish each of my sons to have a Horse to be worth forty dollars, and a saddle worth fifteen dollars when they are twenty one years old, I wish each of my children sons and daughters when they marry to have one cow and calf, one sow and pigs, and bed and furniture, one set of knives and forks, one set of cups and saucers. I wish that at my death, that my Executors to sell all such property as my wife Rebecca Lampley should th at she did not stand in such need of and to put that money to the use of schooling my children and to their benefit otherwise my will and wish is that the court of Dickson County shall have no Jurisdiction over my Estate nor bind Executors to give Security, as I have full confidence in them, and my wish is that at the death of my wife Rebecca Lampley that all of my Estate shall be sold and the money equally divided amongst my children.

Lastly- I do hereby nominate constitute, and appoint my wife Rebecca Lampley and my sons John J. Lampley and William C. Lampley, my true and lawful Executors to this my last Will and Testament to carry the same into execution hereby annulling and revoking all other wills by me heretofore made. In testimony whereof I have hereunto set my hand and affixed my seal this fourth day of January one thousand Eight hundred and fifty two.

```
Signed, sealed and delivered)        Jacob Lampley (seal)
in presence of us            )
Miles X Hutcheson            )
Mark Harris                  )
```

A codicil to my last Will and Testament I wish my daughter Nancy Lampley, and my daughter Zilpha Lampley, to have a tolerably good Home apeice, I wish my dear wife to have six hundred dollars money   what I have heretofore left her, and also all the money that is dur me the 25th December 1855. This my codicil whereunto I set my hand and seal this 7th day of Sept. 1855.

Signed, sealed in the presence of
```
        his
Joseph X Lampley                     Jacob Lampley (seal)
     mark
William Harrison
```

(294)   State of Tennessee, Dickson County Court October term 1855. This day was produced in open Court a paper writing purporting to be the last Will and Testament of Jacob Lampley dec'd which was proven to be such by the oaths of Miles Hutcheson, J. Lampley and William Harrison, subscribing witnesses thereto, and Mark Harris & hand writing were proven by Miles Hutcheson and the court ordered the same to be Recorded.

                                    Tho. McNeilly, Clk.
                                 By Tho. Morris, D. C.

State of Tennessee, Dickson County, County Court Clerks office February 29th 1856. Then was the foregoing last Will and Testament of Jacob Lampley dec'd, Recorded in Will Book A. pages

293 & 294.

Thomas McNeilly, Clk.
By Thomas C. Morris, D. C.

(295) (JESSE WOODWARD'S, Will No. 253)

In the name of God Amen, I, JESSE WOODWARD of Davidson County State of Tennessee, do make and ordain this to be my last Will and Testament.

1st- I recommend my soul to God.

2nd- I devise my worldly goods and substance as followeth:

3rd- Devise the tract of land lying in Dickson County containing two hundred acres by loan to my beloved wife Elizabeth Woodward during her natural life.

4th- I devise my negro man Boston, and my negro woman Mariah my negro boy Henry Allen, my negro girl Juda Ann, my negro girl Betsey, my negro boy Benjamin, my negro boy Jesse, my negro boy Henry Allen, my negro girl Juda Ann, my negro girl Betsy, my negro boy Benjamin, my negro boy Jesse, my negro boy David, and their increase I loan to my wife, Elizabeth Woodward, during her natural life.

5th- I devise all my household & kitchen furniture also all my stock of every description, I loan to my wife, Elizabeth Woodard during her natural life.

6th- I divise my wagon & all my farming utensels I loan to my wife Elizabeth Woodward during her natural life.

7th- I devise, that at the death of my wife, Elizabeth Woodward, all the property that I have loaned to my wife Elizabeth Woodward, during her natural life, I devise to my Brother Benjamin Woodward, during her natural life, I devise to my Brother Benjamin Woodward, during her natural life, I devise to my Brother Benjamin Woodward & his heirs forever.

Lastly- I appoint my Brother Benjamin Woodward the Executor of this my last Will and Testament, hereby revoking all other Wills by me hereto made.

In testimony of which I have hereunto set my hand & seal this 14th day of November 1856.

In presence of
Michael D. Gill
Robert Hill.

Jesse Woodward   (seal)

(296)   Dickson County Court, March Term, March 5th 1856. This day was produced in open Court two papers of writing, one purporting to be the last written Will and Testament of Jesse Woodward dec'd and the other purporting to be the Will of said Jesse Woodward dec'd and it appearing to the court from proof that Michael D. Gill has removed beyond the limits of the State of Tennessee, and that he is one of the subscribing witnesses of said written Will, his hand writing was proven by Warren Jordan, S. V. Davidson and Isaac Juy, and it also appearing to the Court from proof, that Robert Hill the other subscribing witness to said Will is dead, his handwriting was proven by S. Davidson in open court whereupon the Court ordered said Will be recorded.

Tho. McNeilly, Clk.
By Tho. C. Morris, D. C.

State of Tennessee, Dickson County, County Court Clerk's office March 6th 1856. Then was the foregoing last Will and Testament of Jess Woodward dec'd Recorded in Will Book A pages 296,295.

Tho. McNeilly, Clerk.
by Tho. C. Morris, D. C.

We, George B. Woodward, William Woodward and William Waymen, Harriet Woodward, A. Woodward, so state that the non cupative Will of Jesse Woodward was made by him on the 31st day of January 1856, in our presence, to which we were specially required to be witnesses by the Testator himself in the presence of each other, and it was made in his last sickness in the House of his brothers, Benjamin Woodward when he was surprised by sickness from Hence. And the sum is as follows to Wit: It was his Will and desire that his effects should be disposed of after his decease in the following manner:

First- He wishes that his nephew John D. Woodward should have his land, stock of all kind, Household and kitchen furniture during his natural life, and at his death, he asked it to go to his son Jesse Woodward. He then desired that his wife Sarah Woodward should have two negro men to wit: Boston and David, forever. He then desired that his just debts should be paid and that his Brother Benjamin Woodward should have all the rest of his Estate.

Made out by me and signed this the day of February 1856.

W. T. Waymen
Wm. Woodward
Harriet Woodward
A. Woodward
G. B. Woodward

Dickson County Court, March Term, March 8th 1856. This day was produced in open Court two paper and purporting to be the last written will and Testament of Jess Woodward dec'd and the Item pupporting to be the noncupative will of said Jesse Wood-
(297) ward dec'd and thereupon W. T. Waynn, Wm. Woodward, and George B. Woodward, three of the subscribing witnesses thereto to the noncupative will approved in open court, and made oath in due form of law, that they together with the other subscribing witnesses to said noncupative Will, were called upon together by the said Jesse Woodward dec'd to witness same and that the same be directed by him was reduced to writing and attested by them together with the attest witnesses on the 3rd day of February 1856. It is therefore ordered that said Will be recorded.

Tho. McNeilly, Clk.
By Tho. C. Morris D. C.

(298) (ELEANOR SHELTON, Will No.255)

In the name of God Amen. I, ELEANOR SHELTON of the County of Davidson, being of feeble health, but of sound mind and disposing memory, do make, publish this as my last Will & Testament, revoking & making void all other Wills by me at any made.

First- I direct that my funeral expences & all my debts be paid, as soon after my death as possible, out of any money that I may die possessed of, or that may first come into the hands of my Executor.

Second- I give and bequeath to my son William H. Shelton, to my daughter Mary Hains & to my grand children Sarah Agnes Jordun, Lyda Ellison, Hugh Ellison, Eleanor Kkkean, Wm. H. Keelam, Susan Keelum, Lucy Keelum, Y Isabella Keelam my two slaves Sylvia &

Maria, all my stock of Horses, cows, Hogs, all my household and kitchen furniture, the debt due me in Virginia, with all property I may die possessed of, together with all debts due me, to be divided, or at the discretion of my Executor herein after named to be sold for cash or on time, and divided among the above legatees in the following manner, to wit:

Onethird to William H. Shelton, one third to Mary Harris & the other third to be equally divided between the above named children of Lucy Keelum.

Lastly- I do hereby nominate William Harris and Warren Jordan my Executors, in witness whereof I do to this my Will set my hand and seal this the 10th day of December 1833.

Signed, sealed & published)
in our presence & we have sub)   Eleanor Shelton (seal)
scribed our names hereto in the
presence of the Testator, this 10th day of December 1855.
Jesse Jordan
C. G. Lovell

State of Tennessee, Dickson county Court April Term 1856. This day was returned into open Court a paper writing purporting to be the last Will and Testament of Eleanor Shelton Dec'd which was proven to be such by the witnesses thereto and ordered to be recorded.

Tho. McNeilly, Clk.

State of Tennessee, Dickson County, County Court Clerk's Office 10th April 1856. Then was the foregoing last Will and Testament of Eleanor Shelton dec'd, recorded in Will Book A. pages 298,299.

Tho. McNeilly, Clk.
By Tho. C. Morris, D. C.

Every Name Index to Dickson County TN Will Book A 1804-1856

ADAMS, Benjamine Johnson, 29
ADAMS, Cinthy, 29
ADAMS, Hodge, 16
ADAMS, Howell, 16
ADAMS, Howell Collen, 29
ADAMS, John, 33
ADAMS, Lillah, 29
ADAMS, Nancy, 16
ADAMS, Reaves, 28
ADAMS, Samuel, 179
ADAMS, Samuel, 269
ADAMS, Sarah, 29
ADAMS, Sarah H., 269
ADAMS, Thomas, 29
ADAMS, Wm., 16
ADAMS, Wm., 29
ADAMS, Wm., 79
ADCOCK, Dolly M., 154
ADCOCK, Henderson, 154
ADKINSON, Qunties C., 235
ALEXANDER, Jesse, 79
ALLEN, Mariah, 263
ANGLIN, Aaron, 130
ANGLIN, Cornelius, 130
ANGLIN, Elizabeth, 130
ANGLIN, George, 130
ANGLIN, John, 130
ANGLIN, John, 130
ANGLIN, Margaret, 130
ANGLIN, Nancy, 130
ANGLIN, Sally C., 130
ANGLIN, Wm., 130
ARMSTRONG, Geo. W., 277
ARMSTRONG, John, 277
ARMSTRONG, Joseph M., 277
ARMSTRONG, Samuel, 277
ARMSTRONG, Thomas, 277
ARMSTRONG, Wm., 279
ARMSTRONG, Wm., 77
AUSTIN, Abraham J., 251
AUSTIN, Dicy, 93
AUSTIN, Jacob J., 251
AUSTIN, Martha, 251
AUSTIN, May, 85
AUSTIN, Wm. G., 85
BACON, Benedict, 89
BACON, Jane, 89
BACON, Sally, 89
BAILEY, Edwin, 52
BAKER, Absalom, 79
BAKER, Absolom, 38
BAKER, Armstrong, 161
BAKER, Augusta, 161
BAKER, Beckah, 71
BAKER, Benjamine, 38
BAKER, C. A., 156
BAKER, Eave J., 161
BAKER, Felix C., 161
BAKER, Jane, 38
BAKER, John, 38
BAKER, John, 71
BAKER, John A., 38
BAKER, Mary Ann, 161
BAKER, Nancy, 38
BAKER, Nelly, 38
BAKER, Norman F., 161
BAKER, Patsey, 38
BAKER, Rebecca, 71
BAKER, Sally, 38

BAKER, Wm., 167
BAKER, Wm., 71
BAKER, Wm. L., 167
BAKER, Wm. dec'd, 35
BALLARD, Lucy, 278
BALLARS, Heophulers, 279
BALTHROP, Mary, 158
BALTHROP, Willie, 100
BALTHROP, Willie, 158
BARTEE, Jasper B., 264
BARTEE, John H., 263
BATSON, Richard, 117
BATSON, Thomas, 82
BAXTER, J. W., 160
BAXTER, Robert, 90
BEARD, Andrew, 78
BECK, Andrew J., 185
BECK, David C., 185
BECK, Jesse, 197
BECK, Jesse, 206
BECK, Jesse, 211
BECK, Jesse jr., 185
BECK, Jesse sr., 185
BECK, John T., 185
BECK, Judy, 185
BECK, Wm. J., 185
BELL, Blount W., 136
BELL, Blount W., 138
BELL, Elisha, 169
BELL, Elisha, 170
BELL, Elizabeth, 208
BELL, J. P., 170
BELL, Jane, 179
BELL, Jane P., 138
BELL, John I., 136
BELL, John I., 179
BELL, John P., 136
BELL, John P., 138
BELL, Marceanna, 136
BELL, Marcinna, 208
BELL, Mary A., 179
BELL, Mary Ann, 138
BELL, Montgomery, 136
BELL, Montgomery, 179
BELL, Montgomery, 186
BELL, Montgomery, 208
BELL, Nancy S., 136
BELL, Nancy S., 136
BELL, Shadrick, 169
BELL, Shadrick, 169
BELL, Shadrick jr., 169
BELL, Thomas, 169
BELL, Thomas D., 208
BELL, Thomas Drew, 179
BELL, Thomas Drue, 136
BELL, Thomas Drue, 138
BELL, Wm. B., 245
BERRY, M. T., 282
BERRY, Nancy, 283
BERRY, Sarah, 283
BERRY?, Vinna, 284
BETTS, Charles, 215
BETTS, Charles, 217
BETTS, Charles, 217
BETTS, Charles, 222
BIBB, Elizabeth, 162
BIBB, James, 206
BIBB, James, 239
BIBB, John G., 206

BIBB, John M., 162
BIBB, Merior, 66
BIBB, Minor, 162
BIBB, Nancy, 206
BIBB, Robert F., 206
BIBB, V. F., 174
BIBB, Vernon F., 164
BILLUPS, Daniel, 59
BINKLEY, Elisa, 224
BINKLEY, Emaline, 224
BINKLEY, F. M., 275
BINKLEY, Parile, 224
BISHOP, E., 199
BLACK, Elizabeth, 103
BLACK, Mary Malvina, 103
BLACK, Nancy, 103
BLACK, Wm., 103
BLEDSOE, Barney L., 73
BLEDSOE, Barnibas, 72
BLEDSOE, Giles J., 73
BLEDSOE, Giles J., 73
BLEDSOE, Pinkney T., 73
BLEDSOE, Rebecca, 72
BLOUNT, Margaret, 25
BLOUNT, Wm. R., 291
BONDS, Sarah, 47
BOWEN, Christopher, 222
BOWEN, George, 34
BOWEN, John, 216
BOWEN, Mary Ann, 210
BOWEN, Reas, 216
BOWEN, Samuel D., 210
BOWEN, Sarah, 221
BOYD, James H., 159
BOYD, Matilda Ann, 159
BRASHER, Wm., 120
BREEDING, Ephriam, 60
BREEDING, Mary, 60
BREWER, John, 165
BREWER, Mary Ann, 166
BREWER, Sarah Elizabeth, 166
BREWER, Susan, 165
BRINO, Andrew Jackson, 264
BROWN, A. A., 235
BROWN, Asa Madison, 56
BROWN, Asa. A., 56
BROWN, Charles W., 112
BROWN, Charles W., 118
BROWN, Daniel, 183
BROWN, H. R., 213
BROWN, James, 212
BROWN, Jane, 173
BROWN, Jenisha, 56
BROWN, Jim, 183
BROWN, John, 164
BROWN, John, 212
BROWN, John, 268
BROWN, John Humphreys, 56
BROWN, Martha, 212
BROWN, Samuel, 95
BROWN, Solomon, 212
BROWN, Thomas, 173
BROWN, Thomas, 83
BROZZELL, George, 38
BRUER, Patsey, 112
BRUMS, Daniel, 239
BRUMS, Evaline, 239
BRYAN, Davis, 148
BRYAN, John, 148

BUGG, Allen, 29
BUGG, Chanie, 29
BUGG, Dorcas, 29
BUGG, Elizabeth, 29
BUGG, Henry, 30
BUGG, Jermiah, 29
BUGG, John, 29
BUGG, Samuel, 161
BUGG, Samuel, 29
BUGG, Stiles, 30
BUGG, William, 30
BUGG, Willis, 29
BULLION, Thomas, 21
BURKETT, Sarah, 23
BURKETT, Thomas, 24
BURTON, Ambrose, 126
BURTON, Polly, 126
CALDWELL, Abiram, 63
CALDWELL, Abraham, 26
CALDWELL, W., 226
CALVERT, Samuel, 150
CARBON, B. B., 59
CARPENTER, John B., 189
CARPENTER, Mary, 189
CARR, John B., 136
CARR, Muckins, 68
CARR, Mukins, 93
CARROLL, Elizabeth, 141
CARTER, James, 90
CARTER, Wm., 133
CATHEY, Archie, 85
CATHEY, Daniel, 85
CATHEY, George, 85
CATHEY, John, 85
CATHEY, John R., 85
CATHEY, Joshua, 85
CATHEY, Peggy, 85
CATHEY, Samuel Martin, 85
CATSON, Judge, 189
CHAMBERLAIN, D. C., 180
CHAMBERLAIN, D. C., 203
CHEATHAM, J. P., 79
CHERRY, Charles W., 8
CHOAT, Susan J., 201
CHOATE, Eleanor, 114
CHOATE, Isach, 5
CHOATE, John, 113
CHOATE, John H., 114
CHOATE, Peter, 114
CHOATE, Squire J., 114
CHRISTIAN, Jesse G., 16
CLAIBORNE, T. H., 109
CLARK, Benjamin, 277
CLARK, George W., 277
CLARK, Jane, 102
CLARK, Jane, 277
CLARK, Richardson L., 102
CLAUDIAS, David L., 26
CLAUDIAS, Elizabeth David L., 27
CLAYTON, H., 233
CLAYTON, M., 233
CLING, Charles W., 8
COBB, C. C., 209
COCHRAN, Juretha Caroline, 159
COCHRAN, Wm. H., 159
COCKE, Richard, 77
COFF, Elizabeth A., 275
COFFEE, Nancy, 275

Every Name Index to Dickson County TN Will Book A 1804-1856

COLDWELL, A., 106	DANIEL, Woodrow, 82	DICKSON, Peggy, 123	ELLIOTT, Tennessee, 271
COLDWELL, A., 116	DAVIDSON, Abraham, 140	DICKSON, Priscilla, 217	ELLIS, Nancy W., 100
COLDWELL, A., 146	DAVIDSON, Aquilla, 68	DICKSON, Robert, 1	ELLIS, Ransom, 100
COLDWELL, A., 92	DAVIDSON, David, 140	DICKSON, Robert, 123	ELLIS, Thomas, 100
COLDWELL, Abram, 281	DAVIDSON, Elijah, 140	DICKSON, Robert, 2	ELLISON, Hugh, 298
COLDWELL, Abriam Ballard, 281	DAVIDSON, Elizabeth, 102	DICKSON, William, 1	ELLISON, Lyda, 298
COLDWELL, Elizabeth W., 170	DAVIDSON, Elizabeth, 68	DICKSON, William, 2	EMERY, N. R., 249
COLDWELL, Emaline, 281	DAVIDSON, George, 102	DILLAHAY, Nathan, 15	ENGLAND, Betsy, 38
COLDWELL, John, 129	DAVIDSON, Henry, 139	DILLAHUND, Sam, 183	EPPERSON, John, 20
COLDWELL, John Campbell, 281	DAVIDSON, James, 140	DILLIHAY, Nancy, 13	EVANS, Caleb, 134
COLDWELL, Nancy, 281	DAVIDSON, John, 139	DILLIHAY, Sterling, 34	EVANS, JAcob, 87
COLDWELL, Orville Bradley, 281	DAVIDSON, John, 29	DODSON, J. W., 181	EVANS, Jacob, 120
COLDWELL, Polly, 281	DAVIDSON, John, 68	DODSON, James W., 182	EVANS, Jacob, 156
COLDWELL, Thomas Montgomery, 281	DAVIDSON, Joseph, 139	DODSON, Susan, 181	EVANS, Jane, 38
	DAVIDSON, Joseph, 68	DORTCH, Isaac, 232	EVANS, Lewis, 30
COLEMAN, Elizabeth, 129	DAVIDSON, Mary, 140	DORTCH, Martha, 232	EVANS, Margaret, 38
COLEMAN, Tho. J. R., 284	DAVIDSON, Mary?, 129	DOUGLASS, Martha, 42	EVANS, Mary, 156
COLEMAN, W. S., 130	DAVIDSON, Matilda, 140	DRAKE, George, 89	EVANS, Richard, 74
COLEMAN, Wm. S., 115	DAVIDSON, Peggy, 140	DRAKE, Mary, 89	EVERETT, Joel D., 279
COLLIER, Angeline, 188	DAVIDSON, Sarah, 139	DRAKE, Mary, 89	EVERETT, Nancy A., 271
COLLIER, B. A., 228	DAVIDSON, Violet, 140	DRUMMOND, Peggy, 97	EVINS, Franky (f), 239
COLLIER, John C., 164	DAVIDSON, Wm., 140	DRUMMOND, Thomas, 95	EZELL, Jane, 204
COLLIER, John C., 235	DAVIS, Gideon, 213	DRUMMOND, Wm., 96	FARMER, Samuel, 182
COLLIER, John C., 279	DAVIS, Wiley, 164	DRUMMOND, Zachius, 96	FARRAR, Jane, 221
COLMAN, W. S., 203	DAVIS, Wiley, 213	DRUMMONS, Thomas, 96	FELIX, L., 193
COMER, Reuben, 70	DAVIS, Wm. (Col.), 15	DRUMMONS, Zachius, 96	FENLY, J., 170
COOK, Cyntha A., 288	DAVISS, John, 6	DRYE, John, 100	FENTRESS, Wm., 79
COOK, Wm., 150	DAVISS, John, 7	DUDLEY, Mary, 204	FINLEY, Elizabeth West, 138
COOKSEY, George T., 128	DESINPORT?, Chancey, 62	DUDLEY, Nicholas, 131	FINLEY, James, 136
COOKSEY, George T., 267	DICKSON, Abigail, 17	DUDLEY, Willis, 131	FINLEY, Rebecca, 208
COOKSEY, George T., 90	DICKSON, Abigail, 18	DUKE, B. C., 179	FINLEY, Silvester, 209
COOKSEY, Pheba, 129	DICKSON, Abner, 1	DUKE, Charlotte, 167	FINLEY, Thomas, 208
COPELAND, Jenet, 27	DICKSON, Abner, 2	DUKE, Charlotte, 60	FLANNERY, Thomas, 274
CORBUN, Burrell B., 235	DICKSON, Alexander, 48	DUKE, Charlotte G., 167	FOREHAND, Susan Ann, 277
CORLEW, Benjamine, 275	DICKSON, Alexander, 62	DUKE, Green W., 167	FORSYTHE, John, 85
COUNCIL, Lovy, 120	DICKSON, Christopher W., 222	DUKE, Green W., 167	FOSTER, James, 5
CRAFT, George R., 88	DICKSON, David, 1	DUKE, Miry P., 167	FOSTER, Nathan, 63
CRAFT, George R., 89	DICKSON, David, 2	DUKE, Robert, 167	FRANCES, Edward, 10
CRAFT, George R., 89	DICKSON, David, 2	DUKE, Robert, 60	FRANCES, Edward, 8
CRAFT, George R., 89	DICKSON, David, 3	DUNAGAN, W., 246	FRANCES, Gideon, 9
CRAFT, James, 88	DICKSON, Elizabeth, 2	DUNNAGAN, Patsey, 93	FRANCES, John, 9
CRAFT, James, 89	DICKSON, Hugh, 1	DUNNAWAY, Heaven Acary, 81	FRASHER, David, 127
CRAFT, Jesse, 89	DICKSON, Hugh, 2	DUNNEGAN, Ailsey, 31	FREEMAN, Bureall, 126
CRAFT, Jesse, 89	DICKSON, Hugh, 2	DUNNEGAN, Andrew, 31	FREEMAN, Freeman, 126
CRAFT, Margaret, 89	DICKSON, Hugh, 3	DUNNEGAN, Charles, 31	FREEMAN, Hannah, 126
CREWS, Barbara H., 91	DICKSON, J. W., 261	DUNNEGAN, Elizabeth, 31	FREEMAN, Howell, 126
CREWS, Elizabeth T., 91	DICKSON, James, 2	DUNNEGAN, James, 31	FREEMAN, Jeramiah, 126
CREWS, Sarah Ann B., 91	DICKSON, Jane, 1	DUNNEGAN, James, 31	FREEMAN, Wm., 126
CREWS, Vann S., 91	DICKSON, Jane, 2	DUNNEGAN, John, 31	FUNDERBUSS, Mary, 239
CRINK, Davidson, 103	DICKSON, Joseph, 1	DUNNEGAN, John, 93	FUSSELL, Lucy, 93
CROCKETT, Joseph, 159	DICKSON, Joseph, 1	DUNNEGAN, Matilda, 31	FUSSELL, Moses, 93
CROW, Eli, 93	DICKSON, Joseph, 2	DUNNEGAN, Susannah, 31	FUSSELL, W. W., 261
CROW, Elizabeth, 93	DICKSON, Joseph, 2	DUNNEGAN, Wm., 31	FUSSELL, Wm., 93
CRUMPLER, Matthew, 82	DICKSON, Joseph, 217	DUNNING, John, 64	FUSSELL, Wm., 93
CRUMPLER, Raifred, 82	DICKSON, Joseph, 217	EASLEY, Elizabeth, 70	FUSSELL, Wyatt, 31
CUNNINGHAM, James, 140	DICKSON, Joseph, 222	EASLEY, Emialine, 69	GAFFORD, John P., 279
CUNNINGHAM, John, 134	DICKSON, Joseph, 3	EASLEY, James V., 70	GAMBLE, John H., 8
CUNNINGHAM, John, 141	DICKSON, Joseph A., 170	EASLEY, John H., 70	GARRETT, Margaret, 185
CUNNINGHAM, Malisko T., 263	DICKSON, Levin, 17	EASLEY, Moses, 68	GARRETT, Martha Ann, 227
CUNNINGHAM, Malissa T., 264	DICKSON, Lucy, 2	EASON, Calvin W., 32	GARRETT, Phenias, 185
CUNNINGHAM, Nathaniel, 141	DICKSON, Martha, 216	EASON, Joseph J., 32	GARRETT, Sarah, 226
CUNNINGHAM, Nathaniel, 263	DICKSON, Martha, 221	EASON, Taffenons?, 34	GARRETT, Sary, 86
CUNNINGHAM, Sarah, 141	DICKSON, Michael, 3	EATON, Lucy, 89	GARRETT, Wm., 182
CUNNINGHAM, Thomas, 141	DICKSON, Molton, 1	EDWARDS, Lucy Ann, 185	GARRETT, Wm., 226
CUNNINGHAM, Willis, 141	DICKSON, Molton, 2	EDWARDS, Sellman, 251	GARRETT, Wm., 86
DANIEL, James, 158	DICKSON, Molton, 2	EDWARDS, Selman, 128	GARRETT, Wm. sr., 86
DANIEL, James, 291	DICKSON, Molton, 216	EDWARDS, Tempy, 133	GARTON, Elizabeth, 248
DANIEL, Luke Anthony, 148	DICKSON, Pearale (f), 2	EDWARDS, Wm. sr., 32	GARTON, Henry, 213

Every Name Index to Dickson County TN Will Book A 1804-1856

GARTON, Kizzeah, 243	GOODWIN, Sal, 118	HALLIBURTON, Nancy, 73	HOGINS, Morgan H., 143
GENIER, Jennet, 7	GOODWIN, Sally, 118	HAMILTON, Nancy, 141	HOGINS, Morgan H., 144
GENTRY, Anderson, 173	GOODWIN, Wm., 118	HAND, W., 134	HOGINS, Polly Matilda, 144
GENTRY, Anny, 173	GOULD, James, 185	HANDY, Thomas K., 84	HOGINS, Sally, 143
GENTRY, B.? T., 239	GOULD, Martha, 185	HANKS, Milly, 239	HOGINS, Wm., 142
GENTRY, Benjaah?, 173	GOULDING, Rebecca, 204	HANNA, James, 17	HOGINS, Wm. W., 143
GENTRY, Benjah, 147	GRAHAM, Solomon, 32	HARBARD, Martin, 288	HOGINS, Wm. Walker, 142
GENTRY, Benjamin, 150	GRAHAM, Solomon, 32	HARDEMAN, Frank, 165	HOLLAND, Benjamine, 118
GENTRY, Elizabeth, 173	GRAHAM, Solomon, 37	HARDEMAN, Nicholas P., 182	HOLLAND, Delia, 112
GENTRY, Jame?, 173	GRAVES, W. T., 209	HARDEMON, Thomas, 5	HOLLAND, Hardy, 112
GENTRY, Lucinda, 173	GRAY, D., 144	HARDIN, Faustina B., 257	HOLLAND, James, 112
GENTRY, Matthew L., 174	GRAY, David, 111	HARDIN, Genieva J., 257	HOLLAND, John, 112
GENTRY, Thomas, 173	GRAY, David, 152	HARDIN, Joab, 257	HOLLAND, Mark, 112
GENTRY, Wm., 103	GRAY, David, 154	HARDIN, Lorena W., 257	HOLLAND, Mary, 112
GENTRY, Wm., 119	GRAY, David, 172	HARDIN, Minerva, 259	HOLLAND, Sally, 112
GILBERT, Elizabeth, 185	GRAY, David, 243	HARDIN, Sarah Ann, 257	HOLLEY, Edward, 55
GILBERT, Henry Masison, 76	GRAY, David, 66	HARRIS, Buckner, 198	HOLLEY, Sophia, 56
GILBERT, James, 134	GREEN, Gardner, 224	HARRIS, Darrel Y., 48	HOLLY, Edward, 58
GILBERT, James Monroe, 76	GREEN, Wm., 205	HARRIS, E., 142	HOLLY, Edward, 59
GILBERT, Mabel, 134	GREER, John, 163	HARRIS, Lucy, 198	HOLT, James M., 188
GILBERT, Mabel, 76	GRIFFIN, Dose? Ann, 152	HARRIS, Mark, 147	HOOD, Morgan, 143
GILBERT, Nancy, 76	GRIFFIN, Elisa Jean, 152	HARRIS, Mark, 293	HOOPER, Ellinor, 47
GILBERT, Nancy V., 91	GRIFFIN, Isaac, 151	HARRIS, Mary, 298	HOOPER, Wm., 33
GILBERT, Nathan, 133	GRIFFITH, John, 163	HARRIS, Robert P., 48	HORNER, Elizabeth, 93
GILBERT, Nathan, 76	GRIGSBY, Sally, 68	HARRIS, Sally, 142	HORNER, George Wyatt, 93
GILBERT, Nicholas, 133	GRIGSBY, Thomas K., 241	HARRIS, Wm., 298	HORNER, James, 93
GILBERT, Nicy, 77	GROVES, J., 225	HARRIS, Wm. jr., 142	HORNER, Lucy, 93
GILBERT, Rosanna, 133	GROVES, John, 225	HARRISON, Wm., 293	HORNER, Sally, 93
GILBERT, Temperance, 76	GROVES, Joseph, 197	HARVEY, Moses, 268	HOWELL, David, 9
GILBERT, Thomas, 185	GROVES, Mary Frances, 225	HARVY, Elizabeth, 237	HUDSON, Araminta, 189
GILBERT, Thomas, 76	GRYMES, C., 264	HAYNES, Minor B., 162	HUDSON, Baker, 34
GILBERT, Wm., 129	GUERIN, Henry, 257	HAYS, E., 231	HUDSON, Baker, 35
GILBERT, Wm., 133	GUNN, Reuben, 30	HAYS, Elizabeth, 231	HUDSON, Carry M., 34
GILBERT, Wm., 75	GUNN, Wm., 30	HEALEY, Isaiah, 42	HUDSON, Christopher, 66
GILBERT, Wm., 76	GUNN, Wm., 79	HEATON, Robert, 231	HUDSON, Christopher C., 144
GILL, Michael D., 295	GUTHERY, Eliza, 281	HEAVEN, Frances, 115	HUDSON, Cluthlept? (m), 66
GILMORE, James, 102	HAGWOOD, Amy, 141	HEDGES, Charles, 30	HUDSON, Comfort T., 271
GILMORE, Matthey, 102	HAIL, Polly Ann, 142	HEDGES, Polly, 38	HUDSON, Cutbert, 17
GIVEN, Wm., 34	HAINS, Mary, 298	HICKERSON, E.?, 245	HUDSON, Cuthbert, 16
GIVIN, Wm., 20	HALE, N. M., 211	HICKERSON, Ezekiel, 182	HUDSON, J. R., 133
GLANNERY, Isaac, 112	HALE, N. W., 239	HICKERSON, Henry, 267	HUDSON, J. R., 166
GLEAVES, Elizabeth, 223	HALE, Titus, 109	HICKS, A. V., 238	HUDSON, J. R. (Dr.), 188
GLEAVES, Ezekiel S., 223	HALEY, James, 42	HICKS, A. V., 239	HUDSON, John R., 160
GLEAVES, Wm. D., 224	HALL, B. B., 237	HICKS, James, 103	HUDSON, John R. (Dr.), 188
GOODRICH, Alice, 48	HALL, Berrimon, 42	HICKS, James, 119	HUDSON, John R. (Dr.), 189
GOODRICH, Alice, 48	HALL, David, 41	HICKS, John, 119	HUDSON, Judith J., 35
GOODRICH, Charlotte, 47	HALL, Elizabeth, 42	HICKS, John L., 103	HUDSON, Lucy, 65
GOODRICH, Charlotte, 48	HALL, Elizabeth M., 41	HICKS, Winefred, 29	HUDSON, Lucy, 66
GOODRICH, Dorothy, 46	HALL, Henry, 87	HICKS, Zebider, 23	HUDSON, Polly, 117
GOODRICH, Dorthy, 47	HALL, Jesse, 41	HIGHTOWER, Wm., 153	HUDSON, Rebeccca B., 35
GOODRICH, Dorthy, 48	HALL, John, 40	HILL, Isaac, 199	HUDSON, Susan, 66
GOODRICH, George Jackson, 47	HALL, John, 42	HILL, Rebecca, 46	HUDSON, Taffincous? (f), 34
GOODRICH, James, 45	HALL, Joseph, 42	HILL, Robert, 295	HUDSON, Thomas C., 34
GOODRICH, James, 47	HALL, Joseph, 87	HINSON, John, 126	HUDSON, Wm., 34
GOODRICH, James, 48	HALL, Joseph W., 40	HINTON, Elizabeth Boyd, 229	HUDSON, Wm., 74
GOODRICH, Jane, 160	HALL, Joshua, 42	HINTON, John J., 229	HUGES, Isaac, 30
GOODRICH, John, 48	HALL, Martha, 41	HINTON, Rachael Adaline, 229	HUGHES, Edwin Madison, 133
GOODRICH, John, 48	HALL, Mary, 87	HINTON, Richard B., 229	HUGHES, J. Bev., 133
GOODRICH, Patsey, 47	HALL, N. M., 238	HODGES, Wm., 18	HUGHES, Lemuel Horace, 133
GOODRICH, Patsey, 48	HALL, Nancy, 87	HODGINS, Nancy, 35	HUGHES, Lewis T., 235
GOODRICH, Wm. H., 47	HALL, Sary, 87	HOGAN, Daniel, 18	HUGHES, Mary, 5
GOODRICH, Wm. H., 48	HALL, Susainna, 42	HOGANS, A. C., 205	HUGHES, Nancy Newton, 133
GOODWIN, Esaw, 54	HALL, Susan, 87	HOGINS, Abram C., 143	HUGHES, Wm. Granville, 133
GOODWIN, Jesse, 217	HALL, Susanna, 42	HOGINS, Betsey Jane Mary, 144	HUGHS, David, 5
GOODWIN, John, 118	HALL, Wesley, 42	HOGINS, Clary, 143	HULISSIS, Emily, 283
GOODWIN, Lucy, 118	HALL?, Abraham, 42	HOGINS, Eleanor, 143	HULME, Tho., 205
GOODWIN, Peter, 118	HALLEY, Ann, 73	HOGINS, Jim, 143	HUMPHREYS, Benjamine, 59
GOODWIN, Peter, 118	HALLEY, Hamor, 73	HOGINS, Morgan H., 142	HUMPHREYS, Dilly, 55

HUMPHREYS, Horatio, 55
HUMPHREYS, Horatio, 58
HUMPHREYS, Horatio, 59
HUMPHREYS, Janira, 59
HUMPHREYS, Jno., 15
HUMPHREYS, Jno., 71
HUMPHREYS, John, 29
HUMPHREYS, John, 54
HUMPHREYS, John, 71
HUMPHREYS, John Howard, 55
HUMPHREYS, John Howard, 58
HUMPHREYS, John Patterson, 57
HUMPHREYS, Parry W., 40
HUMPHREYS, Stokely, 57
HUMPHREYS, Stokely, 58
HUNTER, Allen, 156
HUNTER, Thomas, 27
HUNTER, Wash, 229
HUNTER, Washington, 252
HUSON, J. R., 139
HUTCHESON, Miles, 293
INGRUM, Jesse C., 235
IVES, James, 23
IVES, Quiring, 23
JACKSON, Burrell, 198
JACKSON, Coleman, 49
JACKSON, Coleman (Dr.), 99
JACKSON, E., 210
JACKSON, Elizabeth, 99
JACKSON, Epps, 210
JACKSON, Epsey Ann, 210
JACKSON, Frances, 49
JACKSON, Isaac, 210
JACKSON, James, 210
JACKSON, Mary, 153
JACKSON, Robert, 210
JACKSON, Sarah, 210
JACKSON, Sarah M., 162
JACKSON, Willis, 153
JACKSON, Wm. M., 210
JAMES, Abah, 75
JAMES, Aby, 44
JAMES, Amos, 45
JAMES, Amos, 75
JAMES, Elijah jr., 45
JAMES, Elijah sr., 45
JAMES, Enoch, 45
JAMES, Enoch, 75
JAMES, Enoch, 90
JAMES, Jamay, 45
JAMES, James, 134
JAMES, James, 288
JAMES, Joshua, 44
JAMES, Joshua, 45
JAMES, Joshua, 75
JAMES, Mary, 288
JAMES, P. N., 288
JAMES, P. S., 188
JAMES, Pharnata, 134
JAMES, Polly, 134
JAMES, Sally, 45
JAMES, Samuel, 134
JAMES, Thomas, 45
JAMES, Wm., 45
JOHNSON, Anny, 116
JOHNSON, Charloty, 117
JOHNSON, Cholaty, 117
JOHNSON, Dunkin, 19

JOHNSON, Isac, 27
JOHNSON, Jacob, 27
JOHNSON, James, 19
JOHNSON, Joel, 117
JOHNSON, Joel S., 117
JOHNSON, John, 116
JOHNSON, Martha Jane, 185
JOHNSON, Patsey, 117
JOHNSON, Patsey, 117
JOHNSON, Polly, 19
JOHNSON, Samuel, 19
JOHNSON, Samuel, 20
JOHNSON, Stephen, 117
JOHNSON, Stephen B., 116
JOHNSON, Stephen B., 117
JOHNSON, Thomas, 117
JOHNSON, Thomas M., 116
JOHNSON, Willie B., 233
JOHNSON, Wm., 117
JOHNSON, Wm., 19
JOHNSON, Wm., 20
JOHNSON, Wm., 239
JOHNSON, Wm., 240
JOHNSON, Wm., 252
JOHNSTON, Johnathan, 10
JONES, Easter, 19
JONES, Edward, 33
JONES, Elizabeth, 19
JONES, Ester, 18
JONES, James Madison, 98
JONES, Jane, 98
JONES, John, 19
JONES, John, 97
JONES, John jr., 98
JONES, Joshua, 98
JONES, Josiah, 98
JONES, Nancy, 19
JONES, Reuben, 18
JONES, Seabum, 19
JONES, Thomas, 19
JONES, Thomas Jefferson, 98
JONES, Wm., 98
JORDAN, Jesse, 298
JORDAN, John P., 246
JORDAN, Warren, 298
JORDEN, Brittannia W., 39
JORDEN, George W., 125
JORDEN, George West, 39
JORDEN, John Augustus, 39
JORDEN, Mary, 39
JORDEN, Robert West, 39
JORDEN, Warren, 198
JORDON, Seth B., 38
JORDUN, Sarah Agnes, 298
JOSLIN, Benjamine, 16
JOSLIN, Elizabeth Jane, 159
JOSLIN, James, 159
JOSLIN, Lewis, 89
JOSLIN, Mary Morgan
 (Margaret?), 159
JOURDAN, Warren, 205
JURNAGIN, Unity, 73
KAMES, Jacob A., 153
KEELAM, Isabella, 298
KEELAM, Wm. H., 298
KEELUM, Lucy, 298
KEELUM, Susan, 298
KELLY, Ebeneyer, 63

KELLY, Rachall, 63
KELLY, Tho. J., 154
KELLY, Thos. J., 257
KERNES, Nicholas, 4
KEYS, Eady, 183
KEYS, Tom, 183
KEYS, Tom, 195
KILLABREW, Mary, 94
KIMBLE, Joseph, 99
KING, James, 20
KING, Wm., 82
KIRAGAN, W., 87
KIRAGAN, Wm., 92
KIRK, James M., 265
KIRK, Mary, 153
KIRK, Polly, 153
KIRK, Wm., 153
KKEAN?, Eleanor, 298
KOEN, Henry B., 87
KOON, Polly, 105
LAIN, Erbin H., 284
LAIN, Rufus C., 284
LAMPLEY, Jacob, 293
LAMPLEY, John J., 293
LAMPLEY, Joseph, 136
LAMPLEY, Rebecca, 135
LAMPLEY, Rebecca, 293
LAMPLEY, Wm. C., 293
LANDON (SLAVE), Mark, 189
LANDRITH, Nancy, 152
LARKINS, Delphia Jane, 281
LARKINS, E. E., 258
LARKINS, G. N., 286
LARKINS, H. C., 179
LARKINS, J. M., 228
LARKINS, Joseph, 286
LARKINS, Marshall, 201
LARKINS, Martha, 240
LATHAM, Bryan, 40
LEE, Amanda, 189
LEE, Samuel B., 189
LEECH, Daniel, 130
LEECH, Daniel, 259
LEECH, Daniel, 267
LEEK, Elizabeth, 148
LEEK, Elizabeth, 148
LEEK, Henry, 147
LEEK, Josiah, 148
LEEK, Meriah, 148
LEEK, Randolph, 148
LEGGET, Henry R., 77
LEIGHT, Michael, 70
LESTER (SLAVE), Edmond, 189
LEWIS, Hugh, 19
LEWIS, John, 16
LEWIS, Wm., 73
LIVINGSTON, Charlotte, 81
LIVINGSTON, Robert, 67
LOFTIS, Cintha, 78
LOFTIS, Fereba, 78
LOFTIS, M., 78
LOFTIS, Martin, 78
LOFTIS, Martin, 79
LOFTIS, Martin, 80
LOFTIS, Milton, 78
LOFTIS, Phebe V., 78
LOFTIS, Pheribe, 79
LOFTIS, Rilla E., 78

LOFTIS, Wm., 78
LOFTIS, Wm., 79
LOFTIS, Wm. Samuel, 78
LOGGINS, James, 130
LOTT (SLAVE), Judia Adonia, 183
LOTT (SLAVE), Leroy, 183
LOTT (SLAVE), Malina, 183
LOTT (SLAVE), Margaret Arabella, 183
LOTT (SLAVE), Mary Jane, 183
LOVEACKS, Tennessee, 29
LOVELL, C. G., 298
LUKE, John, 29
LUMSDEN?, Jesse, 33
LUSTER, Fountain, 186
LUSTER, Sarah Ann, 186
MABIN, John, 26
MACKLIN, Benjamine, 52
MALUGEN, Minerva, 120
MANNER, Joseph, 19
MARABLE, Annie E., 49
MARABLE, Henry, 49
MARABLE, John H., 271
MARABLE, John H., 89
MARABLE, John H., 99
MARALILE, John H., 40
MARIABLE, Ann E., 53
MARIABLE, Henry H., 53
MARSH, Ann, 74
MARSH, Elizabeth, 34
MARSH, Gilbert, 74
MARSH, Mineyard, 74
MARTIN, George, 81
MARTIN, James, 7
MARTIN, Jas., 5
MARTIN, John L., 286
MASON, Rebecca, 49
MASON, Wm., 49
MASON, Wm., 52
MASSIE, Elizabeth, 126
MASSIE, Joel, 70
MASSIE, John, 126
MATHIS, Whitson J., 279
MATLOCK, Luke, 115
MATLOCK, Miriah, 275
MATLOCK, Wm., 275
MATTHEWS, Andrew JAckson, 128
MATTHEWS, Emilla, 128
MATTHEWS, George R., 128
MATTHEWS, Lellia, 128
MATTHEWS, Thomas, 128
MAXWELL, Jane, 12
MAXWELL, Jess, 12
MAY, Jessie, 64
MAY, John jr., 179
MCADOO, D., 67
MCADOO, David, 21
MCADOO, David, 23
MCADOO, David, 24
MCADOO, John, 23
MCADOO, Margaret, 22
MCADOO, Margaret, 24
MCADOO, Mary, 24
MCADOO, Samuel, 23
MCADOO, Samuel, 24
MCCANNON, James W., 79

Every Name Index to Dickson County TN Will Book A 1804-1856

MCCLELLAND, Agness, 21	MOLTON, Patience, 11	NESBITT, Alen, 175	OVERTON, Thomas, 210
MCCLELLAND, Frances, 21	MOLTON, Sarah, 11	NESBITT, Allen, 106	PARADISE, Allice V., 252
MCCLELLAND, James, 20	MOLTON, Sarah Ann, 11	NESBITT, Allen, 116	PARKER, Daniel, 18
MCCLELLAND, James, 21	MOLTON, Sarah Ann Jane, 11	NESBITT, Allen, 145	PARKER, Daniel, 243
MCCLELLAND, Jane, 21	MONTGOMERY, JOhn, 97	NESBITT, Allen, 175	PARKER, David, 17
MCCLELLAND, Jane, 23	MONTGOMERY, John, 222	NESBITT, Allen, 245	PARKER, Hannah, 243
MCCLELLAND, John, 21	MOODY, W. A., 269	NESBITT, Allen, 261	PARKER, Hulda May, 243
MCCLELLAND, Nelson, 21	MOORE, Daniel, 83	NESBITT, Andrew F., 290	PARKER, John, 243
MCCLELLAND, Thomas, 21	MOORE, Daniel, 90	NESBITT, Betsey, 290	PARKER, Moses, 243
MCCLELLAND, Wm., 21	MOORE, Isaiah, 15	NESBITT, Betsy Ann, 290	PARKER, Wm., 243
MCCLURE, Louisa, 231	MOORE, Robert, 87	NESBITT, Catherine M., 290	PARKES, Thomas, 61
MCCLURE, Louisa, 233	MOORE, Tarlton F., 188	NESBITT, Jermiah, 290	PARRISH, N. C., 235
MCCLURE, Robert W., 233	MOORE, Tarton F., 196	NESBITT, John, 145	PASSMORE, David, 103
MCCLURKIN, Hugh, 269	MOREHEAD (SLAVE), Stephen Shelby Daniel, 106	NESBITT, John, 291	PATTERSON, Anna, 141
MCCOLLUM, James, 201		NESBITT, John, 5	PATTERSON, John T., 55
MCCRAY, Sam, 189	MORRIS, Araminta, 224	NESBITT, John C., 290	PATTERSON, John Tapley, 58
MCKEE, James, 38	MORRIS, Joseph, 167	NESBITT, Joseph, 290	PATTERSON, Polly, 123
MCLAUGHLIN, Nancy, 142	MORRIS, Wm., 98	NESBITT, Margaret, 290	PATTERSON, Polly White, 55
MCMURRY, Eably, 81	MORRISON, Betsey, 121	NESBITT, Martha, 290	PATTERSON, Rachel, 122
MCMURRY, Thomas, 125	MORRISON, Elizabeth, 122	NESBITT, Nancy W., 290	PATTERSON, Rachel, 123
MCNEILLY, C., 193	MORRISON, Rachel, 121	NESBITT, Nathan, 235	PATTERSON, Robert, 123
MCNEILLY, James Hugh, 186	MORRISON, Wm., 120	NESBITT, O., 235	PATTERSON, Wm., 123
MCNEILLY, John, 223	MORRISON, Wm., 231	NESBITT, Robert, 145	PEARSALL, Ann, 3
MCNEILLY, Margaret, 193	MORRISON, Wm., 271	NESBITT, Robert, 175	PEARSALL, Edward, 11
MCNEILLY, Robert, 175	MORRISON, Wm., 42	NESBITT, Robert, 175	PEARSALL, Jermiah, 11
MCNEILLY, Robert, 183	MURRELL, Richard, 79	NESBITT, Robert, 5	PEARSELL, Patience, 11
MCNEILLY, Robert, 186	MURRELL, Thomas, 273	NESBITT, Robert S., 290	PENDERGRASS, John Harvey, 246
MCNEILLY, Robert, 275	MYATT, Burwell, 132	NESBITT, Sally, 290	
MCNEILLY, Robt., 222	MYATT, Eldridge, 132	NESBITT, Samuel, 175	PENDERGRASS, Rilly, 246
MCNEILLY, Sophia B., 199	MYATT, Elizabeth, 127	NESBITT, Thomas, 145	PENDERGRASS, Sarah Elizabeth, 246
MCNEILLY, Thomas, 194	MYATT, Elizabeth, 151	NESBITT, Wm. A., 290	
MCNEILLY, Thomas, 211	MYATT, Elizabeth, 171	NEVILLE (SLAVE), Judy, 259	PENDERGRASS, Van Buran, 246
MCNEILLY, Thomas, 275	MYATT, Matthew, 154	NOLEN, Betsey Melinda, 121	PENDERGRASS, Wm. E., 180
MCNEILLY, Thos., 146	MYATT, Polly, 132	NOLEN, Charity, 121	PENDERGRASS, Wm. E., 246
MCNEILLY, Wm. Y., 199	MYATT, Polly, 132	NORRIS, Betsey, 15	PENDERGRASS, Wm. E., 246
MEAD, Sarah, 254	MYERS, Simon, 98	NORRIS, Ellinor, 13	PERRY, Ruffin, 136
MEEK, Adam, 8	NALLY, Edward, 149	NORRIS, Ezekiel, 13	PERRY, Sally, 89
MEEK, Elizabeth, 7	NAPIER, Blunt R., 184	NORRIS, Ezekiel, 15	PHILLIPS, Eleaner, 143
MEEK, Joshua, 7	NAPIER, Cassander, 94	NORRIS, Ezekiel, 48	PHIPPS, Nancy, 204
MEEK, Margaret, 7	NAPIER, Charlotte, 184	NORRIS, Jane, 11	PINEGAR, David, 111
MEEK, Moses, 7	NAPIER, Charlotte Mary, 107	NORRIS, Jesse, 14	PINEGAR, Joseph, 111
MEEK, Moses, 8	NAPIER, E. W., 183	NORRIS, Jesse, 15	PINEGAR, Leonard, 111
MEEKS, Adam, 7	NAPIER, Elias W., 194	NORRIS, John, 12	PINEGAR, Susannah, 111
MERRELL, Thomas, 119	NAPIER, Hannah, 108	NORRIS, John, 13	PINEGAR, Wm., 111
MIDDLETON, Martha, 129	NAPIER, Henry A. C., 189	NORRIS, John, 14	PONDER, Archibald, 131
MILLS, Gilford, 245	NAPIER, Henry A. C., 83	NORRIS, Robert, 12	PORCH, Delia, 260
MINER, James, 206	NAPIER, James R., 107	NORRIS, Robert, 15	PORCH, Henry L., 260
MINOR, Charles, 232	NAPIER, James R., 184	NORRIS, Wm., 11	PORTER, J. W., 237
MINOR, John, 232	NAPIER, Jennetta, 94	NORRIS, Wm., 13	PORTER, John, 140
MITCHEL, George, 173	NAPIER, John W., 186	NORRIS, Wm., 13	PORTER, John, 150
MITCHEL, Samuel, 82	NAPIER, John W., 188	NORRIS, Wm., 15	PORTER, Mary E., 237
MITCHELL, Adelin, 254	NAPIER, John W., 189	NORWORTHY, Susannah, 94	PORTER, Matilda, 280
MITCHELL, Asenatha, 254	NAPIER, Judy, 183	NORWORTHY, Willis, 64	PORTER, Matilda I., 237
MITCHELL, Ballard, 254	NAPIER, Leroy, 184	NOWLES, Elizabeth, 239	PORTER, Mattilda, 237
MITCHELL, Benjamin Franklin, 254	NAPIER, Leroy W., 107	OAKLEY, Joseph R., 286	PORTER, Sam'l S., 163
	NAPIER, Lizzie, 183	OLIPHANT, Adalenen, 210	PORTER, Samuel M., 237
MITCHELL, D., 255	NAPIER, Madison C., 108	ONLY, ___ (m), 188	PORTER, Tilan, 239
MITCHELL, George, 254	NAPIER, Madison C., 184	OUTLAW, Harriet, 88	PORTER, Wm., 237
MITCHELL, John D., 249	NAPIER, Richard C., 184	OUTLAW, Harriett, 89	PORTER, Wm. M., 237
MITCHELL, John D., 254	NAPIER, Richard Claiborne, 106	OUTLAW, Margaret, 88	POWELL, George, 45
MITCHELL, Josephus, 254	NAPIER, Thomas, 189	OVERTON, Elizabeth, 17	PRICHARD, Cary (m), 205
MITCHELL, Martha, 254	NAPIER, Thomas, 189	OVERTON, Elizabeth, 17	PRICHARD, John, 205
MITCHELL, Minor, 254	NAPIER, Wm. C., 186	OVERTON, Gabriel, 17	PRICHARD, Richard, 205
MITCHELL, Sarah, 254	NAPIER, Wm. C., 189	OVERTON, Moses, 17	PRICHARD, Susan, 205
MOLTON, Abraham, 11	NAPIER, Wm. H., 186	OVERTON, Robert, 17	PULLEN, Archibald, 199
MOLTON, Jane, 11	NAPIER, Wm. H., 189	OVERTON, Thomas, 107	PULLEN, Archibald, 45
MOLTON, Jane, 11	NAPIER, Wm. H., 193	OVERTON, Thomas, 109	PULLEN, Archibald, 90
MOLTON, Michael, 11	NAPIER0, John W., 160	OVERTON, Thomas, 194	PULLEN, James C., 199

PULLEN, James C., 238
PULLEN, John A., 199
PULLEN, Nelson B., 199
PULLEN, Polly, 199
PULLEN, Wm. C., 199
RAGAN, Patience, 96
RAGLAND, Martha B., 133
RAPE, Barbra, 239
RAPE, Daniel, 239
RAPE, Gustavus, 239
RAPE, Henry, 10
RAPE, Henry, 239
RAPE, Jacob, 239
RAPE, John, 239
RAPE, Peter, 239
RAWORTH, B., 217
RAWORTH, Egbert, 217
READER, Mary, 103
REAVES, Robert A., 265
RECORD, David, 185
REYNOLDS, Amos, 55
REYNOLDS, Carolina, 57
REYNOLDS, Clarida, 55
REYNOLDS, Clinton, 57
REYNOLDS, Gilly, 81
REYNOLDS, Jane, 123
REYNOLDS, John, 81
REYNOLDS, John, 82
REYNOLDS, John Severe, 57
REYNOLDS, John sr., 81
REYNOLDS, Mark, 42
REYNOLDS, Mark, 81
REYNOLDS, Martha C., 288
REYNOLDS, Nancy, 81
REYNOLDS, Solomon, 123
REYNOLDS, Sophia, 55
REYNOLDS, Susannah, 81
REYNOLDS, Susannah, 82
REYNOLDS, Thomas, 81
REYNOLDS, Wm., 73
REYNOLDS, Wm., 81
RICHARDSON, Amey, 49
RICHARDSON, Amey, 50
RICHARDSON, Amey, 52
RICHARDSON, David Irvin Lebius, 26
RICHARDSON, Edward, 99
RICHARDSON, Eliza, 52
RICHARDSON, Elizabeth, 99
RICHARDSON, Elizabeth J., 139
RICHARDSON, Frances, 25
RICHARDSON, Frances, 50
RICHARDSON, Frances, 52
RICHARDSON, Frankey, 104
RICHARDSON, Hartwell Henry, 99
RICHARDSON, James, 105
RICHARDSON, John, 104
RICHARDSON, John, 105
RICHARDSON, Jorden, 49
RICHARDSON, Jorden, 52
RICHARDSON, Jorden W. A., 99
RICHARDSON, Lebbius Wilkins, 104
RICHARDSON, Lebius, 104
RICHARDSON, Lebius, 281
RICHARDSON, Lebius W., 105
RICHARDSON, Lebius W., 116

RICHARDSON, Mary, 51
RICHARDSON, Mary, 52
RICHARDSON, Mary A., 99
RICHARDSON, Nancy E., 50
RICHARDSON, Nancy E., 52
RICHARDSON, Polly, 50
RICHARDSON, Polly, 52
RICHARDSON, Polly, 99
RICHARDSON, Rebecca, 50
RICHARDSON, Rebecca, 52
RICHARDSON, Rebecca Ann, 99
RICHARDSON, Sally, 29
RICHARDSON, Sally, 50
RICHARDSON, Sally, 50
RICHARDSON, Sally, 52
RICHARDSON, Stephen Daily, 104
RICHARDSON, Stith, 100
RICHARDSON, Stith, 126
RICHARDSON, Stith, 49
RICHARDSON, Stith, 52
RICHARDSON, Stith, 99
RICHARDSON, Thomas, 104
RICHARDSON, Thomas, 105
RICHARDSON, Thomas, 24
RICHARDSON, Thomas, 63
RICHARDSON, Thomas E., 99
RICHARDSON, Thomas J., 25
RICHARDSON, Winnefred, 24
RICHARDSON, Winnifred, 283
RICHARDSON, Wm., 51
RICHARDSON, ____, 99
ROBERTSON, Ann G., 186
ROBERTSON, B. C., 252
ROBERTSON, Benjamin C., 186
ROBERTSON, Benjamin J., 186
ROBERTSON, Benjamine C., 183
ROBERTSON, Benjamine C., 193
ROBERTSON, Benjamine C., 240
ROBERTSON, Benjamine C., 84
ROBERTSON, Christopher W., 186
ROBERTSON, Edward A., 186
ROBERTSON, James, 6
ROBERTSON, John H., 186
ROBERTSON, Martha D., 186
ROBERTSON, Peyton, 109
ROBERTSON, R. C., 229
ROOK, Wm., 267
ROOKER, Caleb, 167
ROSS, George, 88
ROSS, James M., 82
ROSS, James M., 88
ROSS, James M., 89
ROSS, James M., 89
ROSS, Mary T., 169
ROUNDTREE, Jim, 189
RUCKER, Jacob, 130
RUE, Agnes, 73
RUE, Elizabeth, 73
RUSHING, Mary, 46
RUSSELL, Polly F., 34
RYE, Peggy, 96
RYE, Sarah B., 33
RYE, Solomon, 32
RYE, Wm., 33
SAMPLE, Samuel, 8
SANDERS, Benjamine, 82

SANDERS, John, 201
SANDERS, Samuel W., 201
SANDERS, Susan, 201
SANKING, John M., 175
SANSOM, Barbara, 83
SANSOM, David N., 83
SANSOM, Richard D., 83
SANSOM, Wm. C., 83
SCHMITTOU, Frances V. (Dr.), 71
SCHMITTOU, O. L. V., 251
SCOTT, Christian, 94
SCOTT, G. W., 240
SCOTT, John, 37
SCOTT, John, 95
SCOTT, Nehemiah, 79
SCOTT, Wm., 95
SEAL, Elizabeth Jane, 251
SEGG, Wm., 27
SELF, Abraham, 126
SELF, Martha, 126
SELF, Susan, 157
SENSING, Drewsillah B., 245
SENSING, Henry, 245
SENSING, John, 245
SENSING, Margaret Ann, 245
SENSING, McKendrie Gardner, 245
SENSING, Polly Welding, 245
SENSING, Wiley Powel, 245
SENSING, Wm. H., 228
SHARP, Benjamin jr., 109
SHARP, James D., 10
SHELTON, Creel, 128
SHELTON, Eleanor, 298
SHELTON, Patrick, 188
SHELTON, Wm., 120
SHELTON, Wm., 128
SHELTON, Wm. H., 298
SHELTON, Wm. H., 298
SHEWMAKER, Fanny, 74
SHROPSHIRE, Elizabeth, 96
SIKES, John, 148
SIKES, Levina, 148
SIKES, Nancy, 148
SIMMONS, Wm. B., 120
SIMPKINS, P. W., 224
SIMPSON, Elizabeth, 11
SIMPSON, John, 11
SIMPSON, Thomas, 5
SKELTON, Abmr.? B., 264
SKELTON, Abner, 263
SKELTON, Abner, 267
SKELTON, Alford, 263
SKELTON, Archibal, 262
SKELTON, John M., 263
SKELTON, Sarah, 263
SKELTON, Sarah Elizabeth, 263
SLAYDEN, H.? M., 158
SLAYDEN, Hartwell U., 177
SLAYDEN, Jane, 177
SLAYDEN, Wm. E., 120
SMITH, Alley, 81
SMITH, B., 271
SMITH, Bartholemew, 6
SMITH, Bartholomew, 274
SMITH, Bartholomew, 4
SMITH, Bartholomew, 4

SMITH, Dorthy, 272
SMITH, Elisha, 79
SMITH, Gray W., 271
SMITH, Jackson, 271
SMITH, Madison H., 271
SMITH, Mansford, 4
SMITH, Mose, 6
SMITH, Mumford, 79
SMITH, Susanna, 6
SMITH, Thomas C., 79
SMITH, Thomas C., 83
SMITH, W. B., 170
SMITH, Williason E., 271
SMITH, Wm. B., 271
SPEIGHT, Allis V., 252
SPEIGHT, Emily C., 252
SPEIGHT, Wm. D., 240
SPEIGHT, Wm. D., 252
SPEIGHT, Wm. D., 252
SPENCER, Daniel, 136
SPENCER, James, 136
SPENCER, Mary, 136
SPENCER, Thomas, 52
SPENCER, Wm., 136
SPICER, Oliver, 206
STACKER, Martha J., 231
STAFFORD, John, 45
STAFFORD, John, 90
STANFIELD, Elizabeth, 47
STEWART, D., 3
STEWART, Duncan, 3
STEWART, James, 3
STEWART, Jane, 11
STEWART, John, 3
STEWART, Susan, 162
STONE, Bartholomew, 4
STONE, Benjamin, 189
STONE, Dolly, 4
STONE, Dorcus, 4
STONE, Elizabeth, 4
STONE, Hardeman, 4
STONE, John H., 166
STONE, John H., 4
STONE, Marble, 4
STONE, Marble, 4
STONE, Mary, 189
STONE, Solomon, 4
STONE, Solomon, 4
STONE, Susanna, 4
STONE, William sr., 3
STONE, Wm., 4
STONE, Wm., 6
STREET, Abram, 157
STREET, Ailsey, 156
STREET, David, 157
STREET, Jechonias, 156
STREET, Martha, 157
STREET, Moses, 156
STREET, Moses, 157
STRINGFELLOW, Robert, 10
STRONG, Christopher, 214
STRONG, Rosannah, 214
STRONG, Rosannah, 222
STUART, W. T., 226
STURDIVANT, Nancy, 47
SUITHER, Mary, 134
SULIVAN, Owen, 150
SULLIVAN, Nancy, 237

Every Name Index to Dickson County TN Will Book A 1804-1856

SWANSON, Edward, 15
TATOM, Ann, 38
TATOM, Eliza, 104
TATOM, Elizabeth, 25
TATOM, G. W., 161
TATOM, George W., 119
TATUM, Richardson, 37
TAYLOR, Claiborne, 147
TAYLOR, Daniel, 146
TAYLOR, Mary Ann, 147
TEAS, James, 102
THEADFORD, James, 186
THERMAN, Carter, 186
THERMAN, Dock, 186
THERMAN, Elizabeth, 185
THERMAN, James, 185
THERMAN, John, 185
THERMAN, Richard, 185
THERMAN, Wm., 185
THERMAN, Wm. J., 185
THOMAS, James H., 193
THOMAS, John C., 66
THOMAS, May, 67
THOMAS, Nancy, 239
THOMAS, Stephen, 66
THOMAS, Wm., 67
THOMPSON, Charles, 131
THOMPSON, Charles, 131
THOMPSON, James, 131
THOMPSON, John, 131
THOMPSON, Lucy Ann, 186
THOMPSON, Mary, 131
THOMPSON, Nancy, 131
THOMPSON, Richard, 186
THOMPSON, Sally, 131
THOMPSON, Wm., 199
THORNTON, Esther, 79
THORNTON, J., 152
THORNTON, Josiah, 127
THORNTON, Josiah, 78
THORNTON, Josiah, 79
THORNTON, Reuben, 79
TIDWELL, Aquilla, 68
TIDWELL, B., 140
TIDWELL, Benjamine, 268
TIDWELL, Edward, 66
TIDWELL, Edward, 68
TIDWELL, Frances, 135
TIDWELL, Isiah, 180
TIDWELL, James, 135
TIDWELL, John, 136
TIDWELL, John K., 136
TIDWELL, Lucinda, 268
TIDWELL, Mary, 135
TIDWELL, Moses, 268
TIDWELL, Rebecker, 180
TIDWELL, Silas, 268
TIMM, Jane, 161
TUBB, Daniel, 129
TUBB, George, 129
TUBB, George, 129
TUBB, Isaac, 129
TUBB, James, 129
TUBB, Nathan, 129
TUBB, Nathan, 130
TUBB, Richard, 129
TUCKER, Aby, 45
TUCKER, C., 119

TUCKER, James M., 119
TUCKER, Jane, 119
TUCKER, John, 119
TUCKER, Lewis, 119
TUCKER, Louisa, 119
TUCKER, Mary Anne, 119
TUCKER, Wm. C., 119
TURNER, Elizabeth, 64
TURNER, H. W., 125
TURNER, Howard, 64
TURNER, Howard W., 59
TURNER, John, 64
TURNER, Samuel, 64
TURNER, Wm., 64
TURNER, Wm., 82
TYCER, Ellis, 282
TYCER, Levis, 281
UNDERWOOD, Jermiah, 126
VAN, Richard P., 210
VANHOOK, Ashburn, 79
VANLANDINGHAND, Francis, 243
VARNELL, Wm. H., 70
VICKS, Elizabeth, 267
VOORHEIS, J., 153
WALKER, Elizabeth, 265
WALKER, Elizabeth, 288
WALKER, Elizabeth, 91
WALKER, Elizabeth, 92
WALKER, Elizabeth Jane, 283
WALKER, Fanny, 145
WALKER, J. V., 288
WALKER, Jim B., 145
WALKER, John B., 106
WALKER, John B., 92
WALKER, John E., 91
WALKER, John V., 288
WALKER, Martha, 288
WALKER, Martha T., 288
WALKER, Mary, 241
WALKER, Mary S., 91
WALKER, Mary S., 91
WALKER, Sally, 25
WALKER, Sally, 283
WALKER, Sally, 284
WALKER, Sarah R., 91
WALKER, Sarah R., 91
WALKER (SLAVE?), Harry, 88
WALL, Mary, 29
WALLACE, Rebecca, 73
WAUGH, Richard, 97
WAYMEN, Wm., 296
WEAKLEY, Isabella, 223
WEAKLEY, John, 79
WEAKLEY, May, 123
WEAVER, Dorcas, 33
WEAVER, Henry H., 149
WEAVER, Martha dec'd, 33
WEAVER, Richard H., 149
WEST, George, 231
WEST, Isaac D., 231
WEST, Isaac D., 231
WEST, John, 21
WEST, Nancy, 230
WEST, Robert, 125
WEST, Robert, 230
WEST, Robert, 39
WEST, Robert J., 231

WEST, Robert J., 231
WEST, Sally, 21
WEST, Sally, 88
WEST, Sally C., 231
WESTLY, John, 220
WHITALL, Robert, 87
WHITE, Benjamin, 150
WHITE, Chapman, 142
WHITE, Charles, 142
WHITE, Crage (m), 142
WHITE, Daniel, 150
WHITE, David, 150
WHITE, Elizabeth, 150
WHITE, James, 141
WHITE, James, 150
WHITE, James T., 142
WHITE, Jesse, 150
WHITE, John, 142
WHITE, Joseph T., 206
WHITE, Joshua, 150
WHITE, Joshua, 98
WHITE, Martha, 142
WHITE, Martha, 150
WHITE, Mary B., 248
WHITE, Mary B., 254
WHITE, Moses T., 82
WHITE, Nancy, 150
WHITE, Polly, 142
WHITE, R., 239
WHITE, Raney, 150
WHITE, Ruben, 248
WHITE, W. L., 249
WHITE, Wm. S., 246
WHITEHEAD, Drucilla, 73
WHITMILL, D_ny S., 27
WHITTLEDGE, Robert, 59
WHITWELL, Ann, 136
WILEY, Adderson, 127
WILEY, Ann, 127
WILEY, Ann, 152
WILEY, Ann, 171
WILEY, David, 127
WILEY, Ebenezer, 127
WILEY, Ebenezer, 151
WILEY, Eli, 151
WILEY, Garton, 127
WILEY, Jasper, 127
WILEY, Jess, 151
WILEY, Jesse, 127
WILEY, Jonathan, 127
WILEY, Jonathan, 151
WILEY, Josiah, 151
WILEY, Lowson, 127
WILEY, Wm., 127
WILEY, Wm., 151
WILEY, Wm., 171
WILKINS, Alexander, 265
WILKINS, Alexander, 97
WILKINS, N. F., 265
WILKINS, Sarah M., 265
WILLEY, Elizabeth, 115
WILLEY, John, 115
WILLEY, John, 26
WILLEY, John F., 284
WILLEY, Joseph, 64
WILLEY, Martha, 241
WILLEY, Mary, 241
WILLEY, Polly, 115

WILLEY, Polly, 241
WILLEY, Polly, 64
WILLEY, Willis, 240
WILLEY, Wm., 116
WILLIAMS, Aby (f), 134
WILLIAMS, Benjamine, 94
WILLIAMS, Daniel, 94
WILLIAMS, Daniel H., 11
WILLIAMS, Daniel H., 132
WILLIAMS, Daniel H., 94
WILLIAMS, Ester E., 132
WILLIAMS, Henry B. H., 94
WILLIAMS, James, 94
WILLIAMS, John T., 82
WILLIAMS, Joseph, 94
WILLIAMS, Lydia Ann, 225
WILLIAMS, Margaret R., 91
WILLIAMS, Nancy, 170
WILLIAMS, Pernella, 89
WILLIAMS, Richard Nixon, 94
WILLIAMS, Thomas, 170
WILLIAMS, Thos., 94
WILLIAMS, Wesley A., 170
WILLY, Joanirah, 157
WILLY, John W., 240
WILLY, Michael B., 240
WILLY, Willis Carroll, 241
WILSON, Adam, 60
WILSON, James, 61
WILSON, John, 61
WILSON, Joseph, 61
WILSON, Lucerria, 61
WILSON, Margaret, 60
WILSON, Mary, 141
WILSON, Mary Elizabeth, 186
WILSON, Nancy, 61
WILSON, Polly, 81
WOODWARD, A., 296
WOODWARD, Benjamin, 295
WOODWARD, Benjamin, 296
WOODWARD, Elizabeth, 295
WOODWARD, George B., 296
WOODWARD, Harriet, 296
WOODWARD, Jesse, 295
WOODWARD, John D., 296
WOODWARD, Sarah, 296
WOODWARD, Wm., 296
WORK, Andrew, 204
WORK, Andrew, 204
WORK, Branetta J., 288
WORK, Catherine, 204
WORK, John F., 204
WORK, Robert, 204
WORK, Samuel, 204
WRIGHT, John, 38
YARRELL, Mary, 133
YATES, Fannin, 172
YOUNG, Benjamin, 148
YOUNG, Bennet, 149
YOUNG, Mary, 148
ZUTHMAN, Eliza, 186
ZUTHMAN, John, 186

Slave Index to Dickson County TN Will Book A 1804-1856

Note that the surnames listed below represent the slave owners

ADAMS, Mary, 29
ANGLIN, Phebe, 130
ANGLIN, Wm. Henry, 130
ARMSTRONG, Mariah, 277
BELL, Aggy, 170
BELL, Alfred, 170
BELL, Alston, 170
BELL, Ben, 170
BELL, Caroline, 170
BELL, Charity, 169
BELL, Charlotte, 169
BELL, Daniel, 170
BELL, Dency, 169
BELL, Dilsy, 170
BELL, Hannah, 170
BELL, Harriet, 179
BELL, Jim, 169
BELL, Kate, 179
BELL, Kitty (Catherine), 170
BELL, Mary, 169
BELL, Ned, 169
BELL, Nelson, 169
BELL, Paralee, 170
BELL, Patsy, 208
BELL, Rachel, 170
BELL, Tempy, 208
BELL, Venis, 170
BELL, Vergil, 208
BELL, Vester, 170
BELL, Vilet, 170
BELL, Viney, 169
BELL, Wiley, 169
BELL, Wilson, 170
BELL, Wm., 208
BLEDSOE, Dinah, 72
CHOATE, Alsia, 114
CHOATE, Mary, 114
CHOATE, Nancy, 114
CHOATE, Verge, 114
COLDWELL, Amanda, 281
COLDWELL, Ann, 282
COLDWELL, Benjamin, 281
COLDWELL, Ellen, 281
COLDWELL, Flora, 281
COLDWELL, Jeana, 281
COLDWELL, John, 281
COLDWELL, Levena, 281
COLDWELL, March, 281
COLDWELL, Roda, 282
COLDWELL, Sela, 281
COLDWELL, Violet, 281
COLDWELL, Wm., 282
DAVIDSON, Edd, 68
DICKSON, Almyra, 1
DICKSON, Cato, 2
DICKSON, Clarry, 2
DICKSON, Dinah, 1
DICKSON, Harry, 2
DICKSON, Phillis, 2
DICKSON, Reddick, 1
DICKSON, Stephen, 17
DICKSON, Sylvia, 1
DICKSON, Sylvia, 2
DICKSON, Tom, 18

DICKSON, Virgil, 1
DICKSON, Warwick, 1
DODSON, Adaline, 182
DODSON, Fillis, 182
DODSON, Jack, 182
DODSON, Manuel, 182
DORTCH, Jack, 231
EASLEY, Elleck, 69
ELLIS, Milly, 100
FUSELL, Ben, 93
GARRETT, Ben, 226
GARRETT, Jerry, 226
GARRETT, Pheriba, 226
GILBERT, Fanny, 76
GILBERT, Jeffry, 76
GILBERT, Jude, 76
GILBERT, Mary, 76
GILBERT, Monah, 76
GILBERT, Smith, 76
GLEAVES, Calib, 223
GLEAVES, Emily, 223
GLEAVES, Joseph, 223
GLEAVES, Martin, 223
GLEAVES, Mary, 223
GLEAVES, Violet, 223
GOODRICH, Aggy, 46
GOODRICH, Anthony, 46
GOODRICH, Big Peter, 47
GOODRICH, Billy, 47
GOODRICH, Bob, 46
GOODRICH, Cresey, 47
GOODRICH, Edmond, 47
GOODRICH, Ester, 46
GOODRICH, Filda, 47
GOODRICH, Harriett, 47
GOODRICH, Hezekiah, 47
GOODRICH, Jane, 46
GOODRICH, Jefferson, 46
GOODRICH, Jenny, 47
GOODRICH, Linda, 47
GOODRICH, Little Peter, 47
GOODRICH, Lucy, 47
GOODRICH, Mary, 47
GOODRICH, Mereda, 47
GOODRICH, Newborn, 46
GOODRICH, Racoolina, 46
GOODRICH, Ridley, 46
GOODRICH, Rose, 46
GOODRICH, Sally, 47
GOODRICH, Sarah, 47
GOODRICH, Sealy, 47
GOODRICH, Seloy, 47
GOODRICH, Tom, 48
GOODRICH, Young Dave, 47
GOODRICH, clarrica, 48
HALL, Amy, 42
HALL, Brick, 40
HALL, Caty, 41
HALL, Edwarda (m), 41
HALL, Ester, 42
HALL, Hager, 42
HALL, Jamima, 41
HALL, Joe, 41
HALL, Juliet, 41
HALL, Lucinda, 42
HALL, Penny, 40
HALL, Robert, 42
HALL, William, 40
HARDIN, Coleman, 259

HARDIN, Core, 257
HARDIN, John, 257
HARDIN, Judy, 259
HARDIN, Mary, 257
HARDIN, Sawney, 257
HARDIN, Stephen, 257
HIGHTOWER, Nelson, 153
HOGINS, Jack, 143
HOGINS, Lucy, 143
HUDSON, Agnis, 34
HUDSON, Alsy, 35
HUDSON, Arizilla, 34
HUDSON, Bronce, 34
HUDSON, Carry, 34
HUDSON, Charles, 34
HUDSON, Clory, 35
HUDSON, Edith, 34
HUDSON, Eliza, 35
HUDSON, Emanuel, 66
HUDSON, Filda, 34
HUDSON, George, 66
HUDSON, Jacob, 34
HUDSON, Lucinda, 34
HUDSON, Madison, 66
HUDSON, Mary, 34
HUDSON, Mary, 66
HUDSON, Matilda, 34
HUDSON, Nancy, 66
HUDSON, Susan, 34
HUDSON, Thornhill, 34
HUDSON, Viny, 34
HUMPHREYS, Amy, 58
HUMPHREYS, Annaky, 57
HUMPHREYS, Anthony, 58
HUMPHREYS, Brisis, 58
HUMPHREYS, Buckner, 58
HUMPHREYS, Chana, 59
HUMPHREYS, Chonce, 55
HUMPHREYS, Dorcus, 55
HUMPHREYS, Glaster, 55
HUMPHREYS, Joe, 56
HUMPHREYS, Peggy, 57
HUMPHREYS, Sabra, 56
HUMPHREYS, Sara, 56
HUMPHREYS, Scippis, 57
HUMPHREYS, Waynick, 55
JAMES, Fanny, 45
JOHNSON, Elick, 19
JOHNSON, Jenny, 117
JOHNSON, Joe, 117
JOHNSON, Wm. Bedford, 117
JORDON, Britt, 39
JORDON, Charity, 39
JORDON, Gin, 39
LEEK, Anderson, 148
LEEK, Isham, 148
LEEK, Lidia, 148
LEEK, Tyna, 148
LEEK, Yellow Lucy, 148
LOFTIS, James, 78
LOFTIS, Milla, 78
LOFTIS, Peter, 78
LOFTIS, Tony, 78
MARSH, Ceely, 74
MARSH, Nancy, 74
MARSH, Peter, 74
MARSH, Tony, 74
MOLTON, Anneritter, 11
MOLTON, Betty, 11

MOLTON, Penny, 11
MORRISON, Ann, 123
NAPIER, Albert, 189
NAPIER, Amanuel, 183
NAPIER, Andrew Jackson, 183
NAPIER, Angelin, 183
NAPIER, Billy, 188
NAPIER, Bob, 186
NAPIER, Burwell, 188
NAPIER, Carolina, 188
NAPIER, Caroline, 197
NAPIER, Cephus, 188
NAPIER, Charity, 183
NAPIER, Charity, 188
NAPIER, Charles, 106
NAPIER, Clary, 186
NAPIER, Cloe, 107
NAPIER, Cloey, 189
NAPIER, Creecy, 183
NAPIER, Drumica, 189
NAPIER, Eliza, 188
NAPIER, Ephragin, 194
NAPIER, Esther, 188
NAPIER, Evaline, 183
NAPIER, Fanny, 183
NAPIER, Frances, 188
NAPIER, Fred, 189
NAPIER, Georga, 188
NAPIER, Hannah, 107
NAPIER, Henry, 107
NAPIER, Hiat, 188
NAPIER, Ivin Tasberry, 106
NAPIER, Jack, 183
NAPIER, James Monroe, 183
NAPIER, Jane, 188
NAPIER, Jarrato, 188
NAPIER, Judeanna, 188
NAPIER, Judy, 183
NAPIER, Kitty, 186
NAPIER, Lananna, 188
NAPIER, Landon, 189
NAPIER, Landono, 188
NAPIER, Lizza (Elizabeth), 183
NAPIER, Lucy, 188
NAPIER, Mary, 106
NAPIER, Mima, 188
NAPIER, Nancy, 189
NAPIER, Peggy, 186
NAPIER, Perry, 183
NAPIER, Sam, 188
NAPIER, Simon, 183
NAPIER, Solomon, 183
NAPIER, Speedley, 106
NAPIER, Tho. Benton, 183
NAPIER, Wm. Carroll, 183
NESBITT, Harry, 146
NESBITT, Lucy, 175
NESBITT, Mary, 175
NORRIS, Entnum, 12
NORRIS, Entrum, 14
NORRIS, Jill, 12
NORRIS, Jill, 15
NORRIS, Jude, 12
NORRIS, Jude, 13
NORRIS, Rachel, 12
NORRIS, Rachel, 13
NORRIS, Rose, 12
NORRIS, Rose, 13
PARKER, Evaline, 243

Slave Index to Dickson County TN Will Book A 1804-1856

PASSMORE, Jane, 103	SANSOM, Armsted, 83	TURNER, Peter, 64
PENDERGRASS, Lucy, 246	SANSOM, Venis, 83	VICKS, Andrew, 267
PENDERGRASS, Smith, 246	SENSING, Lovey, 245	VICKS, Isham, 267
PORTER, Lewis, 237	SENSING, Richman, 245	VICKS, John, 267
PORTER, Nancy, 237	SHELTON, Maria, 298	VICKS, Sylvy, 267
PULLEN, Adline, 199	SHELTON, Sylvia, 298	VICKS, Violet, 267
PULLEN, Peter, 199	SKELTON, Ellen, 263	WALKER, Deliah, 91
RAPE, John, 239	SKELTON, Henry, 263	WALKER, Horton, 91
REYNOLDS, Gillis, 81	SKELTON, Martha, 263	WALKER, Priscilla, 91
REYNOLDS, Isaac, 81	SKELTON, Patson, 264	WALKER, Tennessee, 91
RICHARDSON, Amey, 49	SKELTON, Wm., 263	WEST, Bill, 231
RICHARDSON, Ben, 25	SMITH, Belfield, 272	WEST, Flora, 233
RICHARDSON, Caster, 104	SMITH, Blount, 271	WEST, Hetty, 231
RICHARDSON, Chancy (f), 104	SMITH, Calvin, 271	WEST, Nancy, 231
RICHARDSON, Charlotte, 25	SMITH, Casandra, 271	WEST, Nelson, 231
RICHARDSON, Claburn, 49	SMITH, Chancey, 271	WEST, Penny, 231
RICHARDSON, Dick, 49	SMITH, Ellis, 271	WEST, Peter, 231
RICHARDSON, Edmond, 49	SMITH, Jimmy, 272	WEST, Sarah Lydia, 231
RICHARDSON, Fairry, 49	SMITH, Mariah, 272	WEST, Sylvia, 231
RICHARDSON, John, 25	SMITH, Martha, 271	WEST, Tom, 231
RICHARDSON, Jude, 49	SMITH, Mary, 271	WEST, Zal (f), 233
RICHARDSON, Julia, 49	SMITH, Nancy, 271	WHITE, Rachael, 150
RICHARDSON, March, 25	SMITH, Nancy, 272	WHITWELL, Cambridge, 136
RICHARDSON, Milly, 284	SMITH, North, 272	WHITWELL, Caroline, 136
RICHARDSON, Phebe, 50	SMITH, Peter, 271	WHITWELL, Drue, 136
RICHARDSON, Tempy, 49	SMITH, Rachael, 272	WHITWELL, Hannah, 136
ROSS, Abraham, 89	SMITH, Raleigh, 272	WHITWELL, Jude, 136
ROSS, Alston, 88	SMITH, Viney, 271	WHITWELL, Lucy, 136
ROSS, Betty, 88	SPEIGHT, Ann, 252	WHITWELL, Patsey, 136
ROSS, Caroline, 88	SPEIGHT, Calebs, 252	WHITWELL, Penny, 136
ROSS, Cassandra, 88	SPEIGHT, Daniel, 252	WHITWELL, Phillis, 136
ROSS, Charity, 88	SPEIGHT, Joe, 252	WHITWELL, Reuben, 136
ROSS, Clarrisa, 88	SPEIGHT, Jordan, 252	WHITWELL, Sam, 136
ROSS, Dave, 89	SPEIGHT, Martha, 252	WHITWELL, Tempy, 136
ROSS, Dick, 88	SPEIGHT, Virgil, 252	WHITWELL, Tom, 136
ROSS, Ealy, 88	STONE, Adam, 4	WHITWELL, Virgil, 136
ROSS, Elijah (boy), 88	STONE, Jenny, 4	WHITWELL, Wm., 136
ROSS, Elijah (man), 88	STONE, Jerry, 4	WILLIAMS, Matilda, 95
ROSS, Gabe, 88	STONE, Jess, 4	WILSON, Henry, 62
ROSS, Haky (f), 89	STONE, Nicy, 4	WOODWARD, Benjamin, 295
ROSS, Hanna, 88	STONE, Pleasure, 4	WOODWARD, Betsey, 295
ROSS, Harriet, 88	STREET, Belfield, 157	WOODWARD, Boston, 295
ROSS, Harry, 88	STREET, Charles, 157	WOODWARD, David, 295
ROSS, Isaac, 89	STREET, Diannah, 157	WOODWARD, Henry Allen, 295
ROSS, Isbel, 88	STREET, Diay, 157	WOODWARD, Jesse, 295
ROSS, Ivvy, 88	STREET, Edmond, 157	WOODWARD, Juda Ann, 295
ROSS, Jim, 89	STREET, Henry, 157	WOODWARD, Mariah, 295
ROSS, Laurel, 89	STREET, Kitty Ann, 157	YARRELL, Martin, 133
ROSS, Lewis, 89	STREET, Mary, 157	YARRELL, Matilda, 133
ROSS, Lilo, 88	STREET, Mirah, 157	
ROSS, Lucy, 88	STRONG, John Westly, 220	
ROSS, MArtha, 88	STRONG, Tennessee, 220	
ROSS, Major, 89	TIDWELL, Anna, 135	
ROSS, Mark, 89	TIDWELL, Calvin, 135	
ROSS, Milly, 88	TIDWELL, Easter, 135	
ROSS, Milly, 89	TIDWELL, Sam, 135	
ROSS, Nan (f), 89	TIDWELL, Taner, 135	
ROSS, Peter, 89	TUBB, Carroll, 129	
ROSS, Phillis, 88	TUBB, Hager (f), 129	
ROSS, Priscilla, 88	TUBB, Mary, 129	
ROSS, Sarah, 88	TUBB, Milly, 129	
ROSS, Serena, 89	TUBB, Nicy, 129	
ROSS, Sigh (m), 88	TUBB, Prince, 129	
ROSS, Yellow Harry, 89	TUBB, Solomon, 129	
ROSS, no name, child of Betty (f), 88	TUBB, Tener (f), 129	
	TUBB, Tom (old), 129	
SANDERS, John, 201	TUBB, Tom (young), 129	
SANDERS, Mary, 201	TURNER, Loviea, 64	

www.ingramcontent.com/pod-product-compliance
Lightning Source LLC
Chambersburg PA
CBHW082122230426
43671CB00015B/2774